LIBRARY OF HEBREW BIBLE/ OLD TESTAMENT STUDIES

571

Formerly Journal for the Study of the Old Testament Supplement Series

ROYAL MOTIFS
IN THE PENTATEUCHAL PORTRAYAL
OF MOSES

Danny Mathews

t&t clark

Published by T & T Clark International
A Continuum imprint
80 Maiden Lane, New York, NY 10038
The Tower Building, 11 York Road, London SE1 7NX

www.continuumbooks.com

Visit the T & T Clark blog at www.tandtclarkblog.com

© Danny Mathews, 2012

Library of Congress Cataloging-in-Publication Data
A catalog record for this book is available from the Library of Congress.

ISBN: HB: 978-0-567-11614-7

Typeset by Forthcoming Publications Ltd (www.forthpub.com)
Printed and bound in the United States of America

CONTENTS

PREFACE

This study originated from a close examination of Exod 7:1 in context of a translation project:

ויאמר יהוה אל משה ראה נתתיך אלהים לפרעה ואהרן אחיך יהיה נביאך

"The Lord said to Moses, "See, I have made you God (אלהים) to Pharaoh, and your brother Aaron will be your prophet."

(author's translation).

A straightforward translation results in a striking description of Moses as "God." A brief investigation of the treatment of this verse reveals that most sources either gloss over this difficult portrayal of Moses or tone it down. For example, translations such as the NRSV typically include a qualifier, such as "like" or "as," that is not present in the Hebrew text. This results in a more metaphorical understanding of the Lord making Moses "like God" and thereby conceals the difficulty from readers not working directly from the Hebrew text. This surprising attribution of the quality of divinity to Moses raises the question of the basic portrayal of Moses in the Pentateuch. The typical understanding of Moses as a "prophet" that is quite ingrained in the collective consciousness of biblical scholars does not appear to be operative here since this category is applied explicitly to Aaron. And the difficulty is not limited to Exod 7:1 since other passages also appear to portray Moses in a super-human light (e.g. Exod 4:16, 21; 34:29–35; Deut 34:7, 11–12). Finally, the various ways Moses is portrayed throughout the Pentateuch, such as military general, law-giver, temple builder, suggest that the typical classification of Moses as a prophet merits re-examination.

This study seeks to argue that royalty as it is generally understood in the ancient Near East provides a more appropriate category that can comprehend these fantastic and varied portrayals of Moses. A brief survey of various monumental inscriptions in the ancient Near East shows that the king shares many of the qualities that are also used to portray Moses such as shepherd, military general, temple builder, law-giver, as well as his humility and even divinity. To establish this argument, this study broadly examines a number of well-documented royal motifs that are used to depict Moses. These will be used as a basis for a fresh re-examination of select sections from the Pentateuch. It must be emphasized from the outset that this study does not intend to offer the final word, or to provide a comprehensive profile of the various motifs used in the portrayal of Moses—each of the fifteen motifs that are briefly surveyed in Chapter 2 of this study could easily be the subject of an extensive monograph. Rather, it is the intention of this study to spark a new line of inquiry that will hopefully result in a re-examination of the portrayal of Moses in the Pentateuch.

This study originated as a dissertation completed under the direction of Dean McBride at Union Theological Seminary and Christian School of Presbyterian Education in Richmond, Virginia (now renamed as Union Presbyterian Seminary). Dean deserves my utmost appreciation for his enthusiastic guidance and his patient, incisive and instructive comments provided throughout each stage of this project. I also wish to express my gratitude to Sam Balentine and Dennis Olson for their careful reading and sage advice on the improvement of this project. Many, many thanks are especially due to Jim Brashler for the countless hours spent on the proofing and editing of this manuscript. Special thanks are due to my graduate assistant Andrew Sowers, who made my life much easier in the formatting of the manuscript for publication. I would also like to express appreciation for the encouragement and guidance and many, many hours of enjoyable and engaging conversation with my fellow student-colleagues from Union, especially Raj Nadella, Aubrey Watkins, and John Herbst, and colleagues from Harding University, especially Dale Manor, John Fortner, Keith Stanglin, Nathan Guy, and Tim Westbrook. This volume is dedicated to Wendi with my thanks for her undeserved understanding and unyielding devotion and support and to our three sons: Taylor, Bailey, and Avery.

ABBREVIATIONS

AB	Anchor Bible
ABD	*Anchor Bible Dictionary*. Edited by D. N. Freedman. 6 vols. New York, 1992
AGJU	Arbeiten zur Geschichte des antiken Judentums und des Urchristentums
Alleg. Interp.	*Allegorical Interpretation* (*Legumallegoriae*)
ANEP	*The Ancient Near East in Pictures Relating to the Old Testament*. Edited by J. B. Pritchard. Princeton, 1954
Ant.	Josephus, *Jewish Antiquities*
BASOR	*Bulletin of the American Schools of Oriental Research*
BETL	Bibliotheca ephemeridum theologicarum lovaniensium
BZAW	Beihefte zur Zeitschrift für die alttestamentliche Wissenschaft
CBQ	*Catholic Biblical Quarterly*
COS	*The Context of Scripture*. Edited by W. W. Hallo. 3 vols. Leiden, 1997–2003
Deut. Rab.	*Deuteronomy Rabbah*
Embassy	*On the Embassy to Gaius* (*Legatio ad Gaium*)
EncJud	*Encyclopaedia Judaica*. 16 vols. Jerusalem, 1972
EstBib	*Estudios bíblicos*
ETR	*Etudes théologiques et religieuses*
Exod. Rab.	*Exodus Rabbah*
FAT	Forschungen zum Alten Testament
FOTL	Forms of the Old Testament Literature
FRLANT	Forschungen zur Religion und Literatur des Alten und Neuen Testaments
HALOT	Koehler, L., W. Baumgartner, and J. J. Stamm, *The Hebrew and Aramaic Lexicon of the Old Testament*. Translated and edited under the supervision of M. E. J. Richardson. 4 vols. Leiden, 1994–1999
Hist.	Herodotus' *Histories*
HSM	Harvard Semitic Monographs
IBC	Interpretation: A Bible Commentary for Teaching and Preaching
Int	*Interpretation*
JAOS	*Journal of the American Oriental Society*
JBL	*Journal of Biblical Literature*
JNES	*Journal of Near Eastern Studies*

JQR	*Jewish Quarterly Review*
JSOTSup	Journal for the Study of the Old Testament: Supplement Series
JSS	*Journal of Semitic Studies*
LCL	Loeb Classical Library
LHBOTS	Library of Hebrew Bible/Old Testament Studies
LXX	Septuagint (the Greek Old Testament)
M. Marq.	*Memar Marqah*
Mos.	*On the Life of Moses* (*De vita Mosis*)
MT	Masoretic Text
NJPS	*Tanakh: The Holy Scriptures: The New JPS Translation according to the Traditional Hebrew Text*
NovTSup	Novum Testamentum Supplements
NRSV	New Revised Standard Version
NT	New Testament
Or	*Orientalia*
OT	Old Testament
OTL	Old Testament Library
Pesiq. Rab. Kah.	*Pesiqta de RabKahana*
Resp.	*Republic (Respublica)*
RGG	*Religion in Geschichte und Gegenwart.* Edited by K. Galling. 7 vols. 3d ed. Tübingen, 1957–65
SAA	State Archives of Assyria
SBL	Society of Biblical Literature
SBLMS	Society of Biblical Literature Monograph Series
SBLWAW	Society of Biblical Literature Writings from the Ancient World
SJT	*Scottish Journal of Theology*
STDJ	*Studies on the Texts of the Desert of Judah*
Tanḥ.	*Tanḥuma*
TDNT	*Theological Dictionary of the New Testament.* Edited by G. Kittel and G. Friedrich. Translated by G. W. Bromiley. 10 vols. Grand Rapids, 1964–76
TDOT	*Theological Dictionary of the Old Testament.* Edited by G. J. Botterweck and H. Ringgren. Translated by J. T. Willis, G. W. Bromiley, and D. E. Green. 8 vols. Grand Rapids, 1974–2006
VT	*Vetus Testamentum*
VTSup	Supplements to Vetus Testamentum
WMANT	Wissenschaftliche Monographien zum Alten und Neuen Testament
WUNT	Wissenschaftliche Untersuchungen zum Neuen Testament
ZAW	*Zeitschrift für die alttestamentliche Wissenschaft*

Chapter 1

"WHO AM I?":
UNRAVELLING THE MYSTERY OF MOSES

1.1. *Introduction*

According to Deut 33:1–29, the final act of Moses before his death was his testamentary blessing of the individual tribes of Israel, who under his leadership have become the united people of the LORD.[1] The heading in Deut 33:1 identifies Moses as "the man of the gods/God" (אִישׁ הָאֱלֹהִים), a title that expresses extraordinary divine empowerment. The blessing's hymnic prologue opens with a celebration of the LORD's march as divine warrior from Sinai to Canaan, accompanied by celestial hosts as well as Israel's tribal militia (vv. 2–3; cf. Judg 5:4–5). Then Moses' contribution as divine agent is praised:

> Moses charged us with the Torah (as) the possession of the assembly of Jacob. Thus he became king in Jeshurun when the leaders of the people, the tribes of Israel, assembled together. (Deut 33:4–5; author's translation)

The simplest way to understand the Hebrew construction at the beginning of v. 5 is to recognize "Moses" as its implied subject. In other words, when Moses promulgated the constitutional Torah for Israel's tribal assembly he consummated his career, becoming Israel's archetypal "king."[2]

---

1. On the form of this chapter as a blessing in the context of a final testament, see Richard D. Nelson, *Deuteronomy: A Commentary* (OTL; Louisville: Westminster John Knox, 2002), 386–87. See also S. Dean McBride, "Deuteronomy, Book of," in *The New Interpreter's Dictionary of the Bible* (ed. Katharine Doob Sakenfeld; 5 vols.; Nashville: Abingdon, 2007), 2:110.

2. Although Moses seems to be the natural subject in v. 5, this view is typically rejected in favor of identifying the antecedent as God, who is the subject of vv. 2–3 or as an impersonal subject (i.e. "There arose a king..."). For a discussion of the interpretive issues, see Jeffrey H. Tigay, *Deuteronomy: The Traditional Hebrew Text with the New JPS Translation* (The JPS Torah Commentary; Philadelphia: Jewish Publication Society, 1996), 322.

Deuteronomy 33 serves as a capstone to the Pentateuch by reviewing concisely the relationship between the three major subjects of the Pentateuch: God, Israel, and Moses.[3] Israel's incomparable divine creator and patron is manifest here in solar phenomena as he leads his armies into Canaan for conquest (see also 33:26–29). Israel, as the unified assembly of various individual tribes (vv. 6–25), is "the beloved one of the LORD," singled out among the nations and entrusted with the Torah (vv. 3–4, 28). Because of God's sovereign and providential work on their behalf, the Israelite tribes are able to enjoy the material blessings of the land in security and safety from their enemies. As a result, Israel is a nation uniquely blessed by God (v. 29).

But in addition to celebrating the normative identities of God and Israel, this climactic hymn of blessing integrates a third major topic: the exaltation of Moses who is described for the first and only time in the Pentateuch as "the man of the gods/God" (cf. Josh 14:6; Ps 90). It is Moses who acts on the LORD's behalf to give the Torah to Israel. And remarkably, it is Moses who is described as Israel's founding "king." This portrayal of Moses in the conclusion to the Pentateuch differs from the typical view of Moses as God's prophet and raises the question of identifying the basic Pentateuchal portraiture of Moses. Is it appropriate to speak of Moses as a "king" according to Deut 33:5? What does it mean to speak of Moses as a "the man of God"? Is he a human being with divine qualities? What is the nature of the relationship of Moses to God and Israel?

It is the purpose of this study to address the literary character and function of the principal portraiture of Moses in the Pentateuch. The thesis that will be argued may be stated succinctly: Pentateuchal authors adapted tropes and traditions, well-attested elsewhere in biblical and other ancient Near Eastern sources, to identify Moses as an exalted, even divinized figure. While other offices or vocations also find support in biblical descriptions of Moses (especially "prophet," "priest," and "judge"), the portrayal of Moses in the likeness of a "king" serves to elevate Moses and to emphasize the preeminence of his work. Moses is depicted throughout the Pentateuch, from Exodus to Deuteronomy, as God's deputized and empowered agent, a role that is represented especially by the designations "servant" and "man of God" in the political and religious formation of Israel.

---

3. See S. Dean McBride, "The God Who Creates and Governs: Pentateuchal Foundations of Biblical Theology," in *The Forgotten God: Perspectives in Biblical Theology; Essays in Honor of Paul J. Achtemeier on the Occasion of His Seventy-Fifth Birthday* (ed. A. Andrew Das and Frank J. Matera; Louisville: Westminster John Knox, 2002), 11–28.

It must be noted here that this portrayal of Moses as a royal figure does not imply that Moses actually fills the office of "king." To use a modern example, an American biographer might portray Benjamin Franklin as "presidential" without implying that he ever held the office of president. Rather, various familiar motifs and traditions that are typically employed to depict kings in the ancient Near East are collected and adapted by Pentateuchal authors to highlight the uniqueness of Moses and his incomparable relationship with God that allowed Moses to act as God's empowered agent to rescue Israel and constitute Israel as a theocratic nation. The best and most exalted way to depict the uniqueness of Moses was through the use of those motifs and traditions that have typically been used to portray the unique status of kings in ancient Near Eastern society.

The Pentateuch and its depiction of Moses resulted from a long and complicated history of composition which is reflected in a composite portrait of Moses that was a product of different writers who assembled various pieces of traditions over time. Since the precise identification and dating of the individual strata of the Pentateuch continue to be the subject of lively and vigorous debate,[4] care will be taken not to limit the conclusions of this study to any particular model of the development of the Pentateuch. This study will seek to show that throughout this process of Pentateuchal formation, however it might be understood, various motifs have been selected and combined in order to portray Moses as an exalted royal figure in a way that is consistent with portrayals of various kings in the ancient Near East. This study will assume the existence of three major tradition complexes—the JE source[5] and the Deuteronomic/

---

4.   A helpful review of modern scholarship on the composition of the Pentateuch is Ernest W. Nicholson, *The Pentateuch in the Twentieth Century: The Legacy of Julius Wellhausen* (Oxford: Clarendon, 1998).

5.   For a convenient presentation of Noth's stratification of the Pentateuch, see Antony F. Campbell and Mark A. O'Brien, *Sources of the Pentateuch: Texts, Introductions, Annotations* (Minneapolis: Fortress, 1993). For a relatively recent presentation of Wellhausen's model, see Richard Elliot Friedman, *Who Wrote the Bible?* (2d ed.; San Francisco: HarperSanFrancisco, 1997), as well as his entry "Torah (Pentateuch)," *ABD* 6:605–21. Despite recent attempts to argue against the existence of a JE source by viewing the materials as a collection of unrelated fragments or blocks of texts or by close alignment with the Deuteronomic traditions, the present study assumes the existence of a discrete JE layer that differs substantially enough from Deuteronomy and the posited stages of the Deuteronomic traditions. See also John Van Seters, "The Report of the Yahwist's Demise Has Been Greatly Exaggerated!," in *A Farewell to the Yahwist? The Composition of the Pentateuch in Recent European Interpretation* (ed. Thomas B. Dozeman and Konrad

Deuteronomistic[6] and Priestly traditions[7] that have been formed during a period of approximately three to four centuries (late tenth century to the middle of the fifth century)—and will suggest how these three tradition complexes can be taken to represent three different stages of the development of this composite portrait of Moses as an example showing that the Pentateuchal portraiture of Moses is consistent with the portrayal of the major kings who reigned throughout this period (Sargon II, Esarhaddon, Nabonidus, and Cyrus) or whose portrayal was widely copied and studied during this period (i.e. Hammurabi). In the end, this study seeks to demonstrate the need to grapple seriously with the portrayal of Moses as a royal figure regardless of the precise model of the composition of the Pentateuch that is employed.

The initial chapter of this study will survey and assess previous studies of Moses in select classical and modern sources in order to explore the reasons why modern scholars have generally undervalued the royal portrayal of Moses. The second chapter will provide a broad overview of the principal portraiture of Moses in the Pentateuch by surveying fifteen motifs. Chapters 3 and 4 will develop eight of these motifs in context of a detailed analysis of select passages from the Pentateuch. The concluding section of this study will critique the portrayal of Moses as "prophet" and will investigate the Pentateuchal designation of Moses as "Servant" and "Man of God."

Schmid; Atlanta: Society of Biblical Literature, 2006), 143–57. Against Van Seters, I would locate the principal shaping of JE (Van Seters' "Yahwist") to the late monarchial period (ninth–eighth centuries B.C.E.) while acknowledging the work to be a composite of older "epic" traditions and supplements. See, e.g., the essay by Frank Moore Cross, "Traditional Narrative and the Reconstruction of Early Israelite Institutions," in *From Epic to Canon: History and Literature in Ancient Israel* (Baltimore: The Johns Hopkins University Press, 1998), 22–52. A detailed response to Van Seters' late dating of JE can be found in n. 21, pp. 29–31.

6. See, e.g., Steven L. McKenzie, "Deuteronomistic History," *ABD* 2:160–68, and Moshe Weinfeld, "Deuteronomy," *ABD* 2:168–83. On a Deuteronomic or proto-Deuteronomic redaction in the Tetrateuch, see, e.g., William Johnstone, "Reactivating the Chronicles Analogy in Pentateuchal Studies, with Special Reference to the Sinai Pericope in Exodus," *ZAW* 99 (1987): 16–37, reprinted in his *Chronicles and Exodus: An Analogy and Its Application* (JSOTSup 275; Sheffield: Sheffield Academic, 1998), 142–67.

7. See Frank Moore Cross, *Canaanite Myth and Hebrew Epic: Essays in the History of the Religion of Israel* (repr., Cambridge, Mass.: Harvard University Press, 1997 [1973]), 291–325, and Joseph Blenkinsopp, *The Pentateuch: An Introduction to the First Five Books of the Bible* (New York: Doubleday, 1992).

1.2. *Moses in Classical Sources*

In a detailed review of Moses scholarship up to 1960, Eva Osswald concludes:

> The history of research shows that M[oses] is still one of the most controversial figures of the OT and that the solution of the problem is strongly dependent upon the prevailing theological and methodological presuppositions of the individual scholar.[8]

A survey of selected studies of Moses in the modern period[9] confirms Osswald's assertion that the interpreter's methodology and theological views shape the way that Moses is perceived, which is a major reason why the royal portrayal of Moses has not been the object of much substantial investigation. Before providing an overview of modern treatments of the figure of Moses, this chapter will provide a general overview of the portrayal of Moses in various Hellenistic Jewish sources to provide a context for a detailed examination of the writings of Philo and Josephus. This overview will demonstrate that an exalted view of Moses as a royal, semi-divine figure was common in Hellenistic Judaism. Of course, even classical scholars are governed by the particular methodologies and presuppositions of their day. But a survey of classical treatments of Moses challenges modern scholarly treatments of Moses and suggests fresh questions that have been largely ignored in the modern period.[10] This survey will focus on selected sources produced

8. "Die Geschichte der Forschung zeigt, dass M. nach wie vor zu den umstrittensten Gestalten des AT gehört und dass die Lösung des Problems in starkem Masse von den jeweiligen theologischen und methodologischen Voraussetzungen der einzelnen Forscher abhängig ist" (Eva Osswald, "Moses," in *RGG* 4:1153).

9. The standard reviews and assessments of Moses scholarship in the modern period include Eva Osswald, *Das Bild des Mose in der kritischen alttestamentlichen Wissenschaft seit Julius Wellhausen* (Berlin: Evangelische Verlagsanstalt, 1962); Rudolf Smend, *Das Mosebild von Heinrich Ewald bis Martin Noth* (Tübingen: J. C. B. Mohr, 1959); George W. Coats, *Moses: Heroic Man, Man of God* (JSOTSup 57; Sheffield: JSOT, 1988), 9–42.

10. Other surveys and studies of classical treatments of Moses can be found in J. G. Gager, *Moses in Greco-Roman Paganism* (SBLMS; Missoula, Mont.: Scholars Press, 1972); Wayne A. Meeks, *The Prophet-King: Moses Traditions and the Johannine Christology* (NovTSup; Leiden: Brill, 1967); David Lenz Tiede, *The Charismatic Figure as Miracle Worker* (SBLDS 1; Missoula, Mont.: Scholars Press, 1972); John Lierman, *The New Testament Moses: Christian Perceptions of Moses and Israel in the Setting of Jewish Religion* (WUNT 173; Tübingen: Mohr Siebeck, 2004); Axel Graupner and Michael Wolter, eds., *Moses in Biblical and Extra-Biblical Traditions* (BZAW 372; New York: de Gruyter, 2007).

between the third century B.C.E. and third century C.E. in order to show that Moses was typically presented in an exalted way as a royal or semi-divine figure.[11]

1.2.a. *The Portrayal of Moses in Early Hellenistic Sources*

The earliest extant portrayal of Moses outside the Old Testament is found in Sirach, composed in Hebrew some time in the third and second centuries B.C.E. In a long poem that praises the leaders of Israel (Sir 44:1–50:24), three glorious figures are singled out: Moses, Aaron, and Phinehas. Aaron, exalted by God, is "a holy man like Moses" and glorified by God (45:6, 20). Phinehas is "third in glory" (45:23–26). But of these three, Moses receives the highest praise:

> From his descendants the Lord brought forth a godly man, who found favor in the sight of all and was beloved by God and people, Moses, whose memory is blessed. He made him equal in glory to the holy ones, and made him great, to the terror of his enemies. By his words he performed swift miracles; the Lord glorified him in the presence of kings. He gave him commandments for his people, and revealed to him his glory. For his faithfulness and meekness he consecrated him, choosing him out of all humankind. He allowed him to hear his voice, and led him into the dark cloud, and gave him the commandments face to face, the law of life and knowledge, so that he might teach Jacob the covenant and Israel his decrees. (Sir 44:23b–45:5)

Here Moses is portrayed in the nexus between God and Israel. He is "glorified by God" and equal in glory to the "holy ones" (lit. אלהים). As a result, Moses is empowered to perform miracles and to be a source of "terror" to his enemies. Moses is able to approach God "into the dark cloud" to "hear his voice" that allows Moses to receive the commandments from God that he transmits and teaches to Israel. The biblical passage underlying this exaltation of Moses in Sir 45:2 is Exod 7:1. Scholars have reconstructed אלהים as the term translated "holy ones."[12] Yet, given the designation of Moses as אלהים in Exod 7:1 (also 4:16), it is better to translate Sir 45:2 as "He made him equal in glory to God."[13]

---

11. Gager, *Moses*, 162. See also Philo, *On the Life of Moses* 1.2.

12. The Hebrew text from the Cairo Geniza is available in Pancratius C. Beentjes, *The Book of Ben Sira in Hebrew: A Text Edition of All Extant Hebrew Manuscripts and a Synopsis of All Parallel Hebrew Ben Sira Texts* (VTSup 68; New York: Brill, 1997).

13. See Larry W. Hurtado, *One God, One Lord: Early Christian Devotion and Ancient Jewish Monotheism* (Philadelphia: Fortress, 1988), 56, and Crispin H. T. Fletcher-Louis, *All the Glory of Adam: Liturgical Anthropology in the Dead Sea Scrolls, Studies on the Texts of the Desert of Judah* (STDJ 42; Boston: Brill, 2002), 136–37.

Another indication that Exod 7:1 underlies Sirach's description of Moses is the glorification of Moses "in the presence of kings" (Sir 45:3), in reference to the role of Moses as "God" to Pharaoh. Larry Hurtado notes that the equation of Moses with "God" in Sirach reflects a widespread use of Exod 7:1 in Palestine and Alexandria before the time of Philo and that "these statements are hints that a body of tradition glorifying Moses in such superlative terms was familiar to the writer."[14]

An exalted portrayal of Moses as a royal and semi-divine figure can also be found in the Jewish writings of Artapanus and Ezekiel the Tragedian at approximately the same time as Sirach (third–second century B.C.E.).[15] On Moses' royal identity, Artapanus[16] writes:

> Raguel[17] wanted to wage war against the Egyptians because he wished to return Moses from exile and thereby establish the throne for his daughter and son-in-law. But Moses would not hear of it because he had regard for his own people.[18]

The rationale for Moses' refusal of royal rule over Egypt is not clear. Does Moses refuse because he is destined to rule his own people instead? In addition to the royal vocation of Moses, Artapanus stresses his super-human nature by equating the name Moses with Mousaios:

> [She] took as her own a child of one of the Jews and named him Moses (Μώϋσος). When he became a man, he was called Mousaios (Μουσαῖος) by the Greeks. This Moses became the teacher of Orpheus.[19]

14. Hurtado, *One God*, 56–57.

15. Their works survive only in the form of quotations from the work *Concerning the Jews* by Alexander Polyhistor, a Roman writer in the mid-first century B.C.E. Portions of this work are preserved in the writings of Eusebius and Clement of Alexandria.

16. For the Greek text and an annotated English translation (as well as discussion of critical issues), see Carl R. Holladay, *Fragments from Hellenistic Jewish Authors*. Vol. 1, *Historians* (Chico, Calif.: Scholars Press, 1983), 189–243. Recent discussions of Artapanus include John M. G. Barclay, *Jews in the Mediterranean Diaspora from Alexander to Trajan (323 BCE–117 CE)* (Edinburgh: T. & T. Clark, 1996), 127–32; John J. Collins, *Between Athens and Jerusalem: Jewish Identity in the Hellenistic Diaspora* (2d ed; Biblical Resource Series; Grand Rapids: Eerdmans, 2000), 37–46; and Rob Kugler, "Hearing the Story of Moses in Ptolemaic Egypt: Artapanus Accommodates the Tradition," in *The Wisdom of Egypt: Jewish, Early Christian, and Gnostic Essays in Honour of Gerard P. Luttikhuizen* (ed. Anthony Hilhorst and George H. Van Kooten; AGJU 59; Boston: Brill, 2005), 67–80.

17. Raguel reflects the Old Greek (Ραγουηλ) spelling of "Reuel" (MT רעואל), the father-in-law of Moses, due to an earlier pronunciation of the phoneme *gh* which has since merged with ע.

18. Holladay, *Historians*, 214–17.

19. Ibid., 208–9.

On the identity of Orpheus, Holladay notes:

> In some traditions Orpheus is the father [of Musaois], in others the master (teacher) of Musaios; in either case, Musaios was usually subordinate to Orpheus. Reversing this traditional order was a small price to pay for the associative value attaching to the name Orpheus… Orphism was not only ancient and widespread, but in Egypt was a serious competitor of the Dionysus cult. By asserting that Moses is the teacher of Orpheus, Artapanus may very well be taking an indirect slap at the Dionysus cult while at the same time asserting the priority, and therefore the superiority of Judaism over Orphism as a religious system possessing "holy writings."[20]

In addition to asserting Moses' superiority to Orpheus, Artapanus also notes the equation of Moses with the god Hermes:

> Moses was loved by the masses, and being deemed worthy of divine honor by the priests, he was called Hermes because of his ability to interpret the sacred writings.[21]

Finally, Moses' superiority over the gods of Egypt is seen through the power wielded through his rod. With this rod, Moses strikes the Nile, causing the flooding of Egypt, which, according to Artapanus, is the origin of the regular flooding of the Nile![22] He later shows Moses' superiority over Isis, "because the earth is Isis and it produced these wonders when it was struck by the rod." As a result, "the Egyptians set up a rod in every temple."[23]

It is important to note, however, that for Artapanus the divinity and power of Moses are not intrinsic to his own being as a full-fledged deity. Rather, Moses is commissioned and empowered by God. Thus, in response to Moses' prayer for the release of his people from suffering, a "divine voice" commissioned Moses to "wage war against Egypt."[24] Later, Moses is freed from prison through a miraculous opening of the doors at night, attributed to the "will of God" in Clement's citation of Artapanus, and Moses declares the name of God into the ear of the king of Egypt, who "fell over speechless. But Moses picked him up and he

20. Carl R. Holladay, *Theios Aner in Hellenistic-Judaism: A Critique of the Use of This Category in New Testament Christology* (SBLDS 40; Missoula, Mont.: Scholars Press, 1977), 224–25.
21. Ibid., 208–11.
22. Ibid., 221.
23. Ibid., 223.
24. Ibid., 217.

came back to life again."[25] Moses later wrote the name on a tablet, which led to the death of a priest who "showed contempt for what was written on the tablet."[26] Upon hearing the "divine voice," Moses used his rod to strike the sea and divide it.[27] Apparently for Artapanus, Moses functions as God's agent, empowered by the rod and his knowledge of God's name.

The exaltation of Moses to a position of royal power as a semi-divine being is brought out forcefully in the Greek drama *Exagoge* written by Ezekiel the Tragedian.[28] In a dream sequence, God gives Moses his throne, diadem, and scepter, apparently so that Moses can act as God's vice-regent. Raguel interprets the dream by predicting that Moses will assume the position of kingship that will give Moses the authority to rule and judge humankind (not just Israel!) and the prophetic ability to "see things past, present, and future." Regardless of the difficulty of interpreting the dream due to the symbolism and fragmentary nature of the drama, it is clear that the drama portrays the heavenly exaltation of Moses to a position of royal power, and that prophecy represents an aspect of this royal power.[29] As we will see, Ezekiel the Tragedian shares basic agreement with Philo in viewing Moses primarily as a semi-divine royal figure with prophecy functioning as an attribute of the royal office (cf. 2 Sam 23:1–4).[30]

The widespread view of Moses as the "leader" (ἡγεμών) and "ruler" (ἄρχων) of Israel is attested by Thallus in the middle to the late first century C.E.:[31]

---

25. Ibid., 219.

26. Ibid., 221.

27. Ibid., 225.

28. An annotated translation, as well as discussions of text, authorship, and dating, can be found in Carl R. Holladay, *Fragments from Hellenistic Jewish Authors.* Vol. 2, *Poets* (Atlanta: Scholars Press, 1989), 301–529. See also Howard Jacobson, *The* Exagoge *of Ezekiel* (New York: Cambridge University Press, 1983), and Pierluigi Lanfranchi, *L'Exagoge d'Ezéchiel le Tragique: Introduction, texte, traduction et commentaire* (Boston: Brill, 2006).

29. For discussions of the different interpretations of the drama, see Hurtado, *One God*, 58–59, and especially the recent detailed discussion of Lierman, *The New Testament Moses*, 90–102.

30. On Philo's use of Ezekiel's work, see Pierlugi Lanfranchi, "Reminiscences of Ezekiel's *Exagoge* in Philo's De Vita Mosis," in Graupner and Wolter, eds., *Moses in Biblical and Extra-Biblical Traditions*, 144–50.

31. Scholars have debated the identity of Thallus as a pagan, a Samaritan, or even as a Hellenistic Jew. See the discussion in Holladay, *Historians*, 343–44.

> For in the time of Ogyges and Inachus, whom some of your poets suppose to have been earth-born, Moses is mentioned as the leader (ἡγεμών) and ruler (ἄρχων) of the Jewish nation.[32]

Through citation of numerous sources, Thallus indicates clearly that his designation of Moses as "leader" and "ruler" of the Jewish people was a common designation of his day:

> For in this way he is mentioned both by Polemon in the first book of his Hellenics, and by Apion son of Posidonius in his book against the Jews, and in the fourth book of his history, where he says that during the reign of Inachus over Argos the Jews revolted from Amasis king of the Egyptian, and that Moses led them. And Ptolemaeus the Mendesian, in relating the history of Egypt, concurs in all this. And those who write the Athenian history, Hellanicus and Philochorus (the author of The Attic History), Castor and Thallus, and Alexander Polyhistor, and also the very well informed writers on Jewish affairs, Philo and Josephus, have mentioned Moses as a very ancient and time-honoured prince (ἄρχων) of the Jews.[33]

Additional evidence for the widespread view of Moses as Israel's "leader" or "ruler" in the first century C.E. includes the designation of Moses as ἄρχων three times in Stephen's speech in Acts 7:27, 35 that is based on the Septuagint version of Exod 2:14.

The exalted view of Moses as a semi-divine and royal figure is attested or assumed at various places in the New Testament.[34] Perhaps the clearest depiction of Moses as a superhuman figure is the account of Jesus' transfiguration (Matt 17:1–13; Mark 9:2–8; Luke 9:28–36). Thus John Lierman comments,

> The account of the Transfiguration may be the strongest NT evidence that the Jews were prepared to view Moses as a supernaturally active figure… active and alive in heaven… The Transfiguration may be taken at face value as evidence merely for a Jewish belief in the availability of Moses, and concomitantly as evidence for viewing Moses as a divine or similarly glorified figure.[35]

And he also says,

32. Ibid., 362–63.
33. Ibid., 363.
34. A detailed examination of the portrayal of Moses in the New Testament within the Greco-Roman and ancient Jewish settings can be found in John Lierman's *The New Testament Moses*. Other studies of the figure of Moses in the New Testament include Meeks, *The Prophet-King*; David M. Hay, "Moses Through New Testament Spectacles," *Int* 44 (1990): 240–52.
35. Lierman, *The New Testament Moses*, 195–96.

The Transfiguration in particular appears to confirm such a view of Moses among the early Christians…describing Moses not only in life but especially at and after his death, as a glorified figure, a spiritual figure, one thought to be active on behalf of his people from beyond the grave.[36]

The view of Moses as "king" or "ruler" is also attested in the New Testament. Wayne Meeks has shown that two distinct traditions, the prophet and the king, have been combined in the portrayal of Moses in traditions he traced throughout various documents from the Greco-Roman world. This view of Moses as a "prophet-king" clarifies the juxtaposition of the prophetic and royal motifs in John 6:14–15, where after the miracle of the manna, the crowd perceives that Jesus is the "prophet who is to come into the world" and then attempts to make Jesus king by force.[37]

The most explicit portrayal of Moses as a semi-divine ruler is found in Luke–Acts. For example, the charge against Stephen of blasphemy against God and Moses in Acts 6:11 indicates the close association between the two and provides the occasion for Stephen's lengthy speech in Acts 7:20–44.[38] Rather than a balanced summary of the various phases in the history of Israel, the figure of Moses occupies one half of the speech (25 of 52 verses), which means that this speech is essentially an exposition of the career and rejection of Moses. In a refutation of the charge of blasphemy against God and Moses, Stephen responds to the Jewish mob by paralleling their rejection of Jesus with the rejection of Moses. In the section on Moses, Stephen applies three titles to Moses— λυτρωτής ("redeemer"), ἄρχων ("ruler"), and δικαστής ("judge")—on the basis of which Lierman concludes that here Moses is identified "explicitly as Israel's sovereign."[39]

The portrayal of Moses as a semi-divine and royal figure is also attested in a poem cited by various Christian writers from the third to

36. Ibid., 230.

37. For a study of the Markan version of this episode, see especially Joel Marcus, *Mark 1–8: A New Translation with Introduction and Commentary* (AB 27; New York: Doubleday, 1999), 381, 385, 389–90. The description of the crowd there as "sheep without a shepherd" may allude to the portrayal of Moses as a shepherd, a common royal designation, in Num 27:16–20 and Isa 63:11. For a detailed discussion, see Lierman, *The New Testament Moses*, 108–10.

38. See the section "Blasphemy of Moses" in Lierman, *The New Testament Moses*, 226–29. Lierman notes that Acts 6:11 uses a single preposition to govern the two objects of blasphemy as an indication that God and Moses are both objects of blasphemy. The close juxtaposition of God and Moses recalls Exod 14:31 and possibly also Num 21:5, 7, where the people spoke "against God and Moses."

39. Ibid., 113.

fifth centuries C.E.[40] This poem contains an address by Orpheus to his child Musaeus. One recension of this poem is referred to as the "Mosaic recension," since it contains additional lines that clearly refer to Moses.[41] John Lierman raises the possibility that the Mosaic version of this poem "describes the divinization of Moses," who is "portrayed in celestial terms, enthroned in heaven."[42] He notes that the poem begins with the reference to the unique privilege of Moses to see God: "For now one among mortals could see the ruler of men." A couple of lines later, this individual is described as one "of the Chaldean race" who was an "expert in following the sun's course and the movement of the spheres around the earth," perhaps a reference to Moses' ability to count the number of stars from the throne in Ezekiel's vision.[43] These clear references to Moses suggest identifying him as the individual who is seated

> on a golden throne, and earth stands under his feet. And he stretches out his right hand upon the extremities of the ocean; and the mountain base trembles with rage... And it is not possible to endure his mighty force. But in every way he himself is heavenly, and on earth brings all things to completion, since he controls their beginning, as well as their middle and end... Now to say anything other than this is not allowed, indeed I shudder at the very thought; from on high he rules over everything in order.[44]

Lierman rightly notes that the divinization of Moses should receive serious consideration and would fit with the emphasis on the divinity of Moses in a wide range of other texts.[45] This poem provides additional confirmation that the depiction of the divinity and royal rule of Moses is a standard feature of the classical sources as late as the fifth century C.E.

This brief overview of the classical sources suggests that an exalted view of Moses as a semi-divine and royal figure was common in the world of Hellenistic Judaism. This exaltation of Moses is part of a widespread exegetical tradition based on texts such as Exod 7:1 (and 4:16) and Deut 33:1, 5. While this overview is limited, it should be noted that this exalted view of Moses is not confined to the period under

40. Carl R. Holladay, *Fragments from Hellenistic Jewish Authors*. Vol. 4, *Orphica* (Atlanta: Scholars Press, 1996), 43.

41. For the text, translation, and commentary of the "Mosaic recension," see ibid., 194–218.

42. Lierman, *The New Testament Moses*, 235–36.

43. Ibid., 235. Lierman also notes parallels to Philo, who describes Moses as a "Chaldean" who learned astronomy from the surrounding nations and Egypt.

44. Holladay, *Orphica*, 195.

45. Lierman, *The New Testament Moses*, 236.

investigation but continues in Samaritan[46] and Rabbinic Judaism.[47] The next two sections will provide a closer analysis of the portrayal of Moses in the writings of Philo and Josephus.

1.2.b. *Philo's Portrait of Moses: The Ideal Hellenistic Philosopher-King*
Assuming a readership of non-Jews and/or Jews with little familiarity with the content of the Pentateuch, Philo (ca. 20 B.C.E.–50 C.E.) wrote *On the Life of Moses* as a preparation for his exposition and explanation of the Pentateuch.[48] Philo's principal purpose is to present Moses as the ideal king. In Philo's own words, the first volume

46. For a more detailed analysis of the portrayal of Moses in Samaritan sources, see the surveys by Meeks, *The Prophet-King*, 216–57, and John MacDonald, "Moses, Lord of the World," in *The Theology of the Samaritans* (London: SCM, 1964), 147–222. It is important to note here that Meeks has shown the presence of the tradition of Moses' enthronement as "God and King" in the Samaritan sources. In particular, he notes the application of royal images to Moses, who, in *Memar Marqah*, a Samaritan theological work from the third to fourth century C.E., at the revelation at Sinai is "vested" with God's name, "crowned with the light" (*M. Marq.* 2.12), and receives a "robe of light" and a rod as a symbol of royal sovereignty (*M. Marq.* 1.2). Meeks notes that the Sinai revelation was also viewed as a deification of Moses (*M. Marq.* 5.3: "He ascended from human status to that of the angels"). A helpful introduction to and exposition of *Memar Marqah* can be found in Robert T. Anderson and Terry Giles, *Tradition Kept: The Literature of the Samaritans* (Peabody, Mass.: Hendrickson, 2005), 265–358.
47. Rabbinic literature includes a number of fantastic portrayals of Moses. Several examples can be found in the tractate *Soṭah* (*b. Soṭah* 11a–14a; many of the features of Moses in *Soṭah* can also be found in *Exod. Rab.* 1.19–26) where Moses was born circumcised and without pain to a 130-year-old mother after a three month pregnancy and was walking and talking at the age of three days. At his birth, the whole house was filled with light, and as an infant he spoke with a child's voice. *Exodus Rabbah* includes a variant version of Moses taking Pharaoh's crown ("He [Moses] used to take the crown of Pharaoh and place it upon his own head, as he was destined to do when he became great") as a midrashic explanation for Moses' speech impediment. On the portrayal of Moses in Rabbinic literature, see the classic studies by Meeks: "Moses as God and King," in *Religions in Antiquity: Essays in Memory of Erwin Ramsdell Goodenough* (ed. J. Neusner; Leiden: Brill, 1968), 43–67, and *The Prophet-King*, 182–90. Meeks shows that the tradition of Moses as a king was a basic assumption in a number of wide-ranging Rabbinic sources rooted in the designation of Moses as a king in Deut 33:5. On the tension between the divine and human natures of Moses, see *Peṭirat Mosheh*, translated in Rella Kushelevsky, *Moses and the Angel of Death* (New York: Lang, 1995).
48. Kenneth Schenck, *A Brief Guide to Philo* (Louisville: Westminster John Knox, 2005), 100.

dealt with the birth and nurture of Moses; also with his education and
career as a ruler (ἀρχή), in which capacity his conduct was not merely
blameless but highly praiseworthy; also with the works which he
performed in Egypt and during the journeys both at the Red Sea and in
the wilderness...further, with the troubles which he successfully sur-
mounted, and with his partial distribution of territories to the combatants.
(*Mos.* 2.1)[49]

In the second volume of Moses, Philo departs from the chronological
scheme of the first volume in favor of a topical portrayal of Moses as
lawgiver (*Mos.* 2.12–65), high priest (2.66–186), and prophet (2.187–
292). It is clear that Philo views these offices as an extension of the
duties of a ruler. Philo concludes the first volume:

We have now told the story of Moses' actions in his capacity of king
(κατὰτὴνβασιλείαν). We must next deal with all that he achieved by his
powers as high priest and legislator, powers which he possessed as the
most fitting accompaniments of kingship. (*Mos.* 1.334)

In other words, Moses' excellence in these three offices provides additional support for viewing Moses as the perfect king.[50] Philo's understanding of the relationship between the offices of king, lawgiver, high
priest, and prophet is not clear. In the opening section of Book 2, he
states that these four functions are "combined in the same person" (*Mos.*
2.3) and "Beautiful and harmonious is the union of these four facul-
ties...to have one is to have all" (*Mos.* 2.7). He later clarifies that these
four roles (kingship, lawgiver, high priest, and prophet) are "four
adjuncts to the truly perfect ruler (ἡγεμών)" (*Mos.* 2.187). Thus the two-
volume work as a whole is apparently structured in such a way as to
present Moses as the perfect king who excels in the act of ruling, giving
legislation, officiating as the high priest, and transmitting prophetic
oracles to the people.

    In the first volume, Philo models Moses after the ideal Hellenistic king
as described by Plato.[51] Philo quotes a line from Plato's *Republic* in the
introduction to the second volume of his *Moses*: "For it has been said,

    49.   Greek and English citations of Philo's *Moses* will be taken from F. H. Colson,
trans., *Philo* (LCL; Cambridge, Mass.: Harvard University Press, 1935).
    50.   Cf. John Hyrcanus, who filled the roles of king, priest, and prophet, accord-
ing to Josephus, *Ant.* 13.299.
    51.   The seminal study is Erwin R. Goodenough, "The Political Philosophy of
Hellenistic Kingship," *Yale Classical Studies* 1 (1928): 55–102. See also Goodenough's chapter "Moses as Presented to the Gentile Inquirer," in his *By Light,
Light: The Mystic Gospel of Hellenistic Judaism* (New Haven: Yale University
Press, 1935), 180–98.

not without good reason, that states can only make progress in well-being if either kings are philosophers or philosophers are kings" (*Mos.* 2.2). Feldman points out that the various subjects of Moses' education in Egypt (including arithmetic, geometry, poetry, music, philosophy, astronomy, and Assyrian literature [*Mos.* 1.23]) "strikingly resemble those of the philosopher-king in Plato's *Republic*."[52]

In the first volume of *Moses*, Philo establishes the credentials of Moses as the king *par excellence* through his genealogy, birth, childhood, education in the Egyptian royal court, and his handsome appearance. Philo, as well as Josephus, portrays Moses as the adopted son of Pharaoh's daughter and heir to the throne of his grandfather. Unlike Josephus, Philo reports that Pharaoh's daughter deceived her father by making herself appear to be pregnant in order to raise Moses as her actual son and legitimate heir to the throne of Egypt (*Mos.* 1.19, 32). As in Josephus, Moses' act of killing an Egyptian (*Mos.* 1.32–46) is interpreted by the king of Egypt, especially at the instigation of his advisers, to mean that Moses intended to seize the throne and "get the kingship before the time comes" (*Mos.* 1.46).

After his perceived birth to Pharaoh's daughter, Moses was often called the "young king" by the general Egyptian population (ὀνέος βασιλεύς, *Mos.* 1.32) and received a royal education (*Mos.* 1.8, 20). Much of Philo's extra-biblical material about the early life of Moses centers around the nature of his education and his qualities of "temperance and self-control" which kept his passions and desires in check (*Mos.* 1.18–31). In particular, Feldman notes that the subjects listed by Philo (arithmetic, geometry, rhythms, harmony, metrical theory, and the whole subject of music) "are the very subjects, indeed in that very order that Plato (*Resp.* 7.521C–531C) prescribes for the higher education of his philosopher-king."[53] Since Philo reflects the tradition that Greek philosophy derived from Moses, he cannot have Moses learning from the Greeks,[54] and instead portrays Moses' education as recollection of the subjects he had already known at an unusually early age. Moses even challenged teachers from various provinces of Egypt as well as Greece with difficult problems (1.21).[55] Taking his cue from Plato that the ideal ruler should have a handsome appearance (*Resp.* 5.473D), Philo expands the description of Moses as טוב ("good, beautiful") in Exod 2:2 by

52. Louis H. Feldman, "Philo's View of Moses' Birth and Upbringing," *CBQ* 64 (2002): 281.
53. Ibid., 273.
54. Ibid., 272–73.
55. As phrased by Goodenough (*By Light*, 182), Moses was "self-taught."

portraying him as having an appearance at birth that was "more than ordinary goodliness" (*Mos.* 1.9) and when the infant Moses was examined by Pharaoh's daughter "from head to foot, she approved of his beauty and fine condition" (*Mos.* 1.15).[56]

Philo also explains the role of Moses as king in two important sections in the first volume of his *Moses*. First, after Moses fled from Egypt and married into Jethro's family, Philo uses the burning bush episode as the event that commissions Moses to be the leader of the Israelite people. Philo explains Moses' vocation as a shepherd in Exod 3 as a training for his future role as king:

> Moses took charge of the sheep and tended them, thus receiving his first lesson in the command of others; for the shepherd's business is a training-ground and a preliminary exercise in kingship for one who is destined to command the herd of mankind... [F]or the chase of wild animals is a drilling-ground for the general in fighting the enemy, and the care and supervision of tame animals is a schooling for the king in dealing with his subjects, and therefore kings are called "shepherds of their people," not as a term of reproach but as the highest honor. (*Mos.* 1.60–61)[57]

As Moses is shepherding the flock, he encounters God at the burning bush, who commissions Moses to be the "leader" (ἡγεμών) who will guide the people from Egypt to "another home" (*Mos.* 1.71).[58]

Between the escape from Egypt and guidance through the wilderness, Philo includes a lengthy exposition of the exaltation of Moses (*Mos.* 1.148–62). The high portrayal of Moses in this section has generated much discussion:

56.   See also the effect of Moses' appearance on Jethro (*Mos.* 1.59) and the Israelite community after Moses' descent from Sinai (*Mos.* 1.59). Feldman ("Moses' Birth," 279) also cites the portrayal of the beauty of Moses in Josephus (*Ant.* 2.224, 231) and Herodotus' portrayal of Cyrus (*Hist.* 1.112).

57.   Cf. *Tanḥ.* on Exod 3:1, which compares the shepherding vocation of David with Moses: "The Holy One, blessed be He, said to him: 'You have been found trustworthy with regard to sheep; now I shall entrust My flock to you that you may shepherd it, as it is said: Thou didst lead Thy people like a flock, by the hand of Moses and Aaron (Ps. 77:21)'" (Samuel A. Berman, *Midrash Tanhuma-Yelammedenu: An English Translation of Genesis and Exodus from the Printed Version of Tanhuma-Yelammedenu with an Introduction, Notes, and Indexes* [Hoboken, N.J.: KTAV, 1996], 323).

58.   It is interesting to note that while Josephus refrains from characterizing Moses as a king, he apparently takes over and expands Philo's designation of Moses as a general and a leader in his version of the burning-bush story.

> For, since God judged him worthy to appear as a partner (κοινωνός) of His own possessions, He gave into his hands the whole world as a portion well fitted for his heir... For if, as the proverb says, what belongs to friends is common, and the prophet is called the friend (φιλός) of God, it would follow that he shares also God's possessions... Again, was not the joy of his partnership with the Father and Maker of all magnified also by the honour of being deemed worthy to bear the same title? For he was named god and king (θεός καὶ βασιλεύς) of the whole nation, and entered, we are told, into the darkness where God was... Thus he beheld what is hidden from the sight of mortal nature, and, in himself and his life displayed for all to see...a model for those who are willing to copy it. (*Mos.* 1.155–58)

Philo's apparent equation of Moses with God is unlikely due to Philo's worldview of the gulf between humanity and God, which is the underlying principle behind his passionate rejection of Gaius Caligula's claim to divinity in his treatise *On the Embassy to Gaius* (*Legatio ad Gaium*). There, Philo famously claimed that "sooner could God change into a man than a man into God" (*Embassy*, 117). And while Philo views Moses as a perfect man—"the greatest and most perfect of men" (*Mos.* 1.1; cf. also *Alleg. Interp.* 3.134); the "holiest of man ever yet born" (*Mos.* 2.192)—Moses is clearly a mortal who faces limitations common to all humans. Feldman notes, for example, that Philo attributes to Moses' human nature his inability to devise a punishment for the Israelite who blasphemed God (Lev 24:10–12; *Mos.* 2.197).[59] Philo tones down any speculation of an apotheosis of Moses upon his death by noting that Moses did die in accordance with his human nature (*Mos.* 2.288–91) without alluding to an escaping from death in Josephus.

However, Philo does describe Moses in the most exalted way possible without violating the transcendent reality of God by closely associating Moses with God (*Mos.* 1.158). Moses is the "heir" and is given the "whole world." He is the "partner" with God and a "friend" to God. Feldman notes that the term "friend" was "bestowed by the emperor upon those who were nearest and dearest" and cites the example of Caligula giving this title to Agrippa.[60] Thus in this passage Moses stands in an intermediary position between human beings and the transcendent God. As God's heir, partner, and friend, he rules as a vice-regent and serves as a model for the people to imitate. So Borgen comments,

59. Louis H. Feldman, "The Death of Moses, According to Philo," *EstBib* 60 (2002): 237.
60. Ibid., 243.

> Moses' kingship made him an intermediary between God and men. His
> life imitates the visionary world and his subjects imitate him. This double
> imitation is a commonplace in descriptions of Hellenistic kingship...
> Thus Philo employs midrashic tradition about Moses' ascent of Sinai and
> interprets it on the basis of Hellenistic kingship theory, while drawing on
> Platonism and Stoicism. These were his ideals for the Jewish nation and
> its universal role in the world.[61]

This view of Moses as divine intermediary fits well within Philo's
Middle Platonic view of reality that modifies the two-tiered view of
Platonism (the world of ideas and the world of senses) by the addition of
a third, supreme level of a transcendent God (borrowed from Neo-
Pythagoreanism's emphasis on a supreme transcendent principle). This
new level provides the pattern for the world of ideas that now functions
as an intermediate level between God and the world of the senses.[62] In
this intermediate level, Stoicism provides the concept of *logos* which for
Philo functions as the image, or agent of the transcendent God. Philo's
view of the divinity of Moses does not mean he equates Moses with the
transcendent God. Rather, the placement of Moses in the intermediate
level as a divine agent fits perfectly within Philo's basic philosophical
and theological worldview.[63] Along these lines Schenck comments,

> It is true that Philo does at times use the word *god* in relation to entities
> other than the supreme God. He can thus refer to the stars and heavenly
> bodies as "visible gods perceptible to our senses" (*Opif.* 27), or even to
> Moses as "god" to the Jewish people (*Mos.* 1.158). But in these instances,
> Philo was clearly using the word in a subordinate, more limited, even
> figurative sense that seems to stand within the parameters of mainstream
> Jewish monotheism.[64]

In a study that investigates the historical problem of early Christian
veneration of Jesus alongside God within the framework of first-century
Judaism, Hurtado argues that while God alone functions as the object of
cultic veneration and devotion, ancient Judaism nevertheless was able to

61. Peder Borgen, "Philo of Alexandria," in *Jewish Writings of the Second Temple Period: Apocrypha, Pseudepigrapha, Qumran Sectarian Writings, Philo, Josephus* (ed. Michael E. Stone; Philadelphia: Fortress, 1984), 268. See also the similar conclusion drawn by Meeks, "Moses," 355.
62. See "Philo's View of the World," in Schenck, *Philo*, 49–72. See also the detailed and informative chapter "Hellenistic-Roman Philosophies," in Everett Ferguson, *Backgrounds to Early Christianity* (3d ed.; Grand Rapids: Eerdmans, 2003), 319–95.
63. More precisely, Feldman ("Death of Moses," 244) claims that Moses functions as an image of the logos in Philo.
64. Schenck, *Philo*, 44.

accommodate a variety of divine beings within this view without violating the traditional monotheistic belief of devotion to the one God.[65] These divine beings include personified divine attributes (wisdom and *logos*), exalted patriarchs (Enoch and Moses), and angels. Hurtado uses the term "divine agency" to describe these heavenly figures who occupy "a position second only to God and acting on God's behalf in some major capacity"[66] in the literature of post-exilic Judaism. And he characterizes a "divine agent" as a chief agent "associated with God in a unique capacity in the manifestation of his sovereignty," who "seems to function more or less as God's grand vizier or chief representative in terms of general authority and power."[67] With regard to Moses, Hurtado concludes that Philo's depiction of Moses in *Mos.* 1.158–59

> represents his own particular interpretation of the image of Moses as God's chief agent and that he is drawing upon a tradition of divine agency in which Moses was the featured figure and was regarded as God's viceroy or grand vizier.[68]

The office of the Hellenistic king provides for Philo a contemporaneous conceptual category to portray Moses as a semi-divine, intermediary agent rooted on the basis of his interpretation of Exod 7:1, which is cited at least ten times in Philo.[69]

1.2.c. *Josephus' Portrayal of Moses*[70]

Of all the illustrious figures in Israel's past, Moses alone receives extended treatment in a preface to Josephus' exhaustive twenty-volume history of the Jews, *The Antiquities of the Jews* (*Ant.* 1.1–26).[71] In this opening section, Josephus portrays Moses as a "lawgiver" or "legislator"

---

65. Hurtado, *One God*.
66. Ibid., 17.
67. Ibid., 20.
68. Ibid., 60.
69. For a detailed discussion of Exod 7:1 (and Exod 4:16) in Philo, see especially Holladay, *Theios Aner*, 108–29.
70. The standard, systematic study of the profile of Moses in the works of Josephus is Louis H. Feldman, "Josephus' Portrait of Moses," *JQR* 82 (1992): 285–328, "Josephus' Portrait of Moses: Part Two," *JQR* 83 (1992): 7–50, and "Josephus' Portrait of Moses: Part Three," *JQR* 83 (1992): 301–30. These three essays are now available in a revised form in Louis H. Feldman, *Josephus's Interpretation of the Bible* (Berkeley: University of California Press, 1998), 374–442.
71. The primary English translation consulted for this dissertation is Louis H. Feldman, *Judean Antiquities 1–4: Translation and Commentary* (Boston: Brill, 2000). Citations of the Greek text are from H. St. J. Thackeray, trans., *Josephus* (LCL; Cambridge, Mass.: Harvard University Press, 1930).

(νομθέτης, *Ant.* 1.6, 15, 18, 20, 23, 24; cf. *Ap.* 2.165) who promulgates Torah as a "constitution" or "polity" (πολιτεία) for the Jewish people.[72] In his attempt to establish Moses as a reliable lawgiver qualified to transmit a polity that far predates the founding of the various states and institutions in Greco-Roman society, Josephus must portray Moses as having a connection with God that is more direct that any other individual. At the same time Josephus wanted to avoid the implication— apparently to refute rumors circulating among even Jewish circles—that Moses had become a divine figure like other Greco-Roman leaders and heroes. Thus Josephus has the contradictory task of portraying Moses as a human being with a divine nature that allows him access to God.

Despite the antiquity of the events that predate the life of Moses and Josephus' obvious bias against supernatural phenomena,[73] Josephus argues that Moses serves as a reliable source by virtue of his direct encounter with God. Otherwise, Moses would have had to fabricate events that occurred in "ages so long and so remote" (*Ant.* 1.16). Thus

> Our lawgiver comprehended His nature worthily and has always attributed to Him deeds befitting His power, preserving the discourse about him pure from every unseemly mythology that is found among others... [T]hat man considered it the most necessary thing of all for the one who intends to regulate his life properly and to prescribe laws for others first to understand the nature of God... For neither would the lawgiver, if he lacked this contemplation, ever have had proper understanding... (*Ant.* 1.15, 19–20)

Josephus does not explain what he means by Moses' contemplation of God's nature. Josephus is not referring to the mere observation of God's creation, which anyone can do.[74] Rather, Josephus' portrayal of Moses enjoying a special encounter with God throughout his work indicates that Moses had a more direct encounter with the nature of God than other humans. In his presentation of God's commissioning Moses as a general and a leader at the burning bush, Josephus suggests that Moses is able to

72. On the description of the Torah legislation as πολιτεία, see *Ant.* 1.5, 10; 4.184, 193–94, 196, 198, 302, 310, and 312; Feldman, *Judean Antiquities 1–4*, xxiv–xxix, 279; S. Dean McBride, "Polity of the Covenant People: The Book of Deuteronomy," *Int* 41 (1987): 229–31.

73. Josephus customarily provides a rational explanation for the miraculous episodes in the Hebrew Bible (e.g. crossing of the sea, quail) and often qualifies his observations with the refrain "But concerning these matters each will decide as it seems best to him" (*Ant.* 1.108; 2.348; 3.81, 322, etc.). See the discussion of this phrase in Feldman, *Judean Antiquities 1–4*, 39.

74. Contra Feldman, *Judean Antiquities 1–4*, 8.

interact with God in a place infused with divine presence. Moses was leading the flock to Sinai, which was pristine pastureland avoided by shepherds "because of the belief that God spent time there" (*Ant.* 2.265). The approach to the burning bush is evidence of Moses' boldness in daring to come to a place to which no man had previously come because of the presence of the Divinity, and it counseled him to go very far from the flame and being a good man and descended from great men, to be content with what he had seen and to pry no further (*Ant.* 2.267).

This episode clearly shows a tension in Josephus. Moses is human and is unable to appear directly before the flame, but he has been able to approach closer than other humans. Moses alone has the ability and boldness to approach God, but only to a point. The voice from the fire "predicted the glory and honor that he would receive from men…" and commissioned Moses to return as "general and leader (στρατηγός καὶ ἡγεμών) of the multitude of the Hebrews and to liberate his kinsmen from the insolence there" (*Ant.* 2.268). This epochal event qualifies Moses as the only person who is able to approach God (*Ant.* 2.267). From this point onward, Moses is now in a position to bring the polity and law to the people on behalf of God and approach God on behalf of the people.[75]

After bringing the two tablets of the law and God's direct proclamation of the ten words to the people, Moses ascends Sinai a second time, and this time he is gone for forty days. The people debated what had happened to Moses, whether he was killed by wild animals or if "he had returned to the Divinity" (*Ant.* 3.96). The phrase "return to the Divinity" (ἀωαχωρέω with πρός τὸ θεῖον) appears again at the death of Moses and once more for Enoch (*Ant.* 1.85). The mourning of the entire population, young and old, dramatically marks the announcement of the impending

---

75. Several extra-biblical additions made by Josephus highlight Moses' role as an intermediary during the wilderness episodes. For example, Josephus expands the manna and quail episode in Exod 16 by including Israel's threat of stoning Moses and narrating how Moses ascended a mountain to ask God to rescue Israel from their hunger. Moses then descends from the mountain saying that "he had come to bring to them from God a deliverance from their present difficulties (*Ant.* 3.24). This episode may well be Josephus' anticipation of Moses' ascension on Mt. Sinai (see Feldman, *Judean Antiquities 1–4*, 237). Josephus heightens the drama of Moses' ascension by describing the mountain's inaccessibility due to "its gigantic size and the precipitousness of the steep slopes," as well as to the "report concerning God as dwelling there" (*Ant.* 3.76). Moses returns from the mountain a few days later, reporting that God has "prescribed a blessed life for you and a well-ordered constitution" (*Ant.* 3.84), which represents a major theme of Josephus' *Antiquities* (Feldman, *Judean Antiquities 1–4*, 251).

death of Moses. Moses himself "was overcome with weeping at what was being done by the people" (*Ant.* 4.322).[76]

Moses then ascended the mountain and when he was alone with Eleazar and Joshua, "a cloud suddenly stood over him and he disappeared in a certain ravine" (*Ant.* 4.326). But Josephus later mentions that Moses intentionally wrote about his own death because "he was afraid that they might dare to say that because of the abundance of the virtue surrounding him he had gone up to the Divinity" (*Ant.* 4.326).

The phrase πρός τὸ θεῖον could mean that Moses was taken up to heaven or "into divine nature."[77] Josephus explains "that it was likely he should be translated by God to himself because of his inherent virtue" (*Ant.* 3.97). While the basic meaning of this phrase is straightforward, scholars have debated precisely what Josephus actually believed. Tabor, for example, noting that Josephus includes a description of the sudden appearance of the cloud upon Moses and his disappearance into a ravine, understands the phrase as a conscious resistance to such contemporary evaluations of other extraordinary figures, whether that of Philo of Moses, the Christians of Jesus or Dionysius of Aeneas and Romulus. But Josephus really wants to have it both ways. He somehow manages to recast his account so that it sounds like just such a scene, with the tears and weeping, the withdrawal, the cloud descending upon Moses and his disappearance, with nothing said of his burial. At the same time, he records that Moses "died," since Moses, remarkably, had written this of himself while still living.[78]

In a later response to Tabor, Begg notes that Josephus' account of Moses' death is consistent with his portrayal of Enoch's returning πρός τὸ θεῖον with no record of his death.[79] Moses' own account of his death, then, merely represents his modesty, "describing himself as sharing the common lot of 'dying,' even though the reality was otherwise" (*Ant.* 3.212).[80] But Begg's argument is not convincing, since Josephus clearly affirms that Moses died and furthermore, Josephus would have made a clear connection between Moses' sense of modesty and his false report of his death. The tension in Josephus' portrayal of Moses as human and

76. Cf. also the description of the weeping of Moses at his death in *Midrash Petirat Mosheh* in Kushelevsky, *Moses*, 215, 217.

77. See Feldman, *Judean Antiquities 1–4*, 472–73 (n. 1112) for a detailed discussion of early Jewish and Rabbinic traditions surrounding the death of Moses.

78. James D. Tabor, "'Returning to the Divinity': Josephus's Portrayal of the Disappearances of Enoch, Elijah, and Moses," *JBL* 108 (1989): 237–38.

79. Christopher Begg, "'Josephus's Portrayal of the Disappearances of Enoch, Elijah, and Moses': Some Observations," *JBL* 109 (1990): 691–93.

80. Ibid., 692.

divine has made it difficult to determine what he actually believed. Most likely, Josephus wants to imply the divinization of Moses but not on the level of an apotheosis like other Greco-Roman leaders and heroes. But Josephus does attest that a belief in the apotheosis of Moses had circulated in the Judaism of his time. According to Talbert,

> Josephus, therefore, knew of a Jewish tradition of the end of Moses' career that spoke of his passing in the same terms as those employed for the legendary heroes of other Mediterranean peoples. At the same time that he included the tradition shaped this way, he explicitly rejected the interpretation of it in the terms of the mythology of the immortals. Though Philo and Josephus responded negatively to the position, certain Jewish circles did portray Moses in categories taken from the Mediterranean concept of the immortals.[81]

In addition to Moses' contemplation of God's nature, his direct relationship with God, and his return to the divinity upon his death, Josephus also hints at the divinity of Moses in the conclusion to Book 3, where he describes the enduring effectiveness of the polity as proof of his "superhuman power" (τῆς ὑπὲρ ἄνθρωπὸν...δυνάμις αὐτοῦ; *Ant.* 3.318) and that the law has caused Moses "to be esteemed beyond his own [human] nature" (*Ant.* 3.320).

Finally, the precise nuance of Josephus' description of Moses, in his account of the construction of the tabernacle, as a θεῖος ἀνήρ in *Ant.* 3.180 ("our lawgiver was a man of God"), is debated. Is Josephus merely describing Moses as a "godly man," as one might say in contemporary English, without any reference to his divinity? In line with Josephus' alleged anti-supernatural presuppositions and his view of Moses as merely human, some scholars have thought that Moses was not being described as divine in a literal sense.[82] Feldman, for example, notes: "[t]hat Josephus was careful to emphasize the fact that Moses was human and not divine may be seen in the fact that on eight occasions (*Ant.* 2.230, 271; 3.98, 180, 297, 316, 317, 320) he goes out of his way, in extra-biblical additions, to refer to Moses as a man."[83] Yet even Feldman seems to admit that "Josephus proves the divine quality of Moses with the cosmic character of the laws given by him,"[84] and thus it is curious that he later asserts that "Josephus has no intention of asserting Moses'

81. Charles H. Talbert, "The Concept of Immortals in Mediterranean Antiquity," *JBL* 94 (1975): 425.
82. So Holladay, *Theios Aner*, 89–100, and Feldman, *Judean Antiquities 1–4*, 279.
83. Ibid., 473.
84. Ibid., 279.

divinity." However, others take this phrase as evidence of Moses' divine status.[85]

In addition to giving his own view of Moses and attesting to a belief in the apotheosis of Moses in Jewish circles, Josephus also refers to the Egyptian belief of the divinity of Moses. In *Contra Apion* (1.279) Josephus claims that the Egyptians considered Moses to be divine (θεῖος). According to Tiede, Josephus is "documenting Moses' role as a benefactor of human civilization by appealing to the Egyptian practice of deifying those who have made a lasting cultural contribution"[86] and "Moses' particular dignity or virtue is best seen in Josephus' statements about him as lawgiver, and it is in this function that Moses approaches divine stature."[87] In sum, Tiede comments,

> Josephus draws a rather grandiose portrait of Moses. If his varied descriptions of this figure are viewed together, Moses appears at a glance to be the sage, lawgiver, miracle worker, prophet, and military genius, and he is even explicitly called a θεῖος ἀνήρ.[88]

A survey of references to Moses in Josephus shows that although Moses is clearly just a man, he has a unique status that is the result of approaching and apprehending God's nature and that qualifies him to be the preeminent lawgiver. In Josephus' conclusion, Moses has "surpassed in understanding all men who had ever lived" (*Ant.* 4.328; cf. 2.229).

While Josephus portrays Moses as a semi-divine lawgiver in his act of authoring the Pentateuch, he shifts to a different portrayal of Moses as a character in his exposition of the biblical books of Exodus to Numbers (*Antiquities* Books 2–3). Josephus presents this new portrayal of the character of Moses in his account of Moses' encounter with God at the burning bush. Here God commissions Moses as στρατηγός καὶ ἡγεμών ("general and leader"). The description of Moses as a "general" may be Josephus' unique portrayal of Moses.[89] This term does not appear in the Septuagint and is used to refer to Moses fifteen times in the *Antiquities*.[90] Thus Feldman comments, "Indeed, it was not as teacher or legislator that the voice from the burning bush bids Moses to act but rather as general (στρατηγός) and leader (ἡγεμών).[91] Josephus anticipates Moses' commissioning as a military general for the Israelites prior to the burning bush

85. Tiede, *The Charismatic Figure as Miracle Worker*, 207–40.
86. Ibid., 211.
87. Ibid., 231.
88. Ibid.
89. Cf. Philo's reference to Moses as a general in *Life of Moses* 1.60–61.
90. For references, see Feldman, *Judean Antiquities 1–4*, 202–3.
91. Ibid., 203.

episode through his inclusion of an extra-biblical account of Moses' campaign against Ethiopia, a more expanded version than that told in Artapanus (*Ant.* 2.238–53).[92] When Ethiopia invaded Egypt, the Egyptians received word from God through oracles and divinations to take the "Hebrew" as their ally. In response, the king of Egypt had his daughter give up Moses to serve as his "general" (στρατηγός). This episode shows how Moses saved (σώζω) the Egyptians from their perennial enemy and also demonstrates his wisdom by bringing baskets full of ibises to destroy the serpents that prevented the Egyptian army from marching directly into Ethiopia. This brilliant strategy permitted a surprise attack on the Ethiopians, driving the army to retreat to the capital city of Saba. Another confirmation of Moses' wisdom occurs when the daughter of the king of Ethiopia (Tharbis) observes the wisdom of Moses during the siege and proposes marriage. Moses accepts the proposal on the condition that the town surrenders.[93]

In addition to the Ethiopian campaign and the commissioning at the burning bush, Feldman presents numerous pieces of evidence to support Moses' generalship, including the portrayal of Israel as soldiers (*Ant.* 4.177), the qualities of "sheer endurance in the face of adversity," courage, and ability to inspire his troops, as well as the leadership of the people through the desert to a safe destination, despite severe difficulties and obstacles on the way.[94] It is not surprising, then, that according to Feldmen in the economium on Moses in *Contra Apion*, which may be viewed as Josephus' summary of the roles of Moses, Josephus begins by portraying Moses as the best general by virtue of his command and his guidance of the people from Egypt and through the desert, including the defeat of their enemies on the way.[95]

For Josephus, Moses' role as a general qualifies and prepares him for the role of king. Meeks notes that while the term for general (στρατηγός) has a military connotation, this office functions more broadly in the Hellenistic world, including roles such as governor or even the office to which Hasmonean leaders were appointed, before later becoming

92. For the source of the Ethiopian account and its relationship to Artapanus, see the detailed discussion in Feldman, "Portrait of Moses: Part Two," 15–19 (n. 113).

93. For a systematic analysis of the virtue of wisdom as a trait of leadership in Josephus' portrayal of Moses, see Feldman, *Judean Antiquities 1–4*, 7–20. Feldman notes that the Ethiopian campaign finds its biblical basis in the description of Moses' marriage to an Egyptian in Num 12:1. He speculates that Moses honored his agreement to marry the Ethiopian princess in contrast to the typical betrayal by the hero in similar Greco-Roman tales.

94. Feldman, *Judean Antiquities 1–4*, 13–28.

95. Ibid., 14.

kings.[96] Despite his disclaimer that he has accurately recounted the details from scripture (*Ant.* 2.247), Josephus includes several extra-biblical events in his presentation of Exod 1–2, mostly derived from the lore of biblical midrashim, in order to portray Moses as a rival king to Pharaoh. First, Josephus narrates a legend that an Egyptian sacred scribe predicted the birth and rise of an Israelite who would opposed the authority of the king of Egypt. This person will "surpass all men in virtue and win everlasting renown" (*Ant.* 2.205). This threat motivated the king of Egypt to order the observation of the labor and delivery by Egyptian midwives and the drowning of every male Israelite child and (Exod 1).

Second, according to Josephus, upon rescuing Moses from the Nile, Pharaoh's daughter (Thermuthis) brought him to the king of Egypt, her father, and requested that he make Moses "my child and successor to your kingdom" on the basis of his divine appearance ($\mu o \rho \phi \acute{\eta}\ \theta \epsilon \tilde{\iota} o \nu$) and because he was "distinguished in intelligence." (*Ant.* 2.232). Then she placed the baby in the arms of the king, and the king placed his crown upon the head of Moses "to please his daughter" (*Ant.* 2.233). Moses responded by throwing the crown to the ground and stomping on it—after which the sacred scribe screamed and proceeded immediately to attempt to kill Moses, since he was the child of his prophecy. But Moses' life was spared when Thermuthis quickly snatched him away. Josephus reports that God, "whose providence was protective over Moses," caused the king to hesitate and that the Egyptians refrained from killing Moses because he was the only legitimate heir to the throne (*Ant.* 2.237). Moses thus grew up in the royal household as the designated heir to the throne of Egypt (*Ant.* 2.236–38).

Josephus then narrates Moses' Ethiopian campaign as the first mani-festation of his destiny to lead the Hebrews. In reaction to this successful campaign, the Egyptians who served under Moses developed a hatred of him and envied his "generalship." They recommended to the king, along with the sacred scribes, that he kill Moses under the pretext that the successful Ethiopian campaign will embolden Moses to seize the throne of Egypt (*Ant.* 2.254). This new development forced Moses to flee to Midian and set the stage for his commission as "general and leader" of the Hebrews at the burning bush.

In conclusion, Josephus presents a carefully structured profile of Moses. With respect to the Pentateuch as polity, Moses is Israel's pre-eminent lawgiver qualified by his close association with God. As a char-acter in the Pentateuch, Moses is Israel's supreme general and leader, exhibiting the qualities of an ideal Hellenistic king. Josephus portrays

96. Meeks, *The Prophet-King*, 134.

Moses as a rival of Pharaoh, a rival who ultimately becomes Israel's military general and ruler. Although Josephus wants to avoid divinizing and worshipping Moses,[97] he presents Moses as a larger than life figure with a superhuman, or semi-divine, nature that allows him access to God. In the conclusion to his detailed analysis of Josephus' portrayal of Moses, Feldman notes:

> It seems surprising that…Josephus, unlike Philo, nowhere refers to Moses as king. This is all the more remarkable inasmuch as Moses, in Josephus' description, seems to bear all the qualities of a Hellenistic king—lawgiver, judge, general, and shepherd of his people. The very fact that his opponents call him "tyrant" would seem to indicate that in Josephus' mind he was the counterpart of "tyrant," namely king.[98]

Although Josephus concludes his presentation of Moses with references to his roles as general and even a prophet, it appears that Josephus closes his work by viewing Moses as a king who "lived, in all, 120 years, of which he ruled ($\check{\alpha}\rho\chi\omega$) for a third part minus one month" (*Ant.* 4.327). Perhaps Josephus wants to equate Moses with all the qualities of a Hellenistic king without referring to him as a king, since for Josephus this would result in reducing and limiting the role of Moses to a specific office,[99] while Moses is much more—"so that in whatever he said one seemed, when he spoke, to be listening to God" (*Ant.* 4.329).

1.2.d. *Conclusion*

An examination of the two principal sources of Hellenistic Judaism, Philo and Josephus, has shown that one aspect of their portrayal of Moses is as a divinized, royal figure that did not conflict with the Jewish monotheistic belief in the one God. More precisely, Moses acts as a divine agent along the lines of a vice-regent who rules with authority and power from God. This high view of Moses provides additional confirmation to the results of the overview of the classical sources, namely that the view of Moses as royal, semi-divine figure is part and parcel of the world of Hellenistic Judaism and is particularly rooted in a number of important biblical texts, including Exod 7:1 and Deut 33:5. A survey of

---

97. Thus Feldman (*Judean Antiquities 1–4*, 473–74) states, "Great as Moses was as a leader, Josephus takes great pains to make sure that he will not be worshipped as a god. This was particularly necessary in view of the frequency of the apotheosis of heroes, such as Dionysius, Heracles…and Asclepius."

98. Feldman, "Portrait of Moses: Part Three," 314–15.

99. Josephus' avoidance of designating Moses as king, perhaps to avoid offending his Roman audience, and his own role as a general against the Romans may have contributed to his emphasis on portraying Moses as a general.

Philo and Josephus in context of the status of Moses in Hellenistic Judaism allows us to retrieve a fuller, more accurate profile of Moses as he is portrayed in the Pentateuch and provides a crucial corrective to the modern tendency to minimize the importance of Moses in the Pentateuch, a topic that will be explored in the next section.

1.3. *Moses in Modern Critical Scholarship*

In contrast to the generally high portrayal of Moses in Philo, Josephus, and other writers of the Hellenistic period, scholars in the modern period have often undervalued the portrayal of Moses as a semi-divine and royal figure in order to identify the figure who, in their view, was more likely to have been the historical founder of Israelite religion. A survey of the various approaches to the figure of Moses in the last two centuries reveals two trends. First, some scholars have focused on the critical task of reconstructing the "historical" Moses who underlies the interpretative traditions (e.g. prophet, lawgiver, priest). Second, scholarly investigations into the traditions about Moses have prioritized the results of their critical methods over the portrayal of Moses in the received text. Specifically, scholars have allowed various source, form, tradition-historical, and, more recently, redactional approaches to discern various layers and stages of tradition underlying the received text. These results have been used to construct a particular portrait of Moses distinct to each "source," "tradition," or "redactional layer," and this usually results in fragmenting the coherent view of Moses in the received form of the text. The following overview of recent scholarship on Moses will be grouped according to these two tendencies.

1.3.a. *Modernizing Moses*

Hugo Gressmann's pioneering 1913 work *Mose und seine Zeit* inaugurated the modern era of research on the figure of Moses and paved the way for the tradition-historical studies of Martin Noth, Gerhard von Rad, and, more recently, George Coats.[100] Gressman employed the tools of form criticism and tradition-historical criticism to probe behind the major

---

100.   Hugo Gressmann, *Mose und seine Zeit: Ein Kommentar zu den Mose-Sagen* (FRLANT 18; Göttingen: Vandenhoeck & Ruprecht, 1913). Convenient and concise surveys of Gressman's contribution include Smend, *Das Mosebild*, 16–19; Osswald, *Das Bild des Mose*, 135–49; Douglas A. Knight, *Rediscovering the Traditions of Israel* (Missoula, Mont.: Society of Biblical Literature, 1973), 84–91; Brian Britt, *Rewriting Moses: The Narrative Eclipse of the Text* (JSOTSup 402; New York: T&T Clark International, 2004), 68–71.

literary sources of the Pentateuch as established a few decades earlier by
Wellhausen (Jehovistic [JE] and Priestly) in order to reach the oldest
forms of the various sagas and legends in the Old Testament.

Among the various legend cycles identified by Gressmann, the larg-
est one spans the birth of Moses and the sojourn in Egypt until his death
and the arrival of Israel at the border of the promised land.[101] Gressmann
discerned two smaller cycles of tradition (*Sagenkränze*) embedded within
this larger cycle: a collection of episodes situated at Kadesh and a cycle
portraying Moses' relationship with Jethro.[102] Using various criteria,
including the presupposition that shorter units of text are more ancient,
Gressman judged these two cycles to be older than the Sinai traditions
and to have been incorporated secondarily into the larger (and younger)
exodus–Sinai–conquest cycle that forms the basic framework of the
received text. Gressman drew the historically minimal conclusion that
Jethro trained Moses to be a priest of the Yahweh cult and that he later
became the founder of the Israelite religion during an extended stay at
Kadesh.

Gressman's method and conclusions are fraught with a number of
difficulties. Like Wellhausen in his study of the written sources of the
Pentateuch, Gressman presupposed a lengthy evolutionary process
from the initial description of an historical event to its expansion and
embellishment through the vehicle of the oral saga. This posited evolutionary process paves the way for two questionable tendencies. First,
Wellhausen's shift away from the received text to hypothetical written
sources is extended further by Gressmann to the pre-literary stage underlying these sources. Second, the evolutionary presupposition results in
minimal historical conclusions without creating a synthesis that takes
adequate account of all the available sources. Douglas Knight notes, for
example, that Gressmann merely uncovered the various layers of tradition without attempting an historical synthesis.[103] Although Gressmann
listed 29 distinct traditions relating to Moses in the first part of his work,
he portrayed Moses simply as a human founder of Israelite religion.
Stripping Moses of his superhuman attributes will become the hallmark
of Moses studies in the modern period. As Smend remarks, "The only
way in which scholarship today can approach a figure such as Moses is
primarily by a process of subtraction... [T]he history of scholarly

---

101.   "Der grösste Sagenkranz...reicht von Moses Geburt und dem Aufenthalt
Israels in Ägypten bis zu Moses Tod und der Ankunft Israels an der Grenze des
gelobten Landes" (Gressmann, *Mose und seine Zeit*, 386).

102.   Ibid., 386–87.

103.   Knight, *Rediscovering the Traditions of Israel*, 85–86.

endeavor around the figure of Moses can actually be described for the most part as a history of such subtractions."[104]

In the wake of Gressman, Elias Auerbach presented his reconstruction of Moses by using the tools of traditio-historical criticism in an effort to separate the legendary materials and to arrive at the historical core of the Moses narrative. Yet his portrayal of Moses remained fairly close to the biblical witnesses, largely due to his assumption that legendary materials may serve a historical function. He viewed Moses variously as "genius," "hero," "leader," "herald and mediator," and "liberator, lawgiver."[105] Moses was seen as a figure parallel to Muhammad. Both functioned as a prophet, army leader, statesman, and political leader. Above all, Auerbach also took the biblical descriptions of the divinity of Moses seriously, describing Moses as a "gigantic figure" and a "superman" who appeared to be "almost immortal" and died only at the command of God.[106] Auerbach's analysis, however, suffers from the weakness of most of the presentations of Moses by remaining at the level of a description of the various roles of Moses without attempting to formulate a synthesis.

In a similar way, Dewey Beegle assumed a fairly confident view of the historical accuracy of the biblical sources and argued that a real historical figure is attested by the biblical witness.[107] Like Auerbach, Beegle basically recapitulated the biblical narrative. Like Philo, he tended to psychologize the characters (e.g. imagining what Moses felt, what his parents thought). And like Josephus, he revised the legendary elements in the biblical text by means of modern, scientific explanations (e.g. by describing the ten plagues as natural disasters). Beegle's concluding portrait of Moses suffers the same weakness as Auerbach's approach by noting the various roles of Moses without producing a synthesis:

> Because of the uniqueness of the role which Yahweh assigned Moses he had to play a number of parts. As the deliverer from Egypt he became the leader of the Israelites. As the mediator of the covenant he became the founder of the community of Israel. As the interpreter of the covenant he became its legislator. As the intercessor for the people he became their

104.   Rudolf Smend, *Yahweh War and Tribal Confederation: Reflections Upon Israel's Earliest History* (trans. Max Gray Rogers; Nashville: Abingdon, 1970), 120–21.

105.   Elias Auerbach, *Moses* (trans. Robert A. Barclay and Israel O. Lehman; Detroit: Wayne State University Press, 1975), 190, 194, 212–16.

106.   Ibid., 194, 170.

107.   Dewey M. Beegle, *Moses, the Servant of Yahweh* (Grand Rapids: Eerdmans, 1972).

priest, and although in his punishment on Pisgah he died because of his own sin, in a sense he died on behalf of them, and thus he set the stage for Yahweh's later acts in behalf of all mankind…. Truly, Moses was the greatest prophet until the coming of him who went still further by atoning for the sins of Israel and all of God's creation.[108]

More than Auerbach, however, Beegle viewed the various roles of Moses to be the result of Moses' "unique role" assigned by God. While Beegle described the various aspects of Moses' "unique role" as deliverer, founder, mediator, intercessor, and priest, he did not provide a clear understanding of the precise nature of this "unique role."

Like Gressmann, George Coats assumed a lengthy pre-literary stage of oral transmission underlying the current form of Exodus–Deuteronomy, and he situated the origin and development of the Moses tradition among the community ("the folk").[109] Unlike Gressmann, however, Coats also employed a synchronic, literary approach that inquired into the shape of Moses in the received text.[110] Thus Coats took seriously the high view of Moses in the Pentateuch and attempted to account for this in his tradition-historical reconstruction.

Coats uncovered two Moses traditions that existed side-by-side in dialectical tension in the received form of the Pentateuch. First, he claimed that a tradition with the characteristic of narrative, which he named "heroic saga," portrayed Moses as a "hero"[111] by narrating his "mighty deeds…in his leadership of the people and the people's response in faith (or rebellion) to that leadership."[112] For Coats, Moses the hero identifies with the people and represents the people to God. The hero brings various benefits to the people in a variety of ways (such as "military might" or "successful intervention").[113] Despite the tendency to elevate the hero to the level of a god in typical Greek heroic traditions such as the deification of Hercules upon his ascent to Olympus, Coats made a strong but dubious claim that the heroic tradition portrayed Moses purely as a man. Coats denied any type of apotheosis within this tradition.[114]

---

108. Ibid., 348.

109. Coats, *Moses: Heroic Man*. Cf. also his *The Moses Tradition* (JSOTSup 161; Sheffield: JSOT, 1993), and *Exodus 1–18* (FOTL; Grand Rapids: Eerdmans, 1999).

110. On Coats's method, see *Moses: Heroic Man*, 36.

111. See Coats's definition of a "hero" in ibid., 38–41.

112. Ibid., 155.

113. Ibid., 40.

114. Ibid., 41.

Second, Coats uncovered another tradition found in cultic confessions of God's mighty acts on behalf of his people. Following von Rad, Coats found the absence of Moses in various cultic confessions to have important tradition-historical significance. Based on these observations, Coats concluded that Moses first appeared as Israel's hero in the narrative folkloric tradition and originally had no role in the earlier cultic traditions. Moses eventually emerged as the dominant figure in the received text through the merging of the two traditions to produce Moses as the "man of God" who is now the means of effecting God's mighty acts on behalf of his people. To support his observation, Coats explored the basic confessional themes uncovered by von Rad and Noth (Exodus, wilderness, Sinai, conquest) and traced the merging of the heroic Moses traditions with the cultic, non-Mosaic confession of God's mighty acts.[115]

Coats represented the most substantial attempt to take seriously the high portrayal of Moses in the Pentateuch. Yet his work is flawed in several respects. The critiques of Noth and von Rad, especially of the tradition-historical method, the formation of discrete traditional themes, and constructing a particular profile of Moses for each theme, applies to Coats as well.[116] The critical view of literary sources accepted by Coats (e.g. dating of "J" to the reign of David or Solomon, and perhaps even the identification of "J" as a discrete, coherent source) can no longer be considered a scholarly consensus.[117] In recent years, scholars are now examining the Assyrian, Babylonian, and Persian periods as possible settings for the biblical portrayal of Moses.[118] In addition, Coats perpetuated a low, minimalist view of the Priestly materials, in which Moses is a non-heroic character who is simply "the speaker for the ritual [of Passover]."[119] Coats failed to acknowledge the heroic portrayal of Moses in the narrative portions of the Priestly source, such as the call of Moses

115. See the chapter "Heroic Man and Man of God," in *Moses: Heroic Man*, 155–78.
116. See the critical discussion and evaluation of Noth and von Rad in the next section.
117. For a review of the issues and bibliography in the vigorous debate about the identity of "J," see Erhard Blum, "The Literary Connection Between the Books of Genesis and Exodus and the End of the Book of Joshua," in Dozeman and Schmid, eds., *A Farewell to the Yahwist*, 89–106, and Jan Christian Gertz, Konrad Schmid, and Markus Witte, eds., *Abschied vom Jahwisten: Die Komposition des Hexateuch in der jüngsten Diskussion* (BZAW 315; New York: de Gruyter, 2002).
118. See especially Eckart Otto, *Die Tora des Mose: Die Geschichte der literarischen Vermittlung von Recht, Religion und Politik durch die Mosegestalt* (Göttingen: Vandenhoeck & Ruprecht, 2001).
119. Coats, *Moses: Heroic Man*, 161, 196.

(Exod 6:2–7:13), the crossing of the sea (Exod 14), provision of manna and quail (Exod 16), and, above all, the apotheosis of Moses (Exod 34:29–35). Indeed, the Priestly characterization of Moses as "God" in Exod 7:1, as well as the apotheosis of Moses in Exod 34:29–35, fits perfectly with the folkloric tendency to elevate the hero to the level of a god. Finally, the possibility of a final "Priestly" shaping and editing of older "JE" materials in Exodus suggests Priestly acceptance and approval of the older heroic saga.[120]

Second, Coats unduly placed the narrative traditions of Moses as hero in tension with cultic confessions of God's mighty acts. It is more likely that generic conventions account for the accent on Moses in narrative settings and on God in cultic settings. Rather than restricting the designation of Moses as "man of God" to the heroic tradition, this designation may represent a basic characterization of the identity and work of Moses as depicted in the Pentateuch as a whole and may reflect the clear portrayal of Moses with both human and divine characteristics that cuts across the discrete sources.

Finally, Coats's description of Moses as a hero is vague and needs more specification. What kind of hero was Moses? The present study will argue that Moses' heroic role is royal. The portrayal of Moses as a king who stands between God and the people satisfactorily accounts for Moses' status as an intermediary without the need to resort to a dialectic opposition and tension as an explanation to account for Moses' dual role as man and god. The Golden Calf narrative and its aftermath in Exod 32–34 does not represent a conflict in tradition between Moses and God, as Coats asserted.[121] Rather, Moses' status as a royal figure places him and God in complementary roles in relation to Israel. The next chapter of this study will show that demonstrating "heroic" feats is one important component of the royal depictions of rulers in the ancient Near East, especially of those rulers who do not assume power through dynastic succession.

In sum, Coats's stated method has led him to posit a false dichotomy, indicated by the subtitle to his *Moses*, namely, *"Heroic Man, Man of God,"* in the traditions underlying the Pentateuch. However, his portrayal of Moses is a major step in the right direction by the acknowledgment of both the divinity and humanity of Moses in the textual portrait. His explanations for these two natures of Moses is ultimately unconvincing, and this study will show that the portrayal of Moses as a royal figure

---

120.   On the priestly redaction of Exodus, see Mark S. Smith, *The Pilgrimage Pattern in Exodus* (JSOTSup 239; Sheffield: Sheffield Academic, 1997), 180–261.

121.   Coats, *Moses: Heroic Man*, 158.

provides more specificity and accommodates both the human and divine nature without resorting to the creation of a dialectic tension. A major weakness of the approaches surveyed in this section is the basic failure to account for the full Pentateuchal portraiture of Moses. Even scholars who appreciate the high view of Moses (i.e. Auerbach and Beegle) still employ historical and tradition-historical tools to revise the text to fit within a scientific world view (Beegle) that ultimately reduces the full portrait of Moses by humanizing him to into a more believable founder of Israelite religion (Gressmann).

1.3.b. *Moses and Methodology*
In addition to the quest for the historical Moses, which has resulted in minimizing the portrayal of Moses in the received text, scholars have also allowed their methodology to shape a particular view of Moses. This section will demonstrate this tendency through an analysis and critique of a limited selection of important scholars, namely, the works of Martin Noth and Gerhard von Rad as well as recent studies by Brian Britt, James Nohrnberg, and John Van Seters.

Like his pioneering predecessors in form and tradition-historical criticisms (Gressmann and Gunkel), Noth assumed the basic Wellhausen view of the composite literary character of the Pentateuch and attempted to account for the formation of the Pentateuch in a more comprehensive way from its obscure oral beginnings to the final completed work.[122] Thus he filled the lacuna that existed between the individual units of tradition identified by Gunkel and Gressman and their combination and configuration into the respective literary sources. In particular, he postulated the existence of a common oral or written source underlying J and E (*Gundlage* = "G"),[123] which he argued is the result of a long process of a combination and merging of five discrete and independent themes.[124]

The themes, listed in order of historical priority, are (1) "Guidance out of Egypt," (2) "Guidance into the arable land," (3) "Promise to the Patriarchs," (4) "Guidance in the Wilderness," and (5) "Revelation at Sinai." They roughly correspond to Gressman's *Sagenkränze*, but Noth gave greater clarity and precision to the perceived relationships between the themes and their eventual combination and crystallization in the

---

122.   Martin Noth, *A History of Pentateuchal Traditions* (trans. Bernhard W. Anderson; Englewood Cliffs: Prentice-Hall, 1972).
123.   See the chapter "The Relationship between J and E and Their Common Basis (G)," in Noth, *Pentateuchal Traditions*, 38–41.
124.   See the chapter "The Major Themes of the Tradition in the Pentateuch and Their Origin," in ibid., 46–62.

literary sources. These themes developed independently among different tribes at various cultic centers and were eventually combined and merged as a part of the formation of the tribal federation of Israel in Palestine. But this is precisely where Noth's method forced him to minimize the pervasive presence of Moses in four of these themes (Exodus, wilderness, Sinai, and conquest). In Noth's view Moses was originally present in only one of these themes, and his presence was extended to the other themes only as a result of a secondary redactional move ("bracketing") at a later stage of the process of the formation of the Pentateuch. Thus Noth's section on Moses is basically a quest to link Moses with one of the four discrete themes underlying Exodus–Numbers.[125] After taking pains to refute the significant evidence for the centrality of Moses in the themes of Exodus, wilderness, and Sinai, Noth associated Moses with the conquest theme ("Guidance into the arable land").

However, this portrait of Moses did not originate in the conquest theme. Rather, on the basis of the mention of Moses' grave in both D and P, as well as its location near Baal Peor, Noth argued for the historical reliability of the testimony about the location of Moses' grave.[126] Thus, for Noth, rather than originating as part of the creative process of the formation of the themes, the portrait of Moses was based on an actual historical person, probably the oldest figure depicted in the tradition-history process of the Pentateuch, with the possible exception of Jacob.[127] According to Noth, Moses may have indeed been the leader of several tribes and may have married a foreign woman. However, Moses has a role in the theme of conquest only because his grave site happened to be located on the route of the Israelites on the way to occupying the land. Traditions about Moses entered into the central area of Palestine and eventually grew among the northern and southern tribes. Noth's conclusions attempted to account for the paradox of Moses' widespread influence textually and geographically on the one hand[128] and his omission in von Rad's formulation of Israel's earliest creeds on the other hand. Thus, by its nature, the traditio-historical method as devised by Noth has questioned the historical reliability of most of the Moses material in the Pentateuch, save for the accounts of his death and burial, with a strong historical probability of his leadership of some tribes and a marriage to a non-Israelite.

125. Ibid., 156–75.
126. Ibid., 171–73.
127. Ibid., 174.
128. Here Noth (ibid.) mentions the presence of the northern Danite sanctuary that claims a Mosaic origin (Judg 18:30) and Moses' connections to the Kenites in the south.

Noth's minimization of the historical Moses did not find much acceptance among scholars. His formulation of the distinct themes of the
Tetrateuch, however, formed a point of departure for studies that sought
to modify or radically revise his approach by locating Moses in a different theme, such the Exodus,[129] Sinai,[130] or in a combination of themes.[131]
We now know that Noth uncritically prioritized narrative over law, and
recent scholarship has corrected this imbalance by examining the
development of the legal corpora in the Pentateuch without reference to
literary sources.[132] Noth also tended to ascribe greater antiquity and
historical reliability to minor characters rather than major characters in
Pentateuchal narratives. Thus Noth gave historical and chronological
priority to Isaac over Abraham.[133] According to this presupposition the
dominance of Moses in the Pentateuch means that Moses was originally
an insignificant and tangential character. For Noth, the appearances of
Moses are mostly secondary and redactional. In a well-known example,
Noth points to the intermediary role played by the foremen in the
negotiations between the Hebrews and Egyptian officials in Exod 5 as
evidence for the secondary insertion of Moses.[134] Noth must also dis-
regard the mention of Moses elsewhere (e.g. Josh 24:5) as secondary.

129.   E.g. Smend, *Yahweh War*; and Horst Seebass, *Der Erzvater Israel und die
Einführung der Jahweverehrung in Kanaan* (BZAW 98; Berlin: Töpelmann, 1966),
82–87. In an earlier work, he places Moses in the Sinai traditions. A detailed analysis and discussion of these sources is not crucial to the basic arguments of the
present study. Here I am dependent on Bernhard Anderson's brief bibliographic
sketch in Noth, *Pentateuchal Traditions*, xxx (n. 37).

130.   E.g. Horst Seebass, *Mose und Aaron, Sinai und Gottesberg* (Bonn:
Bouvier, 1962), 131–34; and Walter Beyerlin, *Origins and History of the Oldest
Sinaitic Traditions* (Oxford: Blackwell, 1965).

131.   E.g. Murray Lee Newman, *The People of the Covenant: A Study of Israel
from Moses to the Monarchy* (New York: Abingdon, 1962), and Georg Fohrer,
Überlieferung und Geschichte des Exodus: eine Analyse von Ex 1–15 (BZAW 91;
Berlin: Töpelmann, 1964). See Fohrer's concise discussion of Moses in *Introduction
to the Old Testament* (trans. David Green; Nashville: Abingdon, 1968), 124–26.

132.   E.g. Frank Crüsemann, *The Torah: Theology and Social History of Old
Testament Law* (trans. Allan W. Mahnke; Minneapolis: Fortress, 1996).

133.   Noth, *Pentateuchal Traditions*, 102–15.

134.   Ibid., 163. In a rebuttal to this observation, Smend (*Yahweh War*, 124–28)
shows how a similar sequence of events in 1 Kgs 12 serves to introduce the installation of Jeroboam as king. Rather than functioning as evidence for a late redactional
insertion, it is possible that Exod 5 serves to present Moses as an "anti-Jeroboam"
type of king. In addition to Exod 5 // 1 Kgs 12, other parallels between Moses and
Jeroboam (e.g. the oppression theme, flight to Midian, and the golden calf incident)
suggest an intentional comparison between the two and will receive extended
reflection in subsequent chapters.

Noth's portrayal of Moses must be judged to be a failure due to allowing his tradition-historical method to dictate his selection and evaluation of criteria by which to evaluate the portrayal of Moses in the Pentateuch.

Moses also plays a secondary role in the work of von Rad, whose well-known identification of Israel's ancient credo in Deut 6:20–24 and 26:5–9 as a cultic confession of God's mighty acts omits any reference to Moses and Sinai.[135] Von Rad points to the expansion of this credo in Josh 24:2–13, including the insertion of Moses and Aaron in v. 5.[136] Thus von Rad labels Josh 24 as a "Hexateuch in miniature," which, when compared with the earlier and shorter credos in Deut 6 and 26, illustrates the tradition-historical process that eventually resulted in the shaping of the current Hexateuch (Genesis–Joshua).[137] In a later work, von Rad fleshes out the implications of his investigations of these three credos for an understanding of the portrayal of Moses in his traditio-historical scheme: a review of the historical summaries in the confessions and hymns reveals right away an incompatibility with the picture given in the Hexateuch, inasmuch as the former, although certainly mentioning Moses (and Aaron) on occasion, nevertheless appear to have absolutely no knowledge of the position of all-powerful leader and mediator accorded to him in the Hexateuch.[138]

Like Noth, von Rad views the series of credos as evidence for a growth and expansion of traditions about Moses. His identification of discrete sources, each with its own particular identity and character, leads him to construct a specific portrayal of Moses in each of the Pentateuchal sources in a clear scheme of progression.[139] And in a method similar to Gressmann, von Rad excavates a minimal view of Moses in the "Yahwistic" source (abbreviated as "J"). He is "no worker of miracles, no founder of a religion, and no military leader."[140] Instead, Moses is merely an "inspired shepherd" called by God to communicate God's will to the community.[141] In the "Elohistic" source ("E"), Moses appears more as a prophetic figure, who later in Deuteronomy ("D") becomes now "the chief of all prophets."[142] In the final source, the "Priestly" document

135. Gerhard von Rad, *The Problem of the Hexateuch, and Other Essays* (Edinburgh: Oliver & Boyd, 1966), 3–6.

136. Ibid., 6–8.

137. Ibid., 8.

138. Gerhard von Rad, *Old Testament Theology*. Vol. 1, *The Theology of Israel's Historical Traditions* (New York: Harper, 1962), 289.

139. Ibid., 291–96.

140. Ibid., 292.

141. Ibid.

142. Ibid., 294.

("P"), Moses is placed outside the category of prophets and is "set apart for intercourse with Jahweh alone…he is separated from men."[143] The posited existence of various literary sources underlying the Pentateuch does not necessarily warrant the construction of a specific portrayal of Moses unique to each source. It may also be possible that the sources are combined in such a way as to present a specific portrayal of Moses that is not unique to any source or tradition.[144]

Von Rad ignores the clear textual descriptions of Moses' apotheosis, viewing Moses as merely a man: "There was nothing divine about Moses… He was the 'man' Moses."[145] Coats notes that this presupposition leads von Rad to ignore the clear portrayal of the heroic role of Moses and that the narratives of Moses function rather as narratives about God:

> Not a single one of all these stories, in which Moses is the central figure, was really written about Moses… [I]n all these stories it is not Moses himself, Moses the man, but God who is the central figure.[146]

This leads von Rad to the ironic statement that Moses will not be the "principal character" in his book titled *Moses!*[147] Von Rad's view creates an unacceptable dichotomy between Moses and God that ignores the exaltation of Moses alongside God in Exodus that will be explored in this study. Finally, as stressed in the survey of Coats in the previous section, von Rad's (and Noth's) tradition and source-critical assumptions can no longer be assumed in the recent and radical changes in

143.   Ibid., 296.
144.   The potential of the Pentateuch to present a new message through the combination of literary sources is admitted even by Noth (*Pentateuchal Traditions*, 250) who states in a concluding chapter, "The question still remains as to whether the combination of the sources…actually did not give rise to something new, which transcended the individual sources…and has not resulted, perhaps unintentionally, in unexpected narrative connections and theological insights, and hence whether in the final analysis the whole has not become greater than merely the sum of its parts."
145.   Gerhard von Rad, *Moses* (World Christian Books; London: Lutterworth, 1960), 10. Von Rad's criterion of the failure to offer worship to Moses can no longer be used to deny a divine nature of Moses in light of the work of Larry Hurtado (*Lord Jesus Christ: Devotion to Jesus in Earliest Christianity* [Grand Rapids: Eerdmans, 2003]), which shows that the belief in the exclusive worship of God alone did not exclude the reality of divine beings (e.g. angels, exalted patriarchs, logos) in Second Temple Judaism.
146.   Von Rad, *Moses*, 8–9. See Coats's assessment of von Rad in *Moses: Heroic Man*, 31–32.
147.   Von Rad, *Moses*, 9.

Pentateuchal criticism.[148] Above all, the portrayals of Moses in von Rad and Noth fail to explain the presence and primacy of Moses located throughout the various traditions. Indeed, the reverse could be argued, that the presence of Moses in the different traditions attests to his historical existence and importance that precede the formation of the various traditions.

Von Rad and Noth have continued Gressman's agenda and have cast a shadow over subsequent scholars (esp. Auerbach and Coats). Thus it is no surprise that Osswald's conclusions to her detailed review of Moses scholarship in the modern period, written in the early 1960s, extols the tradition-historical approach as worked out by Noth. Although she allows for various modifications, her view that Noth's theories hold the key to unraveling the mystery of Moses is obvious:

> By means of the tradition-historical approach, the historical comprehension of Moses becomes more problematic than ever before, if one also cannot agree with Noth's thesis of Moses.[149]

Osswald draws various minimal historical conclusions, which may be taken as representative of scholars working under the agenda and presuppositions of Gressmann and Noth. She views Kadesh as the melting pot for various combinations of Moses traditions and the location of an amphictyony comprising at a minimum the family of Joseph, the priestly tribe of Levi, and the southern tribes.[150] Osswald accepts Noth's observation of the absence of Moses in important events associated with the Exodus tradition, but she also thinks that Moses' connection to Egypt is quite strong and concludes that Moses participated as an interpreter (*Deuter*) of the Exodus at Kadesh.[151]

In addition to Kadesh, Osswald also views Moses' relationship with the Midianites as historical, as well as the original function of Sinai as a pilgrimage sanctuary. Finally, she also thinks that the portrayal of the settings in the wilderness are historically plausible. Based on the multifaceted role of Moses, Osswald designates him as "charismatic leader."[152] Although "he did not establish the nation of Israel," he was a major

---

148. For a survey and critical assessment of recent trends in Pentateuchal studies, see the section "The Problem of the Pentateuch in Current Research," in Nicholson, *Pentateuch*, 95–268.

149. "Durch die traditionsgeschichtliche Forschung ist die historische Erfassbarkeit des Mose problematischer geworden denn je zuvor, wenn man auch der Mosethese Noth nich zustimmen kann" (Osswald, *Das Bild des Mose*, 338).

150. Ibid., 339–40.

151. Ibid., 339.

152. Ibid., 340.

contributor to the Kadesh amphictyony (*Verdienste für die Amphiktyonie von Kadesch*).[153] Despite her minimal historical conclusions, Osswald's designation of Moses as "charismatic leader" portrays Moses as one who is divinely empowered to lead Israel and so it is to be preferred over a simple designation of Moses as prophet or priest.

1.3.c. *Recent Studies of Moses*
Although the tradition-historical conclusions continue to reverberate,[154] in recent years, many critical studies of Moses bracket out the quest to recover the historical Moses and focus primarily on literary and herme-neutical issues (Brian Britt, James Nohrnberg) or view the narratives about Moses as a creative literary composition (John Van Seters). The term "literary" can be understood in two different ways. First, one sense of the term involves the investigation of the origins of the Pentateuch in the Assyrian, Babylonian, Persian, and Hellenistic periods. For example, instead of investigating the importance of the portrayal of Moses in early Israelite history, Otto explores how a literary construct of Moses may have functioned to subvert the prevailing empire of the day (Assyria, Babylon, and Persia).[155] In a similar vein, Van Seters, whose views will be discussed in greater detail below, understands the Tetrateuch as a *de novo* construction of a creative author in the exilic period. He labels this author with the term "the Yahwist," who functions for Van Seters in a role similar to Noth's Deuteronomist. In his view, a pre-literary period of formation, whether written or oral, did not exist and any attempt to use the Yahwist's work for historical reconstruction of the Exodus period is misguided and "a waste of time."[156]

Second, other scholars working with the tools of literary and narrative criticism have begun to focus solely on the literary portrayal of Moses in the received text without paying much, if any, attention to the historical nature and/or formation of the Pentateuch. This approach characterizes two recent monographs on Moses by Britt and Nohrnberg.[157] Both books

---

153.   Ibid.

154.   In addition to Coats, cf. Brevard S. Childs's discussion of Mosaic traditions in *Biblical Theology of the Old and New Testaments* (Minneapolis: Fortress, 1992), 130–42.

155.   Otto, *Die Tora des Mose*.

156.   John Van Seters, *The Life of Moses: The Yahwist as Historian in Exodus–Numbers* (Louisville: Westminster John Knox, 1994), 34.

157.   Britt, *Rewriting Moses*; James Nohrnberg, *Like Unto Moses: The Constituting of an Interruption* (Indiana Studies in Biblical Literature; Bloomington: Indiana University Press, 1995).

bracket out the issue of history and draw upon literary and hermeneutical theories in their interpretation of Moses. Britt, for example, explores how the portrayal of Moses in the Pentateuch and in the history of interpretation (including contemporary novels and film) can shed light on the nature of "scripture, revelation, and biblical tradition."[158] In a move similar to Coats, Britt constructs two opposing views of Moses. First, Britt presents a "biblical" view of Moses, where Moses is an ambiguous and complex figure who does not play a prominent role in the Pentateuch. Then Britt constructs an opposing "post-biblical" portrait of Moses that tends to smooth out the complex biblical portrayal of Moses and accent the uniqueness and heroic traits of Moses against his minimal role in the Pentateuch.[159]

Britt has clearly allowed his method to dictate his selection and interpretation of the evidence. He must minimize the prominence of Moses in the Pentateuch in order to draw a clear contrast of the supposedly "biblical" view of Moses with the "post-biblical" view. Thus "biblical tradition typically limits Moses to the role of a mortal servant of God," and the post-biblical tradition as seen in Philo, Josephus, "would typically magnify Moses at the expense of the text."[160] This move ignores the heroic portrayal of Moses in Exodus–Deuteronomy that has been clearly shown by Coats, whose work receives no discussion at all in Britt's work.[161] Britt is concerned not so much with constructing a view of Moses that appropriately fits the biblical evidence but with an examination of how his particular construction of Moses will inform the larger issues of language, writing, tradition, scripture, and revelation.[162] Britt wants to draw a contrast between two views of Moses and show a pattern of the suppression of the "biblical" view of Moses in the "post-biblical" period so that he can apply Freud's insight that suppressed views are preserved in tradition. However, Britt's overall assessment of the "biblical Moses" depends on an extremely narrow selection of biblical texts regarding Moses' character. Britt fails to account for the heroic portrayal of Moses in the biblical text that provides the starting point for the post-biblical "magnification" of Moses.

---

158.   Britt, *Rewriting Moses*, 2.

159.   Ibid., 5–11.

160.   Ibid.

161.   According to the index, Coats is mentioned only once, on p. 78 (n. 90).

162.   The precise purpose of Britt's book is not clear. My understanding of his perceived contribution is informed by pages 2 and 184–87 of his book.

In contrast to Britt, Nohrnberg's book is focused more on a literary analysis of Moses in the text and recognizes Moses as a "hero" in Exodus and Numbers, although he subdivides Moses' heroic identity into the categories of "traditional hero," "received hero," "legendary hero," and "culture hero." More helpful are his extended and thoughtful reflections on the literary portrayal of Moses in Exodus. These reflections demonstrate how a purely literary approach can provide a corrective to the tendency of historical-critical scholars to miss some basic elements in the received text due to an almost exclusive focus on its pre-literary formation. Although Nohrnberg does tend to be excessive in laying out extended intertextual connections, he has provided a detailed and plausible comparison between Moses and Jeroboam.[163]

Other recent scholars have also fallen into the trap of allowing their method to dictate their portrayal of Moses. This tendency is especially evident in the work of Van Seters, who is concerned to portray Moses as a prophet in his detailed attempt to establish a late "J" source that relies on D and the prophetic traditions as sources. Despite his overriding agenda to view Moses as a prophet in "J," Van Seters notes the obvious portrayal of Moses as a royal figure in his concluding comments on the portrait of Moses in "J":

> J's presentation of Moses as leader...entails accommodation to royal motifs in the birth story, the flight to Midian, the negotiations with Pharaoh for release, and his victory at sea, even though Moses' role in armed struggle is consciously subdued. The revelation of the law...also has its royal aspect, in which the king is recipient of divine law. This role is confirmed in the "shining face" motif and the repeated references to the Israelites as Moses' people. The strong emphasis on the vanguard motif, in which the divine presence accompanies the leader with his people on their journeys, is another royal motif. The itinerary, the movement in stages, the motion of a camp with military organization, all belong to this same milieu.[164]

Although Van Seters's assessment of the royal motifs in J's portrait of Moses appears to rest on a close reading of certain Pentateuchal texts, his discussion of royal motifs attached to Moses is a subsidiary concern to his larger agenda of demonstrating J's portrayal of Moses as a prophet. Yet, the reflections on the royal features of Moses' portrayal that are scattered throughout Van Seters's book provide a useful starting point for a more systematic investigation of the Pentateuchal portrait of Moses.

---

163.   Nohrnberg, *Like Unto Moses*, 288–91.
164.   Van Seters, *The Life of Moses*, 463.

1.4. *Conclusion*

The principal conclusions of this review of the primary Hellenistic Jewish and modern interpretative descriptions of the figure of Moses as he is portrayed in the Pentateuch are, on the one hand, that the classical interpreters (e.g. Philo and Josephus) typically emphasized Moses' exalted status and unique relationship to the deity. On the other hand, critical scholarship of the past two centuries has generally sought to humanize or historicize Moses in order to recover the likely founder of ancient Israelite religion.

Moreover, this survey has shown that modern critical approaches—especially source criticism, form criticism, and traditio-historical analysis—have tended to fragment the biblical portrayal of Moses by concentrating on the identification of discrete sources and traditions. Without denying that the Pentateuch itself and its portraiture of Moses in particular are the result of a complicated history of composition, this study will investigate the way in which the composite portrait in the received form of this literary complex articulates an understanding of his character and status in order to avoid the trap of allowing a specific method to dictate a particular profile of Moses. This study will differ from the newer "literary" approaches of Britt and Nohrnberg by including an examination of the portrayal of Moses in the context of the ancient Near East. An overview of the principal features of the portrayal of Moses in the Pentateuch will be the topic of the next chapter.

Chapter 2

ROYAL MOTIFS
IN THE PENTATEUCHAL PORTRAITURE OF MOSES:
AN OVERVIEW

2.1. *Introduction*

The consistent portrayal of Moses as an exalted figure in the classical sources surveyed in the last chapter is striking. This chapter will investigate the extent to which this view of Moses in the interpretative traditions of Hellenistic Judaism, though primarily based on several passages (e.g. Exod 7:1; 20:21; Deut 33:1, 5), is also true of the Pentateuch as a whole. Furthermore, with our enlarged understanding of the world of the ancient Near East in the last couple of centuries, does the Pentateuch depict Moses in a way that is consistent with the portrayal of ancient Near Eastern kings as opposed to the category of Hellenistic royalty assumed by the classical sources?

To address these questions, this chapter will provide an overview of the various ways Moses is portrayed in the Pentateuch in order to show that the view of Moses primarily as a prophet or covenant mediator cannot comprehend cogently the varied ways he is presented in the Pentateuch. This overview will also show that many of the aspects of the figure of Moses are also features that are frequently used to portray kings in the Old Testament and ancient Near East. Following this overview of the major motifs of the Pentateuchal portrayal of Moses, this chapter will survey the depictions of the Mesopotamian kings Hammurabi, Esarhaddon, Nabonidus, and Cyrus, in an attempt to demonstrate that the "royal" presentation of Moses lies not so much in the use of individual motifs; rather, various motifs, whether royal or not, cluster together to portray Moses as a king.

2.2. *Survey of the Portrayal of Moses in the Pentateuch*

Many of the aspects of the portrayal of Moses are motifs that are familiar to Pentateuchal authors. The concept of a "floating motif" as developed by David Aaron in his recent investigation of the Decalogue will be utilized here.[1] Aaron coins this term to designate an alternate theory of intertextuality as an explanation for the appearance of common elements in different texts. Common elements have usually been explained by positing the literary dependence of one text upon an earlier source text. Intertextuality has thus been largely an enterprise of identifying texts with common elements, determining the chronological priority of the texts, and examining the literary and historical purposes behind the editing and re-use of source texts. Aaron rejects this linear source-redaction model and argues that the common elements in a group of texts result from independent adaptations of well-known motifs. He defines a "floating motif" as a "highly adaptable set of themes that frequently travel together as part of a culture's ideological, linguistic, aesthetic, or literary 'fabric'"[2] and "'floats' among stories and is engaged within a literature for distinct purposes without insisting upon intertextual links within the biblical literature."[3] In order for a motif to exist, it must be repeatable and exist independently of any literary work. "For the various adaptations to make sense, the ideas themselves must exist independently of any specific literary adaptation, literary or otherwise."[4]

To demonstrate the existence of a motif, this chapter will survey and illustrate its repeated and independent use in the Old Testament and ancient Near East. Several of the motifs will be introduced briefly in this chapter and will be explored in detail in subsequent chapters (i.e. the

---

1. David H. Aaron, *Etched in Stone: The Emergence of the Decalogue* (New York: T&T Clark International, 2006).

2. Ibid., 48.

3. Ibid., 62. By way of critique, the term "floating motif" appears to be a tautology, since motifs by definition are "floating." One would not, in contrast, speak of a "non-floating motif." It seems this new term represents a rhetorical attempt to emphasize the portability and adaptability of a motif as an alternate way to approach common elements shared by different passages in the Old Testament. In a similar way, the earlier study of various motifs in the Joseph and Moses accounts by Thomas L. Thompson and Dorothy Irvin uses the term "plot motif" to refer to a single element within a narrative and a "Traditional Episode" to describe a set of common elements within a story; see their "The Joseph and Moses Narratives," in *Israelite and Judean History* (ed. John H. Hayes and J. Maxwell Miller; Philadelphia: Westminster, 1977), 183.

4. Aaron, *Etched in Stone*, 48.

birth and abandonment of Moses, flight and exile, divine commissioning, public emergence and controversy, temple building, lawgiving and covenant making, servant, and succession). Limitations on space mean that the remaining motifs (e.g. beauty and health, the name "Moses," shepherd, divinity, military leader, judge, humility, and intercessor and appeaser) cannot be treated extensively in the present study. They are, however, given a cursory treatment with the intention of demonstrating the breadth of the portrayal of Moses, and will form the basis for the second part of this chapter, which will seek to show that the various motifs that are combined and clustered in the Pentateuchal depiction of Moses are consistent with the depictions of kings in the ancient Near East.

2.1.a. *The Birth and Abandonment of Moses*
Moses is introduced in Exod 2:1–10 as a "beautiful" (טוב) baby born to unnamed Levitical parents. After three months of hiding, he is placed inside a floatable papyrus basket "among the reeds" on the banks of the Nile under the supervision of his sister. The basket is spotted by Pharaoh's daughter, who, out of compassion for the plight of the Hebrew children, adopts him as her son and gives him the name "Moses." As a result, Moses becomes a member of Pharaoh's royal court and assumes the cultural identity of an Egyptian (cf. Exod 2:19).

When compared to other Old Testament figures, an account of the endangerment and rescue of an infant is unique to Moses. The account that most closely resembles Moses is the abandonment and rescue of Joseph in Gen 37.[5] Yet the endangerment and rescue of an infant is a

---

5. The endangerment of Joseph is one of a number of close parallels between the accounts of Joseph and Moses. The endangerments of both resulted from a group plot. In Exodus, the King of Egypt plans the demise of the Hebrew nation in conversation with the Egyptian population: "Look (הנה)! The Israelite people are too numerous for us. Come and let us deal wisely with them so that they may not multiply" (Exod 1:9; cf. vv. 12–14). In a similar way, Joseph's brothers, in response to the threat of Joseph's rule, plot his death: "They said to each other, 'Look (הנה)! That master of dreams is coming!' Come now, let us kill him and cast him into one of the wells…" (Gen 37:19–20). After this initial plotting, Joseph and Moses both suffer the planned fate, but under controlled conditions under the supervision and care of a sibling (i.e. Moses' "sister" [Exod 2:4, 7–8] and Reuben, Joseph's brother [Gen 37:21–22; cf. vv. 26–28]). Both escaped their fate through chance encounters with foreigners (Pharaoh's daughter; Ishmaelites/Midianites) who provide the means for assimilation into Egyptian culture. As a result, Joseph and Moses, both Hebrews, eventually ended up as members of Egyptian families. Both obtained an Egyptian name (Moses, Joseph is changed to Zaphaneth-Paneah [Gen 41:45]), both married a

familiar motif that is widely attested in numerous cultures, including the ancient Near East. These motifs are typically applied to royal, divine, or heroic characters. Two accounts that have circulated during the approximate period of the composition of the Pentateuch have utilized this motif to depict the rise of kings to power, namely, Sargon of Akkad and Cyrus, king of Persia.[6]

An account of the abandonment and rescue of Sargon of Akkad was circulated during the reign of Sargon II (721–705 B.C.E.). According to this account, Sargon was placed by his mother into a reed basket caulked with bitumen and set adrift on the river. The basket was discovered by someone drawing water from the river who then adopted him. This brief account concludes with Sargon's rise to power as king of Assyria and descriptions of his military exploits and conquests, with a blessing on kings succeeding Sargon.

According to Herodotus (ca. 484–425), a cowherder was ordered to expose Cyrus upon his birth to remove him as a threat to the king of Persia.[7] When the cowherder's wife saw "how fine and fair the child was" (μέγα τε καὶ εὐιδές), they placed her child, who was born stillborn

---

daughter of a priest (Joseph marries Aseneth, daughter of Potiphera priest of On (Gen 41:45). Moses marries Zipporah, daughter of Reuel, the "priest of Midian" (Exod 2:16–21). Both fathered two sons and gave each a name related to the struggle in surviving in a foreign environment. Joseph fathers Manasseh ("God made me forget all my hardship") and Ephraim ("God made me fruitful"; Gen 41:50–52). Likewise, Moses fathers Gershom ("I have been a stranger in a strange land"; Exod 2:22; 18:3) and Eliezer ("God of my father was my help"; Exod 2:22 [LXX; Sry; Vul]; 18:3–4). In sum, both narratives share a similar sequence of abandonment, rescue, and rise to an exalted royal position over Egypt and Israel.

6.   The Egyptian account of the birth of Horus, and how his mother placed him among the marshes to hide him from his uncle Seth, has also been compared to Moses. See Gary A. Rendsburg, "Moses as Equal to Pharaoh," in *Text, Artifact, and Image: Revealing Ancient Israelite Religion* (ed. Gary M. Beckman and Theodore J. Lewis; Providence, R.I.: Brown University Press, 2006), 204–8, and Meik Gerhards, *Die Aussetzungsgeschichte des Mose* (WMANT 109; Neukirchen–Vluyn: Neukirchener Verlag, 2006), 244–47. Both accounts feature two female characters. One is the infant's mother who "hides" the infant for protection. The other female character is a close relative who guards the infant. These similarities as well as the Egyptian setting for both warrant a detailed reexamination. This account, however, is found in texts produced well after the formation of the Pentateuch (Jumilhac Papyrus during the Ptolemaic period and Plutarch's *Isis and Osiris* during the Greco-Roman period).

7.   This summary and citations of the English and Greek text are taken from A. D. Godley, trans., *Herodotus* (LCL; New York: G. P. Putnam's Sons, 1931), 139–71.

that day, in a "chest" (ἄγγος), to be devoured by the wild animals in a remote location in the mountains. Cyrus remained in their family until the age of ten, when his true identity was discovered. He was returned to his natural parents and eventually assumed power and overthrew the king of Persia.

An examination of the accounts of Sargon and Cyrus suggests that an episode of an endangered birth is a familiar motif that introduces the child destined for greatness. Following this introduction is the account of his rule. The introduction of Moses as an abandoned and rescued infant, then, plays a similar role to introduce Moses as the one who will rescue and save Israel from Egyptian rule. All three accounts share the similar features of the abandonment of an infant, the adoption of the infant into a different family, and, after the infant reaches adulthood, his emergence as the leader of his people. In sum, in contrast to the depiction of other characters in the Old Testament, the account of Moses begins with the abandonment and rescue of Moses as an infant. This account shares a number of conceptual features with the ancient Near Eastern accounts of the rise of Sargon and Cyrus to power that suggest the portrayal of Moses as a royal-like figure who is destined to lead and rescue Israel from Egyptian rule.[8]

2.1.b. *Beauty and Health*

The canonical presentation of Moses begins and ends with reference to the appearance and health of Moses. At his birth, he is described as "beautiful" (טוב; Exod 2:2).[9] Upon his death, Moses "was one hundred and twenty years old...his sight was unimpaired and his vigor had not abated" (Deut 34:7). Here Moses is presented as one in perfect health on

---

8. See esp. the concise discussion in the section "The Floating Foundling" in William H. C. Propp, *Exodus 1–18: A New Translation with Introduction and Commentary* (AB 2; New York: Doubleday, 1998), 155–58.

9. Cf. Jean Daniel Macchi, "La naissance de Moise (Exode 2/1–10)," *ETR* 69 (1994): 399: "La mère cache son enfant car elle vit qu'*il était beau*. Chaque mère trouve belle sa progéniture, mais ici le terme 'beau' (*ṭôb*) ne renvoie pas exclusivement à des considérations d'esthétique maternelles. En effet, l'idéologie royale attribue fréquemment ce qualificatif aux souverains. Ainsi l'utilisation de ce terme pour Moïse bébé avertit déjà le lecteur du destin extraordinaire qui attend cet enfant" (translation: "The mother hides her child for she sees that *he was beautiful*. Every mother finds her children beautiful, but here the term beautiful [*ṭôb*] does not lend exclusively to considerations of maternal esthetics. In fact, royal ideology frequently attributes this qualifier to sovereigns. Thus the use of this term for the baby Moses already alerts the reader to the extraordinary destiny awaiting the child").

the day of his death who dies rather at "the Lord's command" (Deut 34:5).

This remarkable description of Moses as "beautiful" and in perfect health is a common way to portray royal figures in the Old Testament and ancient Near East. A handsome appearance is an important attribute that is typically noted in the introduction of a royal character. Examples in the Old Testament include *Joseph* ("handsome and good looking," יְפֵה־תֹאַר וִיפֵה מַרְאֶה; Gen 39:6); *Saul* ("a handsome [טוֹב] young man. There was not a man among the people of Israel more handsome [טוֹב] than he; he stood head and shoulders above everyone else"; 1 Sam 9:2); *David* ("He was ruddy, and had beautiful eyes [יְפֵה עֵינַיִם], and was handsome [טוֹב]"; 1 Sam 16:12; cf. 17:42); *Absalom* ("In all Israel there was no one to be praised so much for his beauty [יֹפִי]"; 2 Sam 14:25); *Adonijah* (a "very handsome man [טוֹב תֹאַר מְאֹד]"; 1 Kgs 1:6); *Esther* ("the girl was fair [יְפַת־תֹאַר] and beautiful [טוֹבַת מַרְאֶה]"; Est 2:7); and *Daniel* (who, as part of the "royal family and of the nobility," is described as "without physical defect and handsome [מַרְאֶה טוֹבִי]"; Dan 1:4)[10]

The handsome appearance of a king is richly documented in ancient Near Eastern and classical sources. For example, a number of sources in the Persian period have been collected by Pierre Briant, who concludes that "this theme is especially prominent during periods of dynastic competition among the various candidates for royal power."[11] These descriptions include the portrayal of Darius I by Strabo as "the most handsome of men" and Plutarch's description of Darius III as "the tallest and most handsomest man of his time."

According to Dan 1, the healthy appearance of members of the court results from the affluent lifestyle of the court characterized by ample access to royal food and wine. Another explanation is suggested by Elena Cassin, who connects the ancient Near Eastern king's physical health and vigor to the manifestation of the king's *melammu*, that is, his radiance or light, granted to him by the deity.[12]

---

10. Cf. John J. Collins, *Daniel: A Commentary on the Book of Daniel* (Hermeneia; Minneapolis: Fortress, 1993), 137: "While good looks and beauty are often ascribed to kings (e.g. Ps 45:2), they are also characteristic of boys selected to be eunuchs, according to Herodotus."

11. Pierre Briant, *From Cyrus to Alexander: A History of the Persian Empire* (trans. Peter D. Daniels; Winona Lake, Ind.: Eisenbrauns, 2002), 225.

12. Elena Cassin, *La splendeur divine: Introduction à l'étude de la mentalité mésopotamienne* (Paris: Mouton, 1968), 80.

In addition to Absalom's unparalleled beauty, he is also depicted as one in perfect health. According to 2 Sam 14:25, "from the sole of his foot to the crown of his head there was no blemish in him." This emphasis on perfect health is also mentioned at end of Moses' life. According to Deut 34:7, Moses lived one hundred and twenty years. He has perfect eyesight, and his "vigor" has not abated. The length of Moses' life is the maximum life span for a human being according to Gen 6:3. In sum, the beginning and conclusion of the career of Moses present him as a person who is beautiful and in perfect health throughout his life, a quality that is typically attributed to royal figures in the ancient Near East.

2.1.c. *The Name "Moses"*

Another detail from Exod 2:1–10 that presents Moses as a royal figure is his naming by Pharaoh's daughter and his adoption into the Egyptian royal court. The name "Moses" evokes a number of interpretations that are not necessarily mutually exclusive.[13] There is broad agreement that the name "Moses" is the Hebrew equivalent of the Egyptian *mśy* ("is born") that is followed by the name of a deity in the names of a number of Pharaohs such as Rameses, Thutmose, and Ptahmose.[14]

This Egyptian name, however, is given a Hebrew wordplay by Pharaoh's daughter, meaning "one who draws out." The Hebrew root משה occurs in at least three places. In 2 Sam 22:17 (= Ps 18:16), the reference is to God's salvation from water. Isaiah 63:11 (MT) explicitly connects the word "Moses" with the act of drawing from the water: "He remembered the days of old, the one who draws his people (משה עמו). Where is the one that drew (המעלם) them from the Sea, the one who shepherds his flock?" The Hebrew wordplay of the name "Moses" is based on the act of saving Moses from the fate of Hebrew male infants to die in the Nile and anticipates his destiny to save his people out from the

---

13. Jean Daniel Macchi, "La Naissance de Moise," 401, suggests that the name Moses may be a two-fold etiology that explains his Levitical and Egyptian identity.

14. *HALOT*, 642; J. G. Griffiths, "The Egyptian Derivation of the Name Moses," *JNES* 12 (1953): 225–32. See also Propp, *Exodus 1–18*, 152; Crüsemann, *The Torah*, 59 n. 4; James S. Ackerman, "The Literary Context of the Moses Birth Story," in *Literary Interpretations of Biblical Narratives* (ed. Kenneth R. R. Gros Louis; Bible in Literature Courses; Nashville: Abingdon, 1974), 94; Paul E. Hughes, "Moses' Birth Story: A Biblical Matrix for Prophetic Messianism," in *Eschatology, Messianism, and the Dead Sea Scrolls* (ed. Craig A. Evans; Studies in the Dead Sea Scrolls and Related Literature; Grand Rapids: Eerdmans, 1997), 15–16; Macchi, "La Naissance de Moise," 401; Gerhards, *Mose*, 139–41.

river in Exod 14 (cf. Isa 63:11). In sum, although it is not a "motif," the name "Moses" indicates two aspects of Moses' identity, as an Egyptian and Hebrew. The adoption of Moses into Pharaoh's court and his Pharaoh-like name serves to anticipate his destiny as one who will challenge Pharaoh (see Exod 7:1).[15] In addition, the Hebrew wordplay on his name indicates his destiny as Israel's savior.

2.1.d. *Flight and Exile*

Indications of the royal portrayal of Moses continue to be given in the following section (Exod 2:11–22). The most important and widely documented motif is the flight to security from the threat of the reigning king.[16] According to Exod 2:11–15, Pharaoh attempts to kill Moses after finding out that Moses has killed an Egyptian, presumably one of the taskmasters supervising the Hebrew slaves (cf. Exod 1:11, 13). Moses flees from Egypt and settles in Midian, where he marries into a Midianite priestly family (Exod 2:15–22). There he is commissioned and empowered by God to lead Israel out of Egypt and returns only upon the death of Pharaoh and those seeking to kill him (Exod 3:1–4:20).

The flight and return of a royal figure is a motif that is well attested in the Old Testament and ancient Near East. The account of Moses' flight and return bear a remarkable resemblance with the portrayals of David, Hadad, and Jeroboam I.[17] This motif is also prominent in several ancient Near Eastern biographies and inscriptions, such as the Egyptian "Tale of Sinuhe," the autobiography of Idrimi, and the royal inscriptions of Esarhaddon.[18] These three ancient Near Eastern accounts are located across a broad geographical and chronological range (over a thousand years in Egypt, Levant, and Assyria) and attest the familiarity of the motif of the flight and return of a political fugitive. These accounts show that this motif is typically adapted and applied to a *royal* or *political* figure and is another important indication that Moses is portrayed primarily as a royal figure in the Pentateuch.

---

15. On the presentation of Moses as a rival to Pharaoh in Exod 1–15, see Rendsburg, "Moses." It is curious that Rendsburg does not discuss the relevance of the name "Moses" to his argument.

16. A closer analysis of Exod 2:11–22 can be found in Chapter 3 of the present study.

17. 1 Sam 19:8–2 Sam 2:4; 1 Kgs 11:14–40.

18. A more detailed comparison of these accounts with the portrayal of Moses will be made in Chapter 3 of this study.

2.1.e. *Shepherd*

The importance of the shepherding motif is indicated by its location at the beginning and conclusion of the career of Moses. The commissioning of Moses occurs when he is shepherding the flock of his father-in-law during his sojourn in Midian (Exod 3:1–4:18). Near the end of his life, Moses commands the appointment of a successor for the task of leading the people so "that the congregation of the Lord may not be like sheep without a shepherd" (Num 27:15–17). This motif appears also in the depiction of God leading Israel as God's flock through the agency of Moses and Aaron (Ps 77:20). It is mostly likely Moses and Aaron who are designated as "shepherds" in Isa 63:11 ("Where is the one who brought them up out of the sea with the shepherds of his flock?").

With the exception of Abel, and perhaps Amos (Gen 4:2; Amos 9:14–15), only three specific individuals in the Old Testament are portrayed as shepherds—Joseph, Moses, and David—which suggests that Moses is a royal figure of the caliber of David or Joseph. A close examination of the portrayal of these three figures shows the royal character of the task of shepherding (common terms are underlined in the following quotations).

יוסף...<u>היה רעה את־</u>אחיו <u>בצאן</u>

Joseph...was shepherding the flock with his brothers. (Gen 37:2)

ומשה <u>היה רעה את־צאן</u> יתרו חתן

Moses was shepherding the flock of Jethro, his father-in-law. (Exod 3:1)

<u>רעה היה</u> עבדך לאביו <u>בצאן</u>

Your servant (David) was shepherding the flock of his father. (1 Sam 17:34[19])

The phrasing of shepherding (היה with the participle of רעה and צאן as possession of a family member—e.g. "his brothers," "his father-in-law") occurs in combination only in these three passages.[19] The explicit connection between the duties of shepherding as qualification for battle is made explicit in David's speech to Saul before his fight with Goliath, one of the several episodes of David's rise to royal power (1 Sam 17:34–37).[20] There David justifies his qualification to fight Goliath by noting his

19.   Abraham Even-Shoshan, *A New Concordance of the Old Testament Using the Hebrew and Aramaic Text* (2d ed.; Jerusalem: Kiryat Sefer, 1993), 1084.

20.   1 Sam 17:40 notes that David fights Goliath only with the implements of a shepherd (i.e. "rod," "shepherd's bag," and "sling"). Cf. also the specific duties of shepherding in Ezek 34:1–31 that are applied to both God and human king (lit. "prince," v. 24) with the task of leadership described as feeding the sheep, strengthening the weak, binding the injured, bringing back the strayed, and protecting the sheep.

experience in defending the flock against predators. Moreover, the description of Joseph as the youngest brother entrusted with the care of the flock recalls the similar portrayal of David tending to the care of the flock (1 Sam 16:11; 17:34). Finally, the exact phrasing of their occupation as רעה בצאן, which occurs only in Gen 37:12; 1 Sam 16:11, and 17:34, signals an intentional comparison of Joseph with David as a royal figure. In addition to Joseph and David, a parallel also occurs between Joseph and Moses (Gen 37:2 // Exod 3:1). Both Moses and Joseph are shepherding flocks entrusted in their care. That the depiction of the shepherding vocation of Moses and Joseph uses almost identical phrasing with David provides a warrant for viewing the activity of shepherding as a *royal* vocation for Moses and Joseph.

Another example of the close correspondence between Moses and Joseph is the similar sequencing of the words and phrases in Gen 37:12–14 and Exod 3:1, 4, 10 (underlined in the following quotations):

וילכו אחיו לרעות את־צאן אביהם בשכם
ויאמר ישראל אל־יוסף הלוא אחיך רעים
בשכם לכה ואשלחך אליהם ויאמר לו הנני

Now his brothers went to pasture their father's flock near Shechem. And Israel said to Joseph, "Are not your brothers pasturing the flock at Shechem? Come, I will send you to them." He answered, "Here I am." (Gen 37:12–14)

ומשה היה רעה את־צאן יתרו חתנו כהן מדין
ויאמר משה משה ויאמר הנני
ועתה לכה ואשלחך אל־פרעה

Moses was keeping the flock of his father-in-law Jethro, the priest of Midian; …God called to him out of the bush, "Moses, Moses!" And he said, "Here I am." So come, I will send you to Pharaoh…" (Exod 3:1, 4b, 10a)

The phrase לכה ואשלחך אל occurs only in Gen 37:13 and Exod 3:10.[21] This phrase in conjunction with the herding of sheep (רעה צאן), the exclamation הנני, and the location of Gen 37:12–14 and Exod 3:1, 4, 10 at the beginning of the Joseph and Moses narrative complexes, in addition to the clear verbal linking of Moses to Joseph in Gen 37:2 and Exod 3:1, point to an explicit literary comparison between the two royal characters of Joseph and Moses. Jacob's summoning and sending of Joseph sets in motion a chain of events that results in the abandonment of Joseph in the well and his subsequent royal exaltation among the Egyptians and his family in Egypt. In a similar way, the commissioning and sending of Moses also results in the exaltation of Moses in the sight

---

21. Even-Shoshan, *A New Concordance*, 301.

of the Pharaoh and the Egyptians (Exod 7:1; 11:3; etc.) as well as the Israelite community (Exod 4:16, 31; 14:30, 31, etc.).

In addition to Joseph, Moses, and David, the motif of shepherding has been applied to God as king (e.g. Gen 49:24; Ps 23:1; Isa 40:11) as well as to the royal office, priests, and political leaders in the Old Testament (e.g. Jer 2:8; 3:15; 10:21; 12:10; 22:22; 23:1–8; 25:34–38; 50:6–7; Ezek 34:1–31; Mic 5:5; Nah 3:18; Zech 9:16; 10:2–3; 11:4–17).[22] Many ancient Near Eastern sources indicate the popularity of describing the king as shepherd. Hammurabi is designated as "shepherd" twice in the prologue to his law code and twice in the epilogue. Two of these references stress Hammurabi's divine election."[23] Nebuchadnezzar I is a "just king, faithful shepherd who makes firm the foundations of the land."[24] Nebuchadnezzar II describes himself as "king of Babylon, the loyal shepherd, the one permanently selected by Marduk."[25] After assuming the throne, Esarhaddon described his throne as the "shepherdship of Assyria" given to him by Marduk.[26] Finally, Cyrus "shepherded with justice and righteousness all the black headed people, over whom he (Marduk) had given him victory."[27]

In sum, close parallels of the shepherding activity of Moses with Joseph and David suggest the presentation of Moses as a shepherd is a preview of his royal destiny; it is consistent with the common use of the shepherding motif to describe primarily the activity of kings in the ancient Near East. The use of this motif to portray Moses at the time of his commissioning as well as to characterize his leadership over Israel is another piece of evidence for the portrayal of Moses as a royal figure in the Pentateuch.

---

22. See the entry, "Sheep, Shepherd," by Jack W. Vancil in *ABD* 5:1188–91, who notes the popularity of describing Assyrian kings with this image (p. 1188).

23. "I am Hammurabi, the shepherd, selected by the god Enlil…shepherd of the people, whose deeds are pleasing to the goddess Isthar" and "I am Hammurabi, noble king. I have not been careless or negligent toward humankind, granted to my care by the god Enlil, and with whose shepherding the god Marduk has charged me… The great gods having chosen me, I am indeed the shepherd who brings peace" ("The Laws of Hammurabi," translated by Martha Roth [*COS* 2.131:335–36, 351]).

24. Benjamin R. Foster, *From Distant Days: Myths, Tales, and Poetry of Ancient Mesopotamia* (Bethesda, Md.: CDL, 1995), 198.

25. "Nebuchadnezzar II's Restoration of E-Urimin-Ankia, The Ziggurat of Borsippa," translated by Paul-Alain Beaulieu (*COS* 2.122B:309).

26. Simo Parpola, *Assyrian Prophecies* (SAA; Helsinki: Helsinki University Press, 1997), LXXV.

27. "Cyrus Cylinder," translated by Mordechai Cogan (*COS* 2.124:315).

2.1.f. *Private Commissioning*

The call of Moses in Exod 3:1–4:18 has too often been assumed to be the calling of a prophet.[28] A common justification for this view is the similarities between the divine commissioning of Moses and Jeremiah (Exod 3:1–4:18; Jer 1).[29] To be sure, a number of similarities exist between the two accounts, such as an inability to speak well (Jer 1:6; Exod 4:10), the presence of God promised to both (Jer 1:8, 19; Exod 3:12; 4:12), and the "sending" by God of both (Jer 1:7; Exod 3:10, 12, 13, etc.).[30] Despite these similarities, the nature and purpose of the commissioning is quite different. Moses is not commissioned explicitly as a prophet, and is rather designated as "god" with Aaron as his prophet (Exod 4:16; 7:1) for the purpose of delivering Israel from Egypt (Exod 3:10). In contrast, Jeremiah is commissioned as a "prophet" for the specific task of conveying an unpopular message from God against the nations and the people of Judah (Jer 1:5, 7, 9–10, 17–18).

The commissioning account of Moses rather shares a similar pattern to the commissioning of Gideon and Saul, both of whom are portrayed as royal figures. In all three accounts we have a cry of the people as a result of a crisis. In the case of Moses, Israel cries out due to their harsh slavery in Egypt (Exod 2:23–25; 3:7, 9). In the time of Gideon, Israel cries to the Lord due to the Midianite oppression (Judg 6:6–7). Later, during the time of Samuel, Israel's outcry to the Lord due to the Philistine oppression leads him to command Samuel to anoint Saul to save Israel (1 Sam 9:15–16).

---

28. A recent example is Michael Widmer, *Moses, God, and the Dynamics of Intercessory Prayer: A Study of Exodus 32–34 and Numbers 13–14* (FAT; Tübingen: Mohr Siebeck, 2004), 75–77.

29. Brevard S. Childs, *The Book of Exodus: A Critical, Theological Commentary* (OTL; Philadelphia: Westminster, 1974), 55–56, 59; Van Seters, *The Life of Moses*, 45–46; Propp, *Exodus 1–18*, 229–31. An example of the assumption of Moses as prophet is the statement by Paul E. Hughes that "Although the great classical prophets immediately come to mind when considering this phenomenon—figures like Isaiah, Jeremiah, and Ezekiel—it is with Moses that the first prophetic call narrative in the Hebrew Bible is associated" ("Moses' Birth Story," 10).

30. In his attempt to argue that the Passover sections of Exodus present Moses as a royal figure who exemplifies the ancient Near Eastern model of the sacral king, Ivan Engnell claims that the action of God "sending" Moses does not necessarily indicate the sending of a prophet but may also describe the "sending" of a royal savior (e.g. Gideon; Judg 6:14) or divine leader (lit. the מלאך; Exod 23:20; cf. also the "sending" of the "terror" and "pestilence" in vv. 27, 28). See Engnell's *A Rigid Scrutiny: Critical Essays on the Old Testament* (ed. and trans. John T. Willis; Nashville: Vanderbilt University Press, 1969), 191.

Following the crisis and cry, the accounts of Moses, Gideon, and Saul narrate a basic pattern of a private, divine commissioning and empowerment to deliver Israel. All three are engaged in a routine activity that serves to isolate them for a private encounter: Moses is shepherding the sheep of his father-in-law (Exod 3:1–6); Gideon is threshing wheat in secret (Judg 6:11–24); and Saul's search for his father's lost donkeys eventually results in his anointing by Samuel in secret (1 Sam 9:1–10:1). After the isolating incident, all three are commissioned by God, through an angel or prophet, to the task of saving Israel from their oppression. Each object to their call by drawing attention to their lowly and insignificant status (Exod 3:11; Judg 6:13, 15; 1 Sam 9:21). In response to their objection and by way of reassurance, all three are empowered by God and given signs. God promises to be "with" Moses, designates him as "god" to Aaron and Israel, and equips him with the ability to perform signs to convince Israel to put their trust in Moses (Exod 3:12–4:17; 4:29–31). In a similar way, God promises to be "with" Gideon, who is later possessed by the "spirit of the Lord" that leads him to begin the process of assembling a militia to overthrow Midian. Gideon is also given signs from God to convince him that he will succeed (Judg 6:36–40; cf. 6:17–23). Finally, a series of signs confirms God's choice of Saul to save Israel and that God's presence is indeed "with" Saul (1 Sam 10:1–16). As with Gideon, Saul is empowered by God's spirit (1 Sam 10:6, 10; 11:6; 16:13–14).

To conclude, the call of Jeremiah lacks two important features that are found in the commissioning accounts of Moses, Gideon, and Saul, namely, the indication of a cry due to a crisis and the giving of signs to confirm the divine authenticity of the call. The accounts of the commissioning of Gideon and Saul indicate that the call of Moses follows the basic pattern of the commissioning and empowerment of a royal figure to deliver Israel from their enemies. Jeremiah's commissioning, by contrast, is that of a prophet for the task of proclaiming God's message to Judah and the nations. It is therefore not appropriate to use the commissioning of Moses as a warrant for viewing Moses as a prophetic figure.

2.1.g. *Public Emergence and Controversy*
A major issue raised during the private commissioning of Moses in Exod 3:1–4:17 is the difficulty of securing Israel's trust in the authenticity of Moses' message that God has indeed heard their cry as well as their affirmation of the authority and ability of Moses to deliver Israel (Exod 3:13–18; 4:1–9). The pressing issue in the following segment

(Exod 4:18–5:23) is now for Moses to secure the trust of the people and leaders of Israel in his authority as God's chosen agent. Although Israel initially trusts in Moses when Aaron performs the signs on Moses' behalf, the intensification of their labor results in their refusal to listen to Moses (Exod 4:29–31; 5:9, 20–21; cf. 6:9). Their trust in Moses eventually becomes more secure, especially after the deliverance at the sea and the theophany at Sinai (Exod 14:31; 19:9). The narrative flow of Exod 3–40, presented in the chart appearing the Appendix to the present study, indicates that the commissioning of Moses that is done in private is revealed to the public, disputed, and eventually acknowledged and affirmed in a prolonged process that begins with the return of Moses to Egypt in Exod 4:18 and concludes with Moses' apotheosis in Exod 34:1–35.

This process of an individual assuming publicly the divine authority granted in private can also be discerned in the accounts of several other royal figures in the Old Testament. After Gideon's military defeat of Midian, Israel is ready to affirm him as king (Judg 8:22). Saul's public affirmation as king takes place through several events, including the public presentation by Samuel and Saul's military victory against the Ammonites (1 Sam 10:17–12:24). Likewise, David becomes king over Israel only after a lengthy period following his private anointing that includes his flight and hiding from Saul until Saul's death (1 Sam 19:8–2 Sam 1) and David's consolidation of power over Israel (2 Sam 2:1–5:5). Finally, the same pattern can be discerned in the account of Jeroboam's rise to power. After his private commissioning to be king over north Israel, Jeroboam flees from Solomon to Egypt (1 Kgs 11:26–40). After Solomon's death, Jeroboam assumes power at the end of failed negotiations between north Israel and Rehoboam, Solomon's successor (1 Kgs 12:1–33). Each of these royal figures assumes power or is publicly affirmed as king as the conclusion of a series of events that begins with a time of crisis, the private selection of the ruler, and the controversial emergence of the rule to power.

In addition to the accounts of the four Old Testament figures surveyed here (Gideon, Saul, David, Jeroboam), this pattern can also be discerned in the depictions of the rise to power of various kings in the ancient Near East, especially Esarhaddon and Nabonidus. Since the accounts of these ancient Near Eastern kings are not as well known, they will be summarized in more detail here.

Obedience to the Voice of the Lord and His Servant Moses:
The Narrative Structure of Exodus 3–40

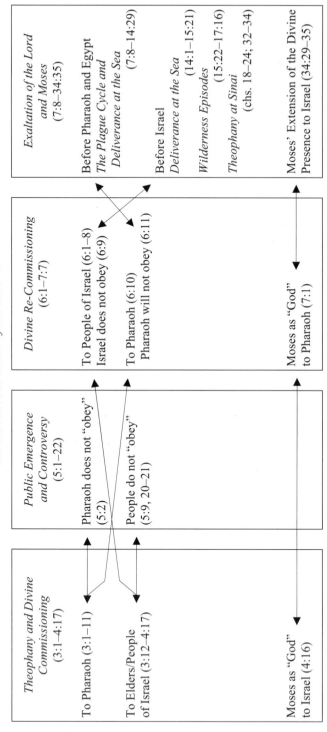

Theophany and Divine
Commissioning
(3:1–4:17)

To Pharaoh (3:1–11)

To Elders/People
of Israel (3:12–4:17)

Moses as "God"
to Israel (4:16)

Public Emergence
and Controversy
(5:1–22)

Pharaoh does not "obey"
(5:2)

People do not "obey"
(5:9, 20–21)

Divine Re-Commissioning
(6:1–7:7)

To People of Israel (6:1–8)
Israel does not obey (6:9)

To Pharaoh (6:10)
Pharaoh will not obey (6:11)

Moses as "God"
to Pharaoh (7:1)

Exaltation of the Lord
and Moses
(7:8–34:35)

Before Pharaoh and Egypt
The Plague Cycle and
Deliverance at the Sea
(7:8–14:29)

Before Israel
Deliverance at the Sea
(14:1–15:21)
Wilderness Episodes
(15:22–17:16)
Theophany at Sinai
(chs. 18–24; 32–34)

Moses' Extension of the Divine
Presence to Israel (34:29–35)

He (Moses) was unequalled for all the signs and wonders that the Lord sent him to perform in the land of
Egypt, against Pharaoh and all his servants and his entire land, and for all the mighty deeds and all the
terrifying displays of power that Moses performed in the sight of all Israel. (Deut 34:11–12)

The autobiographical inscriptions of Esarhaddon (r. 680–669) present a narrative of his rise to power.[31] He was designated as heir to the throne over his older brothers by his father at the command of the Assyrian gods. In response to Esarhaddon's cry in response to hostility and slander from his brothers, the gods Assur and Marduk sent Esarhaddon into exile under their protection. When his brothers, vying for power, instigated civil unrest, Esarhaddon lamented to Assur and Marduk by tearing his garments and raising his hands. Assur and Marduk accepted his prayer and commanded Esarhaddon to go to Nineveh with the gods at his side: "Go without delay! We will go by your side and slay your enemies!" Without waiting to muster and organize his troops, Esarhaddon immediately marched toward Nineveh. When he faced opposition on the way,

> fear of the great gods, my lords, befell them, and when they saw the strength of my onslaught, they went out of their minds... Ištar, the lady of war and battle, who loves my priesthood, stood by my side and broke their bows and disrupted their battle array. They said in their ranks, "This is our king!" and by her august command they crossed over to my side.[32]

Upon reaching Nineveh, Esarhaddon faced the obstacle of crossing the Tigris, and "by the command of Sin and Šamaš...I made all my troops jump across the broad Tigris as if it were a ditch." An oracle sent to Esarhaddon before the crossing reports the words of Ištar: "Have no fear my king!... I will not let you come to shame. I will take you safely across the river."[33] Upon entering Nineveh, Esarhaddon assumed the throne and later attributed his "shepherdship of Assyria" to Marduk. Esarhaddon restored the sanctuaries and reformed the cult that resulted in the blessing of rain, a reversal of Marduk's curse made seven years earlier due to cultic abuses. His rise to power is aptly summarized:

> You duly chose me, Esarhaddon, from amongst my older brothers, placed your sweet protection over me, leveled all my enemies like the deluge, killed all my foes, made me attain my desire, and gave me the shepherd-ship of Assyria to calm the heart of your great godhead and to placate your mind.
>
> At the beginning of my kingship, in my first regnal year, when I magnificently ascended the royal throne, good portents concerning the resettling of the city and the restoration of its sanctuaries occurred to me in heaven and on earth.[34]

---

31. Translations of the Esarhaddon inscriptions are found in Parpola, *Assyrian Prophecies*, LXXII–LXXV and summarized here.

32. Ibid., LXXIII.

33. Ibid., 7–8.

34. Ibid., LXXIV–LXXV.

Likewise, Nabonidus was an unlikely candidate for the throne of Babylon and assumed power only after a series of events. The details of his
rise to power and career have been reconstructed by Paul-Alain Beaulieu
as the result of a painstaking study of a number of extant inscriptions.[35]
Beaulieu's analysis shows that Nabonidus was of a non-royal, non-
Babylonian pedigree. He was from Harran, the location of the sanctuary
to Sin, and was brought with his mother to Babylon, probably as
captives, after Nabopolassar's destruction of Harran.[36] Not belonging to
the royal or upper class, Nabonidus' mother nevertheless won favor in
the Babylonian royal court and later reported near the end of her life that
she introduced her son to Nebuchadnezzar and his son Neriglissar.[37] As a
result of this introduction, Nabonidus was appointed to an office, likely
as a courtier, and lived most of his life as a palace official in Babylon.
After the deaths of Nebuchadnezzar and two of his sons, his successor,
Labashi-Marduk, was assassinated as the result of a palace coup. This
coup resulted in the installation of Nabonidus as king and most likely
included and probably was orchestrated by Nabonidus's son, Belshazzar.[38]

Already an aged man upon assuming control of Babylon, the circumstances of his social status and rise to power are illuminated by
Nabonidus' assertion that "I am Nabonidus, the only son, who has
nobody. In my mind there was no thought of kingship."[39] Nabonidus was
reluctant to assume the throne. He exhibited an openness about his lack
of qualifications to the throne and had a "troubled conscience" about the
legitimacy of his position.[40] A number of inscriptions reveal Nabonidus'
attempt to establish the legitimacy of his rule through the use of various
royal motifs. Marduk has called him by name, a common phrase for
royal legitimation.[41] Nabonidus was elevated to kingship by Marduk and

35. Paul-Alain Beaulieu, *The Reign of Nabonidus, King of Babylon, 556–539 B.C.* (New Haven: Yale University Press, 1989).

36. Ibid., 77.

37. According to the Adad-guppi biographical inscription, on which see ibid., 79.

38. Beaulieu speculates that Belshazzar was the leader of the conspiracy and proposed his aging father to rule the throne, presumably anticipating a brief period of rule that would eventually pave the way for Belshazzar to assume the throne (ibid., 98, 104).

39. Ibid., 67.

40. Ibid., 89. Beaulieu compares Nabonidus' rise to power to the rise of Claudius and his reluctance to rule after the murder of Caligula.

41. Ibid., 113.

referred to himself as "creature of Nabu and Marduk."[42] Nabonidus justified his rise to power by virtue of his superior expertise as a general and
his leadership of the army.

In distinction from his Babylonian predecessors, Nabonidus also
legitimated his rule by situating himself in continuity with the historical
Assyrian empire and the dynasty of Sargon. His fascination with all
things Assyrian is well known. He revived the Assyrian custom begun by
Sargon of Akkad by installing his daughter as high priestess at Ur.[43]
During an excavation of Sin's sanctuary, he ordered the restoration and
reinstallation of a damaged statue of Sargon of Akkad and regular cultic
offerings before the statue. Nabonidus' historical awareness of the
Assyrian rulers is indicated by references to his predecessors and dates of
their rule. Finally, another discovery of the inscriptions of Assurbanipal
led Nabonidus to adopt royal Assyrian titles and epithets. The portrayal
of Nabonidus as reconstructed by Beaulieu shows the continuous effort
of Nabonidus to legitimate his claim to the throne amid persistent
controversy of his non-dynastic assumption to power.

By way of summation, the account of Moses follows the basic pattern
of the public emergence and affirmation of the candidate who has been
privately chosen by the deity. All of the royal figures surveyed here
indicate the common pattern of the process of a non-dynastic candidate
to establish the legitimacy of his rule. The commissioning of Moses
begins the process of establishing his authority over Israel and securing
Israel's affirmation of his status as God's chosen and empowered leader
sent by God to rescue Israel from Egypt.

2.1.h. *Divinity*

During the process of Moses' public emergence in Exod 1:1–7:7, he is
designated twice by God as אלהים:

> You will speak to him (i.e. Aaron) and put words into his mouth, and I
> will be with your mouth and with his mouth so that I will teach you (pl.)
> what to do. He will speak for you to the people. It will happen that he
> will become a mouth for you and you will become God (אלהים) to him.
> (Exod 4:16)

> The Lord said to Moses, "See, I have made you God (אלהים) to Pharaoh,
> and your brother Aaron will be your prophet." (Exod 7:1; author's
> translation)

42. Ibid., 47.
43. Ibid., 71.

These two texts portray Moses acting as "God" to Aaron and Israel (Exod 4:16) and Pharaoh (Exod 7:1) in two specific ways. First, Moses has Aaron as his prophet. The act of putting words into someone's mouth is normally attributed to God (cf. Deut 18:18; Jer 1:9) but here describes Moses' role as "God" who puts his words into the mouth of Aaron, who will speak on behalf of Moses. In addition to speaking on behalf of Moses, Aaron performs signs on behalf of Moses before the people (Exod 4:30) as well as throughout the first half of the plague cycle.[44] After underscoring this point, the plague narrative shifts away from Aaron and focuses exclusively on the conflict between Pharaoh and Moses, shown especially by the fact that God never issues a command to Aaron via Moses to perform a plague in the subsequent accounts of the flies (8:20–30); livestock (9:1–7); boils (9:8–12);[45] hail (9:13–35); locusts (10:1–20); darkness (10:21–29). Completing this cycle is the direct action of God who "strikes" the firstborn of Egypt (11:1–12:32). Moses is portrayed throughout, not as a prophet, but as one on par with Pharaoh, with Aaron as the prophet who speaks and acts on behalf of Moses.[46]

A second way that Moses acts as "God" is his empowerment to perform miracles on behalf of God:

> And the Lord said to Moses, "When you go back to Egypt, see that you perform before Pharaoh *all the wonders that I have put in your power.*" (Exod 4:21)

Elsewhere it is God who performs the signs and wonders to bring Israel out of Egypt (Exod 3:19; 6:1; 7:3; Deut 4:34, 37; 26:8), and these divine activities are clearly attributed to Moses in the concluding verses of the Pentateuch:

---

44. A closer examination of plague cycle reveals that Aaron acts on behalf of God's command to Moses in conflict with the magicians (rod to snake—7:8–13; blood—7:14–25; frogs—8:1–15; and gnats—8:16–19). The first four episodes report a conflict between the "underlings" of Pharaoh and Moses and demonstrate the superiority of Aaron over the magicians. On this, see Moshe Greenberg, "The Redaction of the Plague Narrative in P," in *Near Eastern Studies in Honor of William Foxwell Albright* (ed. Hans Goedicke; Baltimore: The Johns Hopkins University Press, 1971), 243–52.

45. Even here Moses does not receive a divine command to order Aaron to act on his behalf. A close examination of the plague cycle shows that Aaron has an active role in effecting the plague only in conflict with the magicians, which might explain the reference to Aaron in the account of the boils.

46. On this point, see esp. Rendsburg, "Moses."

> He (i.e. Moses) was unequaled for all the signs and wonders that the Lord
> sent him to perform in the land of Egypt, against Pharaoh and all his
> servants and his entire land, and for all the mighty deeds and all the
> terrifying displays of power that Moses performed in the sight of all
> Israel. (Deut 34:11–12)

Exodus 4:1–9, 21 and Deut 34:11–12 make it clear that one aspect of the
divine nature of Moses is his empowerment to perform wonders on
behalf of God to deliver Israel.

In addition to having Aaron as a prophet and the ability to perform
miracles, the close encounter between Moses and God in Exod 33:7–
34:10 results in the divine transformation of Moses, who becomes the
means for extending the divine presence in the midst of Israel (Exod
34:29–35) as the solution for Israel's loss of God's presence due to the
manufacture and worship of the golden calf.[47] The outline of the narrative
of Exod 3–34 shows that the indication of the superhuman nature of
Moses plays a pivotal role in narrative of Exodus. Moses becomes God's
agent, empowered to act on God's behalf to both Pharaoh and Egypt in
the plagues and deliverance at the sea and Israel at the sea, wilderness,
and Sinai. Deuteronomy 34:11–12 summarizes this role of Moses with
respect to Israel and Egypt:

> He was unequalled for all the signs and wonders that the Lord sent him to
> perform in the land of Egypt, against Pharaoh and all his servants and his
> entire land, and for all the mighty deeds and all the terrifying displays of
> power that Moses performed in the sight of all Israel.

The divine nature of Moses is clarified when it is understood as a motif
that is typically used to exalt the king and closely associate him with the
deity. Old Testament texts that indicate the divine or superhuman nature
of kings include the designation of the king as אלהים in 2 Sam 14:17, 20;
Ps 45:6;[48] Isa 9:5; and Zech 12:8.[49] These depictions of Israelite kings fit
within the well-known and documented portrayal of kings in ancient
Near East as a divine being.[50] Perhaps the most famous example is the

47. This section of Exodus will be discussed in more detail in Chapter 4 of the
present study.
48. For a detailed analysis of this designation of the king, see Mark W. Hamilton,
The Body Royal: The Social Poetics of Kingship in Ancient Israel (Boston: Brill,
2005), 50–54, who concludes that "the king of Israel was a godlike figure who
became such at his coronation" (p. 54).
49. See the discussion and cited literature in Mark S. Smith, *The Origins of
Biblical Monotheism: Israel's Polytheistic Background and the Ugaritic Texts*
(Oxford: Oxford University Press, 2001), 157–63.
50. The divine nature of the king has been examined and applied to the Old
Testament in works of the so-called Uppsala circle (e.g. Ivan Engnell, *Studies in*

depiction of Gilgamesh as two-thirds divine and one-third human in the opening description of the incomparable qualities of the king.[51] The Tukulti-Ninurta epic begins with a "hymn of praise"[52] that applies a number of divine epithets and characteristics to the king:

> Glorious is his heroism, it [   ] the dis[respectful] front and rear, incendiary is his onrush, it burns the disobedient right and left. His radiance (*me-lam-mu-šu*) is terrifying; it overwhelms all foes, every pious king of the four world regions stands in awe of him. When he bellows like thunder, mountains totter, and when he brandishes his weapon like Ninurta, all regions of the earth everywhere hover in panic. Through the destiny of Nudimmud, he is reckoned as flesh godly in his limbs, by fiat of the lord of the world, he was cast sublimely from the womb of the gods. It is he who is the eternal image of Enlil, attentive to the people's voice, the counsel of the land, because the lord of the world appointed him to lead the troops, he praised him with his very lips, Enlil exalted him as if he (Enlil) were his (Tukulti-Ninurta's) own father, right after his firstborn son![53]

Propp notes a number of indications of a close connection between king and deity, such as a seventh-century Philistine jar inscription "to Baal and to Padi" (Heb. לבעל ולפדי).[54] In a study of this inscription, Gitin and Cogan speculate that this West Semitic inscription reflects the Neo-Assyrian culture that joins god and king in royal inscriptions.[55]

Divine Kingship in the Ancient Near East [Oxford: Blackwell, 1967], and Geo Widengren, *The King and the Tree of Life in Ancient Near Eastern Religion* [Uppsala: Lundequistska Bokhandeln, 1951]). On the king as אלהים, see "The National God and Royal Ideology," in Smith, *Biblical Monotheism*, 157–60.

51. "Two-thirds of him was divine, and one-third mortal"; see Stephanie Dalley, *Myths from Mesopotamia: Creation, the Flood, Gilgamesh, and Others* (Oxford: Oxford University Press, 1989), 51.

52. Mann (*Divine Presence and Guidance in Israelite Traditions: The Typology of Exaltation* [Baltimore: The Johns Hopkins University Press, 1977], 37–38) credits this designation and the following translation to Lambert.

53. Translation from Foster, *From Distant Days*, 181. Cf. the translation and Akkadian text in Peter Machinist, "Kingship and Divinity in Imperial Assyria," in Beckman and Lewis, eds., *Text, Artifact, and Image*, 160–61.

54. Seymour Gitin and Mordechai Cogan, "A New Type of Dedicatory Inscription from Ekron," *IEJ* 49 (1999): 193–202 (cited in William H. C. Propp, *Exodus 19–40: A New Translation with Introduction and Commentary* [AB 2A; New York: Doubleday, 2006], 262).

55. Gitin and Cogan, "A New Type of Dedicatory Inscription from Ekron," 198. They cite by way of example the cylinder inscription of Sargon II that refers to the training of the new residents of his capital city to "fear god and king" (Akk. *palaḫ ili ú šarri*). For the Akkadian inscription, see Andreas Fuchs, *Die Inschriften Sargon II. aus Khorsabad* (Göttingen: Cuvillier, 1994), 43–44, lines 72–74.

Numerous biblical texts also suggest the close correlation of God with the king, some of which suggest a divine identity of the king.[56]

Elena Cassin provides a substantial discussion of kings sharing some of the aspects of divinity in the ancient Near East.[57] She notes the king's exalted status on the "highest point of the social pyramid" that separates him from the rest of humanity and enables him to receive divine attributes."[58] She then focuses the rest of her discussion on the investigation of the circumstances in which the king possesses the specific attribute of the divine splendor or radiance (lit. *melammu*). The divine brilliance of the king is richly documented in the Mesopotamian world, ranging from Sargon of Akkad, Naram-Sin, Hammurabi to the Neo-Assyrian and Babylonian kings Assurbanipal II, Shalmaneser III, Esarhaddon, and Nabonidus.[59] Cassin notes that at the ascension of Adadnirari II in 911 B.C.E., *melammu* is "the definitive sign of divine favor" that is "granted the sovereign only after he has attained supreme power."[60] Yet before the assumption of power and the actual granting of his *melammu*, Adadnirari describes the royal nature of his birth at which the gods made him physically perfect. The king's *melammu*, that is, his radiance or light, is connected to the king's physical health and vigor and is manifested in his good looks and healthy appearance. The destruction of the king's body thus results in the loss of the king's *melammu*.[61] These observations provide the broad context that shows the royal function of Moses' healthy and beautiful appearance at his birth, his designation as "God" in Exod 4:16 and 7:1, and the ultimate granting of the divine aspect of God's glory to Moses as a result of divine favor that is manifested through his shining face in Exod 34:29–35.

The divine nature of the king has been recently clarified by Peter Machinist, who explores the relationship between king and deity in the depiction of kings in a number of cuneiform inscriptions in the Middle and Neo-Assyrian periods.[62] In these texts, Machinist discerns a number of distinctive royal features that are as old as the late third to the second millennium B.C.E. in southern Mesopotamia (Sumer and Babylon). Some

---

56. E.g. Exod 22:27; 2 Sam 15:21; 1 Kgs 21:13; Prov 24:21. See the list in Propp, *Exodus 19–40*, 262.

57. Cassin, *La Splendeur Divine*, 65–82. This book substantially expands the brief description of the royal quality of *melammu* in the older classic discussion by A. L. Oppenheim, "Akkadian *pul(u)ḫ(t)u* and *melammu*," *JAOS* 63 (1943): 31–34.

58. Cassin, *La Splendeur Divine*, 65.

59. See also Machinist, "Kingship," 169–70.

60. Cassin, *La Splendeur Divine*, 72.

61. Ibid., 80.

62. Machinist, "Kingship."

of the important and widely used features include the divine birth and nurture of the king, the king in the "image" of the god and adorned by divine "radiance" or "effulgence," and the status of the king as the "beloved" and "favorite" of the gods. Machinist concludes that the long history of these features attests to their importance in legitimating kings.[63]

Machinist provides careful reflection on the problematic and complicated relationship between the human king and deity. The features he uncovers suggest that the king has a divine nature and a place in the divine realm. But the king is not thereby elevated to a status equal to the gods. Rather, the king has a subordinate position in the divine pantheon and "was not so fully a god as other members of the pantheon were."[64] Machinist concludes that the most fundamental role of the king in the Assyrian sources is

> "representative / administrator" of the gods…as the primary nexus between heaven and earth: the lynchpin that allows the two realms to communicate with and sustain each other. Viewed from heaven, the king is the principal divine emissary to his earthly community; viewed from earth…he is the principal emissary of his community before the pantheon. Such a dual view was not unique to Assyria; it is probably to be found, in one formulation or another, in virtually every tradition of human kingship.[65]

Divinity, then, is a motif that serves to elevate the king out of the mundane realm and to qualify the king to be the intermediary between the gods and the human community. This view of the king explains the nature and work of Moses in the Pentateuch. Pentateuchal authors have elevated Moses to the sphere of divinity by depicting Moses as the "nexus" between God and Israel. To be sure, Moses still remains fully human and is not totally identified or equated with God. Rather, Moses becomes God's representative, or agent, who is empowered to speak and act on God's behalf. In order to reflect this cautious portrayal of Moses as a divine figure with a special, unique relationship with God, it may be more appropriate to speak of Moses with terms such as "semi-divine" or "super-human."

In sum, despite the prevailing and persistent view of Moses as a prophet, this category cannot adequately account for the figure of Moses in the Pentateuch. A number of passages present Moses as a figure who is more than a human being. Moses is designated as אלהים (lit. "God") in Exod 4:16 and 7:1. His close encounter with God in Exod 34:6 (lit.

63. Ibid., 183.
64. Ibid., 186.
65. Ibid.

"the Lord passed across his face") results in his transfiguration (Exod 34:29–35).

2.1.i. *Military Success*

One role that challenges the standard portrayal of Moses as a prophet, priest, or covenant mediator is that of a military leader. From Israel's exit from Egypt and entrance into the land, Israel is portrayed as an organized army under the leadership of Moses (Exod 13:18; Num 33:1) and described with the military term "hosts" (צָבָא; Exod 6:26; 7:4; 12:17, 37, 41, 51). Under Moses' leadership, Israel defeats a number of nations and kings, including Egypt (Exod 13:17–14:31), Amalek (Exod 17:8–16), Sihon and Og (Num 21:21–34; Deut 2:24–3:7), and Midian (Num 25:16; 31:1–54). Actions as a military commander also include the sending out of spies (Num 13:1–33; 21:32), distributing conquered lands in Transjordan to Reuben and Gad (Num 32:33), and the anticipated conquest of Canaan that is later delegated to Joshua (Exod 34:11; Num 13–14; 27:16–18; Deut 3:21–22, 28; 32:1–8).

Success as a military leader is a typical way to portray kings in the ancient Near East who assumed the throne after a significant military victory and whose military might ensured the peace and stability of the kingdom. In addition to the military success of Esarhaddon and Nabonidus,[66] other examples include the praise of Tukulti-Ninurta, "No one of all kings was ever rival to him, no sovereign stood forth as his battlefield opponent"[67] and the description of the military campaign of Nebuchadnezzar I:

> He undertook the campaign in July. With the heat glare scorching like fire, the very roadways were burning like open flames!… The finest of the great horses gave out, the legs of strong men faltered. On goes the preeminent king with the gods for his support, Nebuchadnezzar presses on, nor has he a rival. He does not fear the difficult terrain, he stretches the daily march![68]

An examination of these texts leads to the more precise observation that the ultimate cause of Israel's success in battle is attributed to God with Moses as the means by which God accomplishes victory. The victory at the sea, for example, is accomplished by Moses' outstretched hand

---

66. Summarized previously in §2.1.g of the present chapter.

67. Foster, *From Distant Days*, 181.

68. Ibid., 203. For other examples of the military successes of the king, see also the discussion of Hammurabi, Esarhaddon, Nabonidus, and Cyrus later in this chapter. For the Persian period, see the section "The Good Warrior" in Briant, *From Cyrus to Alexander*, 225–32.

(Exod 14:21, 26–27; with the staff in v. 16; cf. Exod 17:9–12). This role of Moses as God's agent is indicated especially by his designation as God's "servant" in Exod 14:31:

> The Lord saved Israel that day from the Egyptians; and Israel saw the Egyptians dead on the seashore. Israel saw the great work that the Lord did against the Egyptians. So the people feared the Lord, and *believed in the Lord and in his servant Moses*.

The close association between Moses and God in context of military victory is quite typical of the relationship between the king and deity.

One common way to depict the close association between the king and deity in the ancient Near East is through the vanguard motif. For example, in the Tukulti-Ninurta epic, Aššur (with a "devouring flame") and Enlil lead the Assyrian army in vanguard with the king marching behind them as his "helpers" in battle.[69] This Assyrian king is the "agent" of the gods, commissioned to punish the king of Babylon.[70] In a similar way, the military exploits of Tiglath-Pileser I is portrayed as a hunter: "[Who curbs] foes, trampler of his enemies, [who hunts] mountain donkeys, flushes the creatures of the steppe, [The Hunter]: Assur is his ally, Adad is his help. Ninurta, vanguard of the gods, [go]es before him."[71]

According to Thomas Mann, the vanguard motif explains the portrayal of Israel marching behind the Lord who guides them in the form of a pillar of cloud and fire.[72] Yet Mann's parallels can be further extended to Moses, whose leading the army of Israel behind the Lord closely parallels the role of the king leading his army into battle behind his deity. Mann's observation that "we are dealing with the exaltation of the Lord and Moses as the Lord's representative and leader for Israel"[73] can be refined more precisely as the exaltation of the Lord and Moses as the Lord's viceroy of Israel. The numerous examples collected by Mann show that this pattern of the exaltation of a king and his deity as the result of a significant military victory is well-known in the literature and culture of the ancient Mesopotamian world.

---

69. Mann, *Divine Presence*, 41, 131.

70. So Peter Machinist, "Literature as Politics: The Tukulti-Ninurta Epic and the Bible," *CBQ* 38 (1976): 456. In this essay, Machinist shows that Tukulti-Ninurta's closeness with the gods, his divine nature, and his role as divine agent are expressed through a number of royal titles and epithets, including "the governor of Enlil" and "the viceroy of Aššur."

71. Foster, *From Distant Days*, 206.

72. Mann, *Divine Presence*, 131.

73. Ibid., 134.

In sum, success in battle publicly affirms the legitimacy of both king and deity. Furthermore, this exaltation of the king is at the same time the exaltation of the king's deity, who chooses an individual to be king and then accompanies the king as vanguard of the army. In this way, we see that Moses and God are jointly exalted after the defeat of the Egyptians at the sea.

2.1.j. *Temple Building*
The activity of Moses building and staffing a cultic sanctuary receives the most attention in Exodus (Exod 25:1–31:18; 35:1–40:38; cf. Lev 8–9; Num 20:22–29). He receives the plan for the sanctuary from God on Sinai (Exod 24:15–31:18; esp. 25:8–9), makes arrangements to acquire materials and securing workers and craftsmen (Exod 35:20–36:7), sets up and dedicates the sanctuary (Exod 40:1–33), blesses the people after its completion (Exod 39:43), and installs Aaron and his son as priests (Lev 8–9). The construction and staffing of cultic centers and oversight of temple personnel is a prominent responsibility exercised by kings in the Old Testament (e.g. 2 Sam 7; 1 Kgs 6–8; 12:25–33) and the ancient Near East.[74] Victor Hurowitz has shown that the account of constructing the portable sanctuary in Exodus and the temple in 1 Kgs 5–10 both follow the typical building genre that includes these features: divine command to build, acquisition of materials and workers, dedication, and blessing of the king.[75] The close correspondences between the account of the building of the tabernacle with other building accounts in the Old Testament and ancient Near East suggest that Moses is acting in the role of a king who receives divine instruction to build the sanctuary, arranges and oversees the construction, and blesses the people. This activity is clearly a responsibility reserved for the king and is perhaps the strongest argument for the Pentateuchal portrayal of Moses as a royal figure.

2.1.k. *Lawgiving and Covenant-making*
The portrayal of Moses as the lawgiver is perhaps the most popular and well-known aspect of Moses' role. The various legal materials collected in the Pentateuch are given to Israel through Moses (i.e. the Decalogue (Exod 19:25–20:17), the Book of the Covenant (Exod 20:22–23:33), Leviticus (cf. Lev 1:1–2; 27:34), and Deuteronomy (cf. Deut 4:44–45;

---

74. Victor Avigdor Hurowitz, *I Have Built You an Exalted House: Temple Building in the Bible in the Light of Mesopotamian and North-West Semitic Writings* (JSOTSup 5; Sheffield: JSOT, 1992). For example, note "[Nebuchadnezzar], king of Babylon, who sets [in order a]ll cult centers, who maintains regular offerings" (Foster, *From Distant Days*, 198).

75. Hurowitz, *I Have Built You an Exalted House*, 64, 112.

5:1). Throughout Israel's journey in the wilderness, Moses promulgates various laws and issues a variety of legal and cultic instructions (e.g. Exod 15:26; 16:1–36; 18:16, 20; numerous passages in Numbers such as ch. 15; 27:1–11, 28–30). In addition to promulgating law, a related activity that Moses engages in is covenant-making with Israel (Exod 24:3–8; Deut 29) and God (Exod 34:10).

Lawgiving and covenant-making are generally attributed to kings in the ancient Near East. The three extant ancient Near Eastern law codes (Ur-Namma, Lipit-Isthar, and Hammurabi) attest that the king is the source of the law.[76] The extant ancient Near Eastern treaties show that establishing pacts is typically done between kings as a means of ensuring stability and peaceful relationship between their kingdoms. A substantial number of extant treaties are made between a powerful overlord and a weaker vassal king that provides a possible explanation of the covenant made between God and Moses regarding Israel in Exod 34:10.[77] The people of Israel are bound to the covenant through their submission to Moses' authority and relationship to God in a way similar to the relationship between citizens of a vassal state to the overlord. Hence, a clear grasp of the nature of lawgiving and covenant-making in the ancient Near East shows the inadequacy of understanding Moses as a "covenant mediator." Rather, Moses is portrayed as a royal figure who acts as an intermediary between God and Israel.

2.1.1. *Judge*

A number of texts portray Moses as a judge who arbitrates disputes and cases. In response to Moses' attempt to intervene in the fighting between two Hebrews, one of the Hebrews asked Moses, "Who made you a ruler and judge over us?" Another text portrays Moses as the highest source of authority in Israel (Exod 18:12–27 // Deut 1:9–18). After the Israelites arrive at Sinai, Moses "sat as judge" for the entire community (v. 13). Upon the advice of Jethro, Moses eventually appointed judges to decide minor cases while reserving major cases for himself.

---

76. See Roth, *Law Collections*, and the discussion in Chapter 4 of the present study.

77. Contra Joshua A. Berman, who quickly dismisses the possibility of viewing Moses in the role of a king and claims that "The covenant is never cast as a treaty between God and Moses" (*Created Equal: How the Bible Broke with Ancient Political Thought* [New York: Oxford University Press, 2008], 42). In addition to Exod 34:10, the role of Moses is comparable to kings who have established a covenant with the people, such as Josiah (2 Kgs 23:1–3), and especially Esarhaddon, whose extant vassal treaty receives no mention here. A more detailed study can be found in Chapter 4 of the present study.

> Moses chose able men from all Israel and appointed them as heads over the people, as officers over thousands, hundreds, fifties, and tens. And they judged the people at all times; hard cases they brought to Moses, but any minor case they decided themselves. (Exod 18:25–26)

Moses' actions in deciding individual cases while establishing and maintaining oversight of the judicial system are consistent with the understanding of the king as the supreme judge of the land in the ancient Near Eastern and Old Testament. A well-known example is Solomon's judgment of the sharp dispute between two mothers, each of whom claimed custody of a child (1 Kgs 3:16–28). In reaction to Solomon's wise discernment of the child's true mother, Israel "stood in awe of the king, because they perceived that the wisdom of God was in him, to execute justice" (v. 27).

In addition to personal oversight over difficult cases, the king also has the authority to establish a judicial system to arbitrate the majority of ordinary cases. For example,

> He (King Jehoshaphat) appointed judges in the land in all the fortified cities of Judah, city by city, and said to the judges, "Consider what you are doing, for you judge not on behalf of human beings but on the Lord's behalf; he is with you in giving judgment. Now, let the fear of the Lord be upon you; take care what you do, for there is no perversion of justice with the Lord our God, or partiality, or taking of bribes."
>
> In Jerusalem Jehoshaphat appointed certain Levites and priests and heads of families of Israel, to give judgment for the Lord and to decide disputed cases. They had their seat at Jerusalem. He charged them: "This is how you shall act: in the fear of the Lord, in faithfulness, and with your whole heart; whenever a case comes to you from your kindred who live in their cities, concerning bloodshed, law or commandment, statutes or ordinances, then you shall instruct them, so that they may not incur guilt before the Lord and wrath may not come on you and your kindred. Do so, and you will not incur guilt. See, Amariah the chief priest is over you in all matters of the Lord; and Zebadiah son of Ishmael, the governor of the house of Judah, in all the king's matters; and the Levites will serve you as officers. Deal courageously, and may the Lord be with the good!" (2 Chr 19:5–11)

In another text, Absalom takes advantage of the failure of David to fulfill his responsibility as "judge in the land" as well as to establish and oversee a judicial system (2 Sam 15:1–6). For four years, Absalom stationed himself near the gate to Jerusalem. During this time, he lamented the lack of an existing judicial system: "See, your claims are good and right, but *there is no one deputed by the king to hear you*"… and took it upon himself to decide the cases of "every Israelite who came to the king for judgment" (vv. 3, 6). Absalom exploited the lack of justice in David's kingdom to build support for his rebellion against David (2 Sam 15:6–12).

The understanding of the king as the highest source of justice in the land is well known and documented throughout the ancient Near East.[78] One example is the account of an anonymous Babylonian king in the seventh or sixth century B.C.E. This fragmentary text provides a number of examples of injustice that required the intervention of the king, including oppression of the poor by the weak, lack of due process for the poor, orphan, or widow, bribing judges, and charging exorbitant interest.[79] Following these situations of injustice is a description of the king as judge:

> For the sake of due process he (the king) did not neglect truth and justice, nor did he rest day or night! He was always drawing up, with reasoned deliberation, cases and decisions pleasing to the great lord Marduk (and) framed for the benefit of all the people and the stability of Babylonia. He drew up improved regulations for the city, he rebuilt the law court.[80]

This text mentions the responsibility of the king both to decide individual cases as well as to oversee the establishment of courts of law. In sum, the depiction of Moses judging individual cases as well as appointing judges to decide minor cases is consistent with the basic responsibility of the king as the agent of justice in the Old Testament and ancient Near East.

2.1.m. *Humility*
According to Num 12:3, "the man Moses was very humble, more so than anyone on the face of the earth." The attitude of humility is also attributed to the king in Zech 9:9:

> Rejoice greatly, O daughter Zion!
>   Shout aloud, O daughter Jerusalem!
> Lo, your king comes to you;
>   triumphant and victorious is he,
> humble and riding on a donkey,
>   on a colt, the foal of a donkey.

The humility of the victorious king is indicated by the riding of a donkey instead of a mule, the usual mode of royal transport (cf. 2 Sam 13:29; 18:9; 1 Kgs 1:33). Saul's objection to his commissioning to be king draws attention to his humility:

    78. Cf. Moshe Weinfeld, "Judge and Officer in the Ancient Israel and in the Ancient Near East," *Israel Oriental Studies* 7 (1977): 65–88.
    79. "The King of Justice," translated by Benjamin R. Foster (*From Distant Days*, 208–11).
    80. Foster, *From Distant Days*, 209.

> Saul answered, "I am only a Benjaminite, from the least of the tribes of Israel, and my family is the humblest of all the families of the tribe of Benjamin. Why then have you spoken to me in this way?" (1 Sam 9:21)

Other indications of the humility of the king include the objections of Moses and Gideon and the prayers of David and Solomon (2 Sam 7:18; 1 Kgs 3:7–9).[81]

The quality of humility also appears in various depictions of ancient Near Eastern kings. Lipit-Ishtar (ca. 1934–1924 B.C.E.) is the "humble shepherd of Nippur."[82] Hammurabi describes himself as humble in the prologue to his law code, "He whom the god Sin created, enricher of the city of Ur, humble and talented."[83] Nebuchadnezzar II in his own words (605–562 B.C.E.) is "king of Babylon, the humble one, the submissive one, the pious one, the worshipper of the lord of lords, the caretaker of Esagil and Ezida, the legitimate heir of Nabopolassar, king of Babylon, I."[84] A text chronicling Esarhaddon's rise to power in 681 B.C.E. emphasizes his humility in contrast to the arrogance of his brothers:

> I spoke with my heart and puzzled my head, asking myself: "Their deeds (i.e. those of Esharddon's brothers) are haughty; they trust in their own decision. What will they bring about in their godlessness? By means of prayers, lamentations and humble gestures I implored Assur, the king of the gods, and the merciful Marduk, to whom treachery is an abomination, and they accepted my plea.[85]

We have also noted the unexpected rise of Nabonidus to power and his reluctance in assuming the throne.[86] Thus the evidence suggests that humility is a well-known motif that has been applied to Moses in Num 12:3.[87] Later we will note that this is just one of several royal motifs used to portray Moses in Num 12.[88]

---

81. These objections will be examined in Chapter 3 of the present study.
82. "Lipit-Eshtar," translated by Douglas Frayne (*COS* 2.95:247).
83. "The Laws of Hammurabi," translated by Martha Roth (*COS* 2.131:336).
84. "Nebuchadnezzar II's Restoration of the Ebabbar Temple in Larsa," translated by Paul-Alain Beaulieu (*COS* 2.122A:309).
85. Martti Nissinen, *Prophets and Prophecy in the Ancient Near East* (SBLWAW 4; Atlanta: Society of Biblical Literature, 2003), 138.
86. See the previous summary in §2.1.g, above.
87. On Moses' humility as a royal trait, see esp. J. Roy Porter, *Moses and Monarchy: A Study in the Biblical Tradition of Moses* (Oxford: Blackwell, 1963), 16, and the additional examples cited there (esp. n. 45).
88. See the discussion in §5.3 of the present study.

2.1.n. *Intercessor and Appeaser*

A number of passages throughout the Pentateuch portray Moses as an intercessor who addresses God in an attempt to change the state of affairs of a third party.[89] The third party is normally Israel (Exod 5:22–23; 14:15[?]; 32:11–14, 30–34; 33:12–34:10; Num 14:13–25; 21:7; Deut 9:18–20, 25–29), but elsewhere Moses intercedes for Pharaoh throughout the account of the plagues (Exod 8:8–13, 29–31; 9:28–33; 10:17–18) and for Miriam (Num 12:13). These numerous instances of intercession place Moses in a category with Samuel (1 Sam 7:5; 12:19–23) and Jeremiah as prominent intercessors in the Old Testament (Jer 7:16; 14:11–12; 15:1).

This association of Moses with Jeremiah and Samuel has led a number of scholars to conclude that intercession is primarily a prophetic function and is another feature of Moses as a prophet.[90] This view has been challenged by Samuel Balentine through a detailed analysis of conventional terminology associated with intercession.[91] He concludes that while intercession is indeed prominent in Jeremiah, it is not exclusively a prophetic responsibility since it is exercised by a variety of non-prophetic characters.[92] For the purpose of the present study, it is important to note that a number of these characters are kings or royal figures, such as David (2 Sam 24:17), Solomon (1 Kgs 8:22–53), and Hezekiah (2 Chr 30:18). A somewhat different example is Mordecai, who is from the family of Saul (Est 2:5). He received "high honor" in Persia through his elevation to a position of power that is "next in rank to King Ahasuerus" (Est 10:2). With his new status, he "sought the good of his people and interceded for the welfare of all his descendants" (v. 3).

In addition to these examples in the Old Testament, a number of ancient Near Eastern texts portray the king praying to the gods for the welfare of the nation. For example, Van Seters calls attention to Moses' response to the people's fearful reaction to the Sinai theophany, "Do not be afraid; for God has come only to test you and to put the fear of him upon you so that you do not sin" (Exod 20:20).[93] He notes the close

---

89. Studies on Moses as intercessor include Erik Aurelius, *Der Fürbitter Israels: Eine Studie zum Mosebild im Alten Testament* (Stockholm: Almqvist & Wiksell International, 1988); J. Muilenburg, "The Intercession of the Covenant Mediator (Exodus 33:1a, 12–17)," in *Words and Meanings* (ed. Peter R. Ackroyd and Barnabas Lindars; Cambridge: Cambridge University Press, 1968), 159–81; Widmer, *Moses*.

90. Recently, Widmer, *Moses*, 72–86.

91. Samuel E. Balentine, "The Prophet as Intercessor: A Reassessment," *JBL* 103 (1984): 161–73.

92. Ibid., 164.

93. Van Seters, *The Life of Moses*, 264–66.

correspondence in concept and phrasing between Moses' response with two prayers of Nabonidus. In these prayers, Nabonidus prayed to Sin on behalf of the people:

> "Establish from heaven the fear of Sin, the lord of the gods, in the heart of his people. May they not commit any sin and may their foundations be firm."

> "[O Sin], establish the fear of your great godhead in the heart of your people, so that they do not commit any sin against your great godhead. May their foundations be as firm as heaven."[94]

Paul-Alain Beaulieu speculates that Nabonidus was occupied with the prospect of "sin" against Sin and thus delayed the reconstruction of his sanctuary due to "the evil conduct of the citizens of Babylonia, who purportedly 'faulted' against Sin's godhead."[95] Based on the close similarities between Exod 20:20 and the prayers of Nabonidus, Van Seters argues that Nabonidus functions like Moses as "an intermediary or intercessor in his prayer on behalf of the people."[96]

Another example is the lamentation of Nebuchadnezzar I (1124–1103 B.C.E.) made while Marduk's statue was removed by Elam:

> [Nebuchadnezzar's] prayers went up to Marduk, lord of Babylon,
> "Have mercy on me, in despair and pros[trate]
> Have mercy on my land, which weeps and mourns,
> Have mercy on my people, who wail and weep!
> How long, O lord of Babylon, will you dwell in the land of your enemy?
> Turn your face towards Esagila which you love!"[97]

Here, Nebuchadnezzar prays to Marduk not only on his behalf but also on behalf of his nation. In response, Marduk states that he will give Elam to Nebuchadnezzar and commands Nebuchadnezzar to relocate his statue from Elam to Babylon.[98] Another composition reports the successful defeat of Elam and return of Marduk's statue:

> [On account of] my most distressing lamentations,
> my ardent prayers, my entreaties
> and the prostration that I performed in lamentation
> before him daily, his profound (?) heart (?) took pity,
> and he relented, [Marduk it was?] who resolved
> to go to the "New City."

94. Ibid., 265 (citing Beaulieu, *Nabonidus*, 64).
95. Beaulieu, *Nabonidus*, 64–65.
96. Van Seters, *The Life of Moses*, 265–66.
97. Foster, *From Distant Days*, 202.
98. Ibid.

He, having set forth from the evils of Elam,
  having taken the road of jubilation,
  the path of gladness, and the way (that signified his)
  hearing and acceptance of their prayers.
The people of the land looked upon his lofty, suitable,
  notable form, as they acclaimed his brilliance,
  all of them paying heed to him.
The Lord entered and took up his comfortable abode.[99]

These two accounts share interesting resemblances to Moses' intercession to God after the golden calf incident. Deuteronomy adds the detail that Moses was lying prostrate before God for forty days and nights in attempt to intercede for Aaron and Israel (Deut 9:18–21, 25–29). And the prayers of both Nebuchadnezzar and Moses resulted in successfully restoring the deity's presence with their people. Other examples include a number of short prayers of Sargon II (721–705 B.C.E.), each directed to a different deity and located at a different temple in his newly constructed capital city. In these prayers, Sargon requests blessings upon the nation, including prayers to Adad for rain, Assur and Nabu for protection, and Ea for wisdom and water.[100]

These examples from the Old Testament and ancient Near East do not necessarily suggest a royal portrayal of Moses, but we have surveyed enough texts to conclude that intercession is a privilege exercised by kings on the basis of their favored status with their respective deity and that the portrayal of Moses as intercessor is consistent with the various royal motifs attributed to Moses that has been surveyed in this chapter.

2.1.o. *Succession by Joshua*
The transfer of authority over Israel from Moses to Joshua receives much attention in the Pentateuch. The account of this transfer is present in two versions underlying the received text. The Priestly account is found in Deut 34:9; Num 27:12–23; 32:28; 34:17. The Deuteronomic tradition is represented by Deut 1:38; 3:21–23, 28; 31:1–8, 14–23; Josh 1:1–9.[101] In a study of the Deuteronomic texts, Norbert Lohfink has discerned a genre of installation (*Amtseinsetzung*). A short representative example is Deut 31:23:

99. Ibid.
100. Ibid.
101. J. Roy Porter, "The Succession of Joshua," in *Reconsidering Israel and Judah: Recent Studies on the Deuteronomistic History* (ed. Gary N. Knoppers and J. Gordon McConville; Winona Lake, Ind.: Eisenbrauns, 2000), 140, originally published in *Proclamation and Presence: Old Testament Essays in Honour of Gwynne Henton Davies* (Richmond: John Knox, 1970), 102–32.

> Then the Lord commissioned Joshua son of Nun and said, "Be strong and bold, for you shall bring the Israelites into the land that I promised them; I will be with you."[102]

Lohfink identifies three elements of this genre illustrated here with reference to Deut 31:23: formula of encouragement ("be strong and bold"), statement of task ("for you shall bring the Israelites into the land..."), and formula of support ("I will be with you.").

Dennis McCarthy expands Lofink's study by including a number of texts within this genre and offering more precise conclusions. These texts include 1 Chr 28:10, which narrates David's appointment of Solomon to the task of building the temple upon his death, 2 Chr 19:5–7, which describes Jehoshaphat's installation of judges, and 2 Chr 32:6–8, which reports Hezekiah's installation of generals to fight Assyria.[103] Another passage that is especially relevant to this study is the succession of David by Solomon in 1 Kgs 2:1–12 which shares close correspondences to Joshua's succession of Moses. According to these texts, the act of installation is done by the king. This act of installation occurs in one of two different ways.[104] First, the king appoints and encourages individuals for a specific office or task, such as military leaders or judges. Second, the king appoints and provides a charge to a successor to his throne, as we see in the case of David designating Solomon as his successor.

A more detailed examination of Joshua's succession of Moses is provided by J. Roy Porter.[105] He notes that the succession of Joshua closely parallels David's speech to Solomon in 1 Kgs 2:1–5 (// 1 Chr 22:1–23:1, 28–29):

> When David's time to die drew near, he charged his son Solomon, saying: "I am about to go the way of all the earth. Be strong, be courageous, and keep the charge of the Lord your God, walking in his ways and keeping his statutes, his commandments, his ordinances, and his testimonies, as it is written in the law of Moses, so that you may prosper in all that you do and wherever you turn. Then the Lord will establish his word that he spoke concerning me: 'If your heirs take heed to their way, to walk before me in faithfulness with all their heart and with all their soul, there shall not fail you a successor on the throne of Israel.'"

102. Norbert Lohfink, "The Deuteronomistic Picture of the Transfer of Authority from Moses to Joshua: A Contribution to an Old Testament Theology of Office," in *Theology of the Pentateuch: Themes of the Priestly Narrative and Deuteronomy* (Minneapolis: Fortress, 1994), 234–47, originally published as "Die deuteronomistische Darstellung des Übergangs der Führung Israels von Moses auf Josue," *Scholastik* 37 (1962): 32–44.

103. Dennis J. McCarthy, "An Installation Genre?," *JBL* 90 (1971): 32–34.

104. Ibid., 37.

105. Porter, "The Succession of Joshua."

This account of Solomon's succession shares several elements with Joshua's succession in Josh 1:1–9. First, both deal with the pressing issue to appoint a successor to take office immediately upon the death of the current leader. Next, both accounts stress the importance of the leader to observe the law of Moses for a successful and prosperous leadership:

> Keep the charge of the Lord your God, walking in his ways and keeping his statutes, his commandments, his ordinances, and his testimonies, as it is written in the law of Moses, so that you may prosper in all that you do and wherever you turn. (1 Kgs 2:3)

> Only be strong and very courageous, being careful to act in accordance with all the law that my servant Moses commanded you; do not turn from it to the right hand or to the left, so that you may be successful wherever you go. This book of the law shall not depart out of your mouth; you shall meditate on it day and night, so that you may be careful to act in accordance with all that is written in it. For then you shall make your way prosperous, and then you shall be successful. (Josh 1:7–8)

Finally, both accounts contain an encouragement formula: "be strong, be courageous" (1 Kgs 2:1) // "be strong and courageous" (Josh 1:6, 9; cf. v. 7). In a detailed comparison of Josh 1:1–9 with 1 Kgs 2, Porter notes that the command to keep the law is an element of the installation formula "only when this is employed for a king, since it is not found when the formula is used for admission to another office."[106] Porter concludes that the account of Moses' succession by Joshua utilizes a formula to depict the transfer of office from a king to his successor.[107] He argues that the purpose of this formula is to "install Joshua into the same office Moses had held" and that "Moses and Joshua are depicted as prototypes of the Israelite king."[108]

2.3. *Clustering of Motifs*

The preceding survey has shown that the individual motifs are inter-related and rarely occur in isolation. For example, the superhuman nature of the king is associated with his military successes (i.e. the vanguard motif) and oversight of temples and cult. The king's military successes, in turn, are related to the responsibility of the king to maintain justice and peace in his realm. Along these lines, David Aaron argues that specific motifs can be clustered or combined into a group.[109]

---

106. Ibid., 151.
107. Ibid., 151–57.
108. Ibid., 143, 153.
109. Aaron, *Etched in Stone*, 176.

> We speak of a motif as involving a matrix or cluster because biblical motifs rarely travel alone as singular ideas. Rather, they are most frequently complex, involving discrete parts, such that the cluster has a meaning that transcends the individual motival elements. Indeed, once a given theme or idea gets embedded within a motival cluster, it only rarely functions independently.[110]

For example, he thinks that Judg 8, 1 Kgs 12, and Exod 32 independently incorporated and adapted six distinct "motival elements" as part of a single floating motif that Aaron labels "the golden icon motif."[111] Elements of this motif include conflict over leadership, acquisition of spoils from war, the use of the spoils to construct a golden icon, and a judgment against the sinful icon.[112] One text provides a very ancient example of the clustering of the motifs of humility, shepherding, overseer of the cult, close association with the deity, and the king as agent of justice:

> I, Lipit-Eshtar (ca. 1934–1924 B.C.E.), humble shepherd of Nippur, true farmer of Ur, unceasing (provider) for Eridu, *en*-priest suitable for Uruk, king of Isin, king of the land of Sumer and Akkad, favorite of the goddess Eshtar, a storehouse of the…offerings of the gods Enlil and Ninlil, in Isin, my royal city, at the palace gate,

> I Lipit-Eshtar, son of the god Enlil, when I established justice in the land of Sumer and Akkad, built (it).[113]

The rest of this section will show how various individual motifs, many of which have been identified so far, are typically combined and clustered in the depiction of four famous rulers in the ancient Near East: Hammurabi, Esarhaddon, Nabonidus, and Cyrus.

2.3.a. *Hammurabi*

Numerous copies of Hammurabi's law code were published and placed in the major cities of Hammurabi's empire during his reign (1792–1750 B.C.E.). Fifty extant copies as well as the famous diorite stela now located in the Louvre attest to the widespread copying and scribal study

---

110.   Ibid., 50.

111.   Ibid., 234–37.

112.   The "golden icon" motif is mentioned here by way of example and is not fully endorsed in the present study. David Aaron has helpfully drawn attention to connections with the Gideon account in Judg 8 and has highlighted the topic of leadership as a central concern. Yet he unduly excludes idolatry which is clearly an important topic, and connections between Exod 32 with 1 Kgs 12 are fairly close to suggest a literary relationship rather than independent adaptations of a motif.

113.   "Lipit-Eshtar," translated by Douglas Frayne (*COS* 2.95:247).

of the law code as late as the Neo-Babylonian period.[114] Close similarity in both the content and sequencing of the laws in the Covenant Code with Hammurabi's code suggests that Pentateuchal authors were familiar with the royal depiction of Hammurabi and adapted royal motifs in the depiction of Moses' reception and promulgation of the law.[115] Along these lines, Van Seters describes Moses as the "Jewish" Hammurabi.[116] Among the numerous titles and epithets ascribed to Hammurabi, his designation as "shepherd" is perhaps the most important, appearing twice in the prologue and twice in the epilogue. Two of these references stress Hammurabi's divine election. He is the "shepherd, selected by the god Enlil" (prologue) and "with whose shepherding the god Marduk charged me." Hammurabi describes himself as "humble" (*ašru*). Various references claim his divine election and empowerment for military success. Thus, "with the mighty weapon which the gods Zababa and Isthar bestowed upon me, with the wisdom which the god Ea allotted to me, with the ability which the god Marduk gave me, I annihilated enemies everywhere." A later description of the god Zababa suggests the vanguard motif: "May the god Zababa, the great warrior, the firstborn son of the Ekur temple, who travels at my right side, smash his weapon upon the field of battle."

The exalted status of Hammurabi is indicated by the numerous references to the light emanating from him. The gods Anu and Enlil called Hammurabi by name to "rise like the sun-god Shamash over all humankind, to illuminate the land" for the purpose of establishing justice. Similar descriptions include the "solar disk of the city of Babylon, who spreads light over the lands of Sumer and Akkad," his creation by "the god Sin," his status as the "beloved brother of the god Zababa." Hammurabi "surrounds the Emeteursag temple with splendor (*melemmē Emeteursag*)," is the "pious one, who prays ceaselessly for the great gods," and is the one "whose prayers the god Adad acknowledges,

114.   See "The Laws of Hammurabi," translated by Martha Roth (*COS* 2.131:335–53); Van Seters, *Law Book*, 56–57; Kenton L. Sparks, *Ancient Texts for the Study of the Hebrew Bible: A Guide to the Background Literature* (Peabody, Mass.: Hendrickson, 2005), 422–23.

115.   See especially David P. Wright, "The Laws of Hammurabi as a Source for the Covenant Collection (Exodus 20:23–23:19)," *Maarav* 10 (2003): 11–87. See also Bruce Wells's refutation of Wright's view of a direct connection between the two works ("The Covenant Code and Near Eastern Legal Traditions," *Maarav* 13 [2006]: 85–118) and Wright's response ("The Laws of Hammurabi and the Covenant Code: A Response to Bruce Wells," *Maarav* 13 [2006]: 211–60).

116.   Van Seters, *Law Book*, 57.

appeaser of the heart of the god Adad." He is remarkably described as "god of the kings" (*ilu šarrī*).[117]

The full range of the responsibilities of Hammurabi is also indicated by his role in supervizing and restoring the various sanctuaries and cultic practices throughout his empire. Thus, he "organizes the magnificent rituals for Isthar and the guardian of the temple of Hursagkalamma" and he is "the pious one who does not fail in his duties to the Ezida temple, the god of kings."

The framing of the laws with narrative suggests the rhetorical purpose of establishing the authority and eternal legacy of Hammurabi throughout his newly expanded empire.[118] That authority is based on the king's "accomplishments, justice, and religiously sanctioned authority," and was especially indicated by the long curse section that is devoted to preventing the effacement of Hammurabi's name and the alteration of his laws (cf. Deut 4:2; 12:32).[119] In a similar way, transmission of the legal materials through Moses points to the authority, sufficiency, and eternal legacy of the Mosiac Torah that is grounded in the authority of Moses as God's chosen and empowered "king."

In sum, the prologue and epilogue present an elaborate exaltation of Hammurabi through the clustering of royal motifs. Some of them are similar to those linked with Esarhaddon, namely, Hammurabi's divine commissioning, his military successes, and his restoration of sanctuaries. Hammurabi enjoys a favored status from the gods, he is empowered by the gods for military successes, and he is supreme among all the kings of the land, and even semi-divine himself. This special status includes effectiveness in prayer to appease the gods and supervision of the temple and rites.

2.3.b. *Esarhaddon*

The autobiographic inscriptions of Esarhaddon have been previously summarized in the section on the public emergence of the king.[120] There we noted Esarhaddon's controversial rise to power over his older brothers by the will of the deities Assur and Marduk who marched with Esarhaddon and provided him with military victory. After assuming

---

117. Although this is a straightforward reading of *ilu šarrī*, this epithet has troubled scholars who have proposed alternate interpretations, including emending the text. See the discussion and cited literature in Roth, *Law Collections*, 140 (n. 1).

118. On this see esp. James W. Watts, *Reading Law: The Rhetorical Shaping of the Pentateuch* (Biblical Seminar 59; Sheffield: Sheffield Academic, 1999).

119. Ibid., 40–49.

120. See the previous discussion in §2.2.g in the present chapter.

power, Esarhaddon restored and reformed the cultic sanctuaries that were responsible for securing Marduk's blessing of rain.

These inscriptions provide the historical context for the approximately fifty extant oracles delivered to Esarhaddon. One oracle describes the establishment of Assur's covenant with Esarhaddon, most likely at his coronation after his rise to power in 681 B.C.E.[121] This oracle describes in more detail the divine response to the king's cry to defeat his enemies. Assur hurled down fire to devour the enemies and rained hailstones and filled the river with the blood, and concludes, "Let them see (it) and praise me (knowing) that I am Assur, lord of the gods." The oracle then describes the establishment of the reign and the king "shines as brilliantly as the sun." Finally the oracle concludes with the presentation of the "covenant tablet of Assur" that is read aloud in the king's presence at the meal of the covenant, where the act of drinking is designed to cause remembrance of Ištar and thus keep the covenant Ištar made "on behalf of Esarhaddon."

Here the oracle describes a period of instability as a "disruption of cosmic harmony"[122] and as a divine punishment against Assyria that is resolved only upon Esarhaddon's assumption of power. There is also the typical pattern of the exile of the divinely chosen leader who returns in power upon the death of the reigning king accompanied by the Assyrian deities who cause a military defeat of his enemies and a miraculous crossing of the river. After the assumption of power, a covenant between the king and the deity is established, followed by a covenant meal. Finally, upon installation, the king immediately begins to restore the sanctuaries and reform the cult, which results in the reversal of the divine curse through the beginning of regular rain. The king is portrayed in various roles: shepherd, political fugitive, military leader accompanied and empowered by the deity, priest (e.g. "Ištar who loves my priesthood"), temple builder and overseer of the cult, and intercessor. In addition, the humility of Esarhaddon also resemble the attitude of Moses. The king is the one who "calms the heart" of Marduk and "placates" his "mind," which recalls Moses in Exod 32–34 and Num 12. The reign of Esarhaddon has ushered in an era of peace and stability for Assyria. Thus Parpola characterizes Esarhaddon as a "saviour king…comparable to David, Cyrus, and Zerubabbel."[123] Finally, the vassal treaty of Esarhaddon shows his concern for a peaceful transfer of rule upon his death in order to avoid a repeat of the violent nature of his assumption to the

---

121.   Parpola, *Assyrian Prophecies*, 22–27.
122.   Ibid., LXXIV.
123.   Ibid., XLIV.

throne. He imposed a loyalty oath upon a mass gathering of the Assyrian population as well as nine vassal states four days later in 672 in order to insure a smooth succession of his son Assurbanipal to the throne in Assyria and his son Shamash-shum-ukin in Babylon.[124]

In sum, a cluster of motifs appear in the various documents produced during the reign of Esarhaddon that include his divine commissioning by the Assyrian deities (esp. Marduk), exile and controversy with his brothers, assumption of power through a miraculous military victory, restoring the neglected sanctuaries of Marduk in Assyria, and arranging a peaceful transition of power upon his death.[125]

2.3.c. *Nabonidus*

The rise of Nabonidus to power over Babylon has been previously summarized with reference to Beaulieu's reconstruction of his career from a study of extant inscriptions.[126] There it was noted that Nabonidus was an unlikely candidate for king in almost every respect due to his old age, his non-royal, Babylonian pedigree, and his worship of Sin. After assuming power, Nabonidus justified the legitimacy of his rule by virtue of his commissioning by Marduk and his excellence as a military general. He also portrayed himself in the mold of an Assyrian king by adopting Assyrian royal titles and epithets.

Numerous building inscriptions attest that during his reign, Nabonidus restored cultic centers that had been destroyed by Assyria. A main concern and strategy behind Nabonidus's rise to power is a concurrent promotion of Sin and displacement of Marduk to the top of the Babylonian pantheon. Nabonidus made plans discreetly to restore Sin's sanctuary at the beginning of his reign that was eventually executed upon his return from his ten-year sojourn in Arabia. In the context of his temple building, one finds the use of the vanguard motif and depiction of the exalted nature of Nabonidus:

124. D. J. Wiseman, *The Vassal-Treaties of Esarhaddon* (London: British School of Archaeology in Iraq, 1958). Close connections have been discerned between the Vassal Treaty of Esarhaddon and Deut 13 and especially in the content and sequence of the curses in Deut 28:23–25. See Moshe Weinfeld, *Deuteronomy 1–11: A New Translation with Introduction and Commentary* (AB 5; New York: Doubleday, 1991), 7.

125. A number of these motifs lead Otto, *Die Tora des Mose*, 20–22, to note that the pattern of events underlying the inscriptions and oracle resembles the basic sequence of events in the Moses narrative. Otto concludes that the reign of Esarhaddon provided a point of reference for the composition of a version of the Moses narrative in the seventh century B.C.E.

126. See the discussion in §2.2.g of the present chapter.

(O Samas), cause the radiance (*me-lam-mu*) of your rays, lordly features, and royal brilliance, to march at my side for plundering the land of my enemy. May I overwhelm the country of my foes. May I slay my opponents… I am indeed a king provider who restores the sacred places and completes the (rebuilding of) sanctuaries forever. At the mention of my prestigious name, may all my adversaries be afraid and quiver, may they bow down at my feet…[127]

It is to be noted here that the vanguard motif is used in conjunction with both military success and temple building (cf. Exod 13:21; 14:31; 33:1–6, 16; 34:9). However, in contrast with the successful exaltation of Inanna and Marduk in the past, Nabonidus' attempt failed due to the opposition of the people. In addition to his roles as temple builder and military leader, Van Seters also calls attention to the intercessions of Nabonidus on behalf of his people.[128]

In sum, the rise and career of Nabonidus shows the standard clustering of royal motifs. Here we have the special divine commissioning and empowerment, the controversial nature of Nabonidus' emergence as king, his role as general, and his sustained effort in building and restoring numerous sanctuaries.

2.3.d. *Cyrus*

Similar royal motifs can also be discerned in the portrayal of Cyrus, Nabonidus's rival king in the neighboring kingdom of Persia, in the Cyrus Cylinder. Cyrus rose to power throughout most of the reign of Nabonidus and eventually exiled Nabonidus after his conquest of Babylon in 539 B.C.E. The Cyrus Cylinder begins with a narrative segment that details a sequence of events that roughly corresponds with the main contours of the Exodus account.[129] The cylinder begins with the rise to power of Nabonidus, unnamed but described as an "incompetent" king, and details his cultic abuses and imposition of corvée labor (cf. Exod 1:8–14). As a result, Marduk heard the people's cries,[130] searched, and then selected Cyrus as king by calling out his name and pronouncing his name to be king over all and to "shepherd" with justice and righteousness (cf. Exod 2:23–25; 3:1–4:18). Marduk then orders Cyrus to march to Babylon, leading an army of vast size with Marduk going

127. Beaulieu, *Nabonidus*, 144–45.
128. See §2.2.n in the present chapter.
129. This section depends on the translation of the Cyrus Cylinder by Mordechai Cogan in *COS* 2.124:314–16.
130. The situation is close to the Exodus account. In neither account do the people cry out to their god. Rather, their cries due to their oppression are heard by the deity who then acts by choosing and commissioning a savior.

alongside Cyrus as a "companion and friend" (cf. Exod 33:11). The account concludes with Cyrus' "saving" Babylon without a fight and his joyful reception and praise by the local population (cf. Exod 14:1–15:21)

The narrative account is followed by an autobiographical report of Cyrus' rescue of Babylon and his return of the deities to their temples. The cylinder portrays Cyrus as the agent chosen by Marduk to deliver Babylon from the evil king and to provide for the return of Marduk to his restored sanctuary in Babylon. It is likely that the cylinder, composed on the model of earlier Assyrian royal inscriptions,[131] serves as a dedication to the restored Marduk sanctuary.[132] The portrayal of a non-Babylonian as the agent of Marduk and savior of Babylon corresponds to a similar view of Cyrus as Yahweh's anointed servant in Deutero-Isaiah (Isa 44:24–45:1).

This brief examination of the depiction of Cyrus in the Cyrus Cylinder has shown the clustering of a number of royal motifs: Cyrus' divine selection by Marduk as Marduk's agent to liberate Babylon as well as to establish justice and righteousness; Cyrus' role as general with Marduk as vanguard; and the restoration of Marduk's sanctuary after Cyrus' conquest of Babylon. In addition to these adaptations of familiar royal motifs, we also encounter more specific parallels between the depiction of Cyrus and Moses. Both accounts use the basic sequence of the corvée, cry of the people, commissioning of the king as the agent of the deity, liberation of the people, and restoration or construction of a sanctuary for the deity. Both figures are "friends" of the deity, who accompanies each leader as vanguard of a vast army[133] and accomplishes victory against the empire without fighting a battle.

2.4. *Conclusion*

This survey allows us to conclude that Pentateuchal authors have utilized and adapted traditional features of royal portraiture attested in ancient Near Eastern sources to depict Moses. Furthermore, it is likely that Pentateuchal authors were familiar with the standard clustering of the individual royal motifs which formed the basis for their portrayal of Moses. The examination of the clustering of royal motifs in the four

---

131.   Indicated especially by the reference to a discovery of Assurbanipal's inscription at the end of the cylinder. See Briant, *From Cyrus to Alexander*, 43–44.

132.   See the discussion and cited literature in Sparks, *Ancient Texts*, 397–98.

133.   In contrast to the Cyrus Cylinder, the community led by Moses, described with the military term "hosts" (Exod 6:26; 7:4; 12:17, 37, 41, 51), is given a large number of 600,000 men (Exod 12:37).

ancient Near Eastern kings surveyed here suggests that the purpose for the way these kings are depicted is to justify their sovereignty through divine election and heroic feats, either in context of non-dynastic accession to power or the establishment and expansion of an empire. The next two chapters of this study will expand in more detail eight of the individual motifs that have been surveyed in this chapter and will explore how these motifs are utilized to depict Moses through a close reading of selected texts from the Pentateuch.

Chapter 3

"I HAVE MADE YOU GOD TO PHARAOH": THE PORTRAYAL OF MOSES IN EXODUS 1:1–7:7

3.1. *Introduction*

This chapter will examine in greater detail the first four of the eight royal motifs introduced in the preceding chapter, namely, the birth, flight, private commissioning and divine empowerment, and public emergence of Moses as God's designated royal leader of Israel.

3.2. *The Birth of Moses (Exodus 2:1–10)*

Various features of Exod 2:1–10 suggest a royal destiny for the rescued infant, including the beautiful appearance of Moses and the name "Moses," which is a common element in names of various Pharaohs of Egypt.[1] These features complement Moses' adoption into the Egyptian royal family as a son to Pharaoh's daughter, and by extension, a grandson to Pharaoh. Most importantly, scholars have long noted a thematic connection between the birth of Moses and other accounts of the abandonment and rescue of an infant. Donald Redford and Brian Lewis have provided a close analysis of numerous "infant-exposure" tales attested in ancient and modern sources.[2]

Lewis catalogues and summarizes 72 examples[3] of the infant-exposure motif, which "has been applied to gods, kings, and culture heroes."[4] In particular, the majority of the accounts (62 out of 72) are applied to an

---

1. See the §§2.1.b, c of the present study.
2. D. B. Redford, "The Literary Motif of the Exposed Child," *Numen* 14 (1967): 209–28; Brian Lewis, *The Sargon Legend: A Study of the Akkadian Text and the Tale of the Hero Who Was Exposed at Birth* (Cambridge, Mass.: American Schools of Oriental Research, 1980).
3. Lewis' statistical analysis must be cautiously evaluated since several of the sources he cites reuse the infant-exposure motif. In particular, the references to Moses' abandonment story in the Talmud and in Josephus inflate the evidence, since these narratives are literarily dependent on Exod 2:1–10.
4. Lewis, *The Sargon Legend*, 149.

individual with a royal or noble descent. He also discovered that a similar majority of the sources (62 out of 72) "refer to specific accomplishments of the hero, or allude, in a general way, to the source of his fame."[5] These accomplishments take one of two forms: "the accomplishment of noteworthy deeds of various nature and the elevation of the hero to the throne."[6] In thirty-two versions of the tale, the infant is exposed in a small receptacle (box, basket, or chest), which, if set adrift on water, was caulked.[7]

Since the discovery of the Sargon Birth Legend in the 1870s, scholars have noted various correspondences between these two accounts.[8] Lewis translates the first portion of the account as follows:

1. Sargon, strong king, king of Agade, am I.
2. My mother was a high priestess, my father I do not know.
3. My paternal kin inhabit the mountain region.
4. My city (of birth) is Azupirānu, which lies on the bank of the Euphrates.
5. My mother, a high priestess, conceived me, in secret she bore me.
6. She placed me in a reed basket, with bitumen she caulked my hatch.

7. She abandoned me to the river from which I could not escape
8. The river carried me along; to Aqqi, the water drawer, it brought me.
9. Aqqi, the water drawer, when immersing his bucket lifted me up.
10. Aqqi, the water drawer, raised me as his adopted son.
11. Aqqi, the water drawer, set me to his garden work.
12. During my garden work, Ištar loved me (so that)
13. 55 years I ruled as king.[9]

Despite the formal differences between the Sargon Birth Legend, drafted as a royal autobiography,[10] and the account of the birth of Moses, a third-

5. Ibid., 249.
6. Ibid., 250.
7. Lewis (ibid., p. 212) cites eight examples of caulking the infant's craft.
8. For a brief review of research, see ibid., 149, 263–66, and Tremper Longman, *Fictional Akkadian Autobiography: A Generic and Comparative Study* (Winona Lake, Ind.: Eisenbrauns, 1991), 54–55. The classic comparison between the two accounts is Gressmann, *Mose und seine Zeit*, 1–16. Recent studies include Otto, *Die Tora des Mose*, 12–17, and Gerhards, *Mose*, 149–240. For a fascinating narrative analysis of Exod 2:1–10 based on a detailed comparison with the Sargon birth story in order to make an argument that the Old Testament narrative exhibits the quality of egalitarianism not found in the ancient Near East, see Chapter 5 in Berman, *Created Equal*. In light of the detailed description of royal ideology in his Chapter 1, it is curious that Berman's detailed comparison of Moses with Sargon fails to lead him to an obvious conclusion that Moses might be portrayed as a royal figure like Sargon.
9. Lewis, *The Sargon Legend*, 24–25.
10. On the Sargon Birth Legend as a representative of the genre of fictional Akkadian autobiography, see Longman, *Fictional Akkadian Autobiography*, 52–60.

person narrative, the points of contact between the two accounts are obvious. Both were born to anonymous parents with a priestly connection.[11] More precisely, Sargon's mother was a high priestess, and both of Moses' parents were members of the priestly tribe of Levi.[12] The anonymity of Moses' parents is unusual, especially when compared to other birth narratives in the Hebrew Bible. Perhaps this anonymity is due to the dependence on the Sargon Birth Legend[13] as well as the focus on the naming of Moses as the conclusion of 2:1–10.[14]

Although the motivations for the abandonment are different for Moses and Sargon, both accounts agree on the secret nature of the birth. Moses was hidden for three months and was abandoned because he could not be hidden any longer. Sargon was born in secret and was presumably abandoned immediately. Both were placed in reed baskets caulked with bitumen and abandoned in the river. The nature of the exposure, however, is fundamentally different. Sargon's craft was carried down the river until he reached "Aqqi, the water drawer," who then pulled Sargon out of the river with his bucket. In contrast, Moses was not set adrift in the river. Instead, the miniature vessel was stationed among the reeds at the bank of the river under the protective watch of Moses' older sibling.

Both infants were discovered by chance. Aqqi unintentionally raised Sargon out of the river during the course of his normal activity of drawing water. Pharaoh's daughter was bathing within sight of Moses' basket and sent a servant to retrieve it. After their chance discovery, both infants were subsequently adopted as sons. Aqqi raised Sargon as his son until Sargon attracted the notice of Ištar as he was working in the garden. Moses, however, was adopted as Pharaoh's daughter only after he was weaned by his Hebrew mother (Exod 2:10).

Finally, the narrative of the abandonment of both infants is the opening act of a larger drama in which both are portrayed as kings. According to Van Seters, the motif of the abandonment and rescue of an infant is "only the opening scene or introduction to the narration of the leader's rise to power."[15] Propp notes a parallel between the divine election of both leaders as they are engaging in the delegated agricultural

11. But cf. Exod 6:20.
12. Literally "house of Levi" in Exod 2:1.
13. So Otto, *Die Tora des Mose*, 12.
14. So Van Seters, *The Life of Moses*, 28: "Since Moses is not identified at birth it was hardly appropriate for the author to give the names of his parents. This makes the naming of Moses at the end not so much an etymological etiology as a literary device by which the deliverer is discovered."
15. Ibid., 29.

tasks of gardening and shepherding.[16] The account of Sargon's exposure and rescue (lines 1–13) is followed by reports of his actions as the king who establishes his rule over the "black headed people" (lines 14–15) and engages in military expedition and conquest (lines 16–21). The remaining lines consist of a blessing on the kings succeeding Sargon.[17] While the function of the abandonment account as a preview of the royal destiny of Sargon is obvious and widely recognized, scholars generally resist deducing a comparable function for Moses.[18] Otto's failure to acknowledge this parallel leads him to the vague formulation, "Both infants have an important mission to fulfill as adults in the horizon of [their] respective political theologies."[19] Close similarities between both accounts, especially the descriptions of constructing and caulking the reed receptacle, suggest that the Sargon Birth Legend was familiar to the author of Exod 2:1–10.[20]

16. Propp, *Exodus 1–18*, 155–56. The portrayal of Sargon and Moses engaging in the tasks of gardening and shepherding is not arbitrary. Ištar's love of gardeners is well known (see the discussion in Otto, *Die Tora des Mose*, 15) and Moses' job of shepherding previews his royal task of shepherding the people of Israel (cf. Num 27:16–21).

17. See the discussion in Longman, *Fictional Akkadian Autobiography*, 55–57.

18. Thus Otto fails to draw the logical conclusion that Moses is also portrayed as a royal figure (Otto, *Die Tora des Mose*, 17). Similarly Gerhards (*Mose*, 126) concludes, "He is above all not a royal figure, and also not one who had a function in the royal system, as David [did] as a follower of Saul" ("er ist überhaupt keine königliche Gestalt, auch keine, die wie David als Gefolgsmann Sauls eine Funktion in einem königlichen System innehätte"). It is granted that Moses is not portrayed as an actual king like David, but this does not preclude the possibility of a royal portrayal of Moses in the Pentateuch.

19. Otto, *Die Tora des Mose*, 15: "Beide Kinder haben als Erwachsene eine im Horizont der jeweiligen politischen Theologie wichtige Mission zu erfüllen."

20. It is beyond the scope of this study to identify more precisely the setting and function for the use of the Sargon Birth Legend in Exod 2:1–10. A number of scholars have concluded that the author of Exod 2:1–10 likely made use of the Sargon Birth Legend, which circulated throughout the Neo-Assyrian Empire during the reign of Sargon II (between 721–705 B.C.E.) to legitimate the dynastic establishment of his throne (Lewis, *The Sargon Legend*, 106; Longman, *Fictional Akkadian Autobiography*, 57–58; Otto, *Die Tora des Mose*, 15–17). Despite a recent attempt by H. Zlotnick-Sivan ("Moses the Persian? Exodus 2, the 'Other' and Biblical 'Mnemohistory'," *ZAW* 116 [2004]: 189–205) to establish a direct connection between Exod 2:1–10 with Herodotus' account of Cyrus' birth, the connections between the two are typical and general and most likely due to an independent adaptation of the motif of the abandonment of a baby slated for a great destiny. She fails to account for the closer connections between Exod 2:1–10 and the Sargon Birth Legend and thus makes an unwarranted assumption that Moses' birth account has more in common with the account of Cyrus' birth.

3.3. *Ruler, Judge, Savior, and Deliverer: Moses' Flight and Sojourn in Midian (Exodus 2:11–22)*

A frequent motif is the flight or exile of an individual destined to become king. The motif of the hero's "flight" is prominent in the portrayals of Moses, David,[21] Hadad, and Jeroboam I in the Old Testament, and is a component of the biographies of Sinuhe and Idrimi as well as the inscriptions narrating Esarhaddon's rise to power. The transition from one ruler to another creates a situation of a struggle for power that results in the flight of a potential rival who will later return and assume control after the death of the current ruler.

The flight of Moses and his subsequent return after the death of Pharaoh closely follows a pattern of the flight and return of a royal figure that is attested in the profiles of Solomon's adversaries Hadad and Jeroboam in 1 Kgs 11:14–40. This passage narrates three episodes of the rise of kings in Edom (11:14–22), Aram (11:23–25), and Israel (11:26–40) who will all oppose Solomon. The outer frame of this series, the rise of Hadad in Edom and Jeroboam in Israel, provides the closest parallels to the flight of Moses to Midian and his return in Egypt. Van Seters finds numerous parallels between Moses and Hadad.[22] Like Moses, Hadad escapes a situation of genocide (instigated by David) by fleeing to the safety of Egypt, where he grows up as an adopted son in Pharaoh's household. Hadad likewise returns to his people (Edom) after the death of a king (David), at which point Hadad assumes the throne of Edom and becomes an adversary of Solomon. Van Seters could have also noted that

---

Propp (*Exodus 1–18*, 159–60) speculates that the Sargon Birth Legend and the story of Moses' abandonment both share similarities with the flood accounts of Atra-ḫasīs and Gen 6–9, respectively. The former account describes the construction of a vessel of reed and pitch to save Atra-ḫasīs. The term for Moses' vessel (תבה) provides a possible link to the Genesis flood account. Yet this is the only firm link between the two otherwise different accounts. It is more likely that Exod 2:1–10 was composed with reference to the Sargon Birth Legend and that the vague conceptual connections between Exod 2:1–10 and Gen 6–9 result from their independent familiarity (indirectly in the case of Exod 2:1–10) with the Atra-ḫasīs flood account.

21. On the comparison of the flights of David and Moses, which will not be discussed here, see Gerhards, *Mose*, 125–27. It is striking that the detailed comparisons between Moses and Sargon, in addition to the comparison of David with Moses, do not lead Gerhards to the obvious conclusion of a royal portrayal of Moses in Exod 2, a view he rejects ("er ist überhaupt keine königliche Gestalt," p. 126). In his discussion of the figure of Moses (pp. 129–36), he emphasizes the passivity of Moses, viewing him as a prophet and "tool" ("Werkzeug") of God in critique of kingship.

22. Van Seters, *The Life of Moses*, 32–33.

both requested permission from their fathers-in-law to return to assume a position of leadership, which suggests that Pharaoh and Reuel played a similar role in the respective Hadad and Moses accounts. Thus in a foreign setting Hadad marries Pharaoh's sister-in-law, fathers a child, and is provided a house and a food allowance from Pharaoh.

Jeroboam's flight is the opening scene in the account of his rise to power. Jeroboam is a citizen of the northern Israelite tribe of Ephraim (1 Kgs 11:26). He is a servant (עבד) of Solomon and placed by Solomon as a supervisor over the forced labor (סבל; cf. סבלות in Exod 1:11; 2:11; 5:4; etc.) of the "house of Joseph." Thus both Jeroboam and Moses were closely associated with a royal government that imposed oppressive forced labor on their own people. After their true loyalty became publicly known, their lives are threatened by the reigning king; both flee to a place of security outside the kingdom and both return to assume a position of power after the king's death. The flight of Moses in the face of Pharaoh's attempt to take his life follows the pattern of the flight and return of a royal figure destined to become king that is well attested in the Hebrew Bible and ancient Near East.

Outside the Old Testament, the motif of the flight of a political fugitive is a component of several ancient Near Eastern biographies and narratives, namely, the popular Egyptian "Tale of Sinuhe," the auto-biography of Idrimi, and the royal inscriptions of Esarhaddon. The "Tale of Sinuhe" narrates how Sinuhe, an Egyptian royal official, flees from Egypt immediately after receiving news of the death of the king of Egypt.[23] He eventually settles in the highlands in the Syro-Palestinian region where a local ruler gives him his eldest daughter as a wife and a region to rule as a "vizier," according to Sinuhe's account to the king of Egypt. Sinuhe eventually returns home at the request of the king of Egypt, is added as a member to the king's royal house, and lives the rest of his days in luxury. The building of Sinuhe's pyramid and construction of his statue in the conclusion of the tale stresses the necessity of an Egyptian to die in Egypt.[24]

---

23. On Sinuhe, see the discussion and cited literature in Sparks, *Ancient Texts*, 254–56. The discussion here is based on the translation by Miriam Lichteim (*COS* 1.38:77–82).

24. In addition to the motif of the flight and return of a political fugitive, this tale utilizes a number of other royal tropes such as narrating an important episode of the duel that serves to publicize the identity of the hero in a manner similar to David's contest against Goliath. Other features that are remarkably similar to Moses include the flight of Sinuhe that marks the transition into an assimilation into another culture by marriage to a local ruler and the tension between the ethnic identity of Sinuhe as an "Asiatic" or "Egyptian."

Idrimi was the king of the city-state Alalakh (located on the coast and north of Ugarit in Aram/Syria) around 1500 B.C.E. His autobiography was actually composed several hundred years later (ca. 1200 B.C.E.) as a memorial glorifying his heroic deeds as a famous dynastic founder in order to legitimate the current king.[25] The approximately one hundred lines of text inscribed on the small statue of the king[26] present an overview of the stages leading to Idrimi's rise to power and the major events of his reign. The Idrimi inscription adapts a number of royal motifs that will be explored later in this study, namely, the role of a treaty or covenant as the means for the overlord to establish his vassal as king over a region of the overlord's realm, the king's military successes, building projects, and cultic duties.[27]

Pertinent to our discussion here is the motif of the flight, sojourn, and return of a political fugitive. The inscription begins with the flight of Idrimi from his hometown in Aleppo. The reason for the flight is not stated, but is probably due to an unsuccessful revolt by Idrimi or his father. After fleeing from Aleppo, Idrimi embarks on an extended sojourn that takes him to several locations over the course of seven years, including dwelling among the "Hapiru" warriors in Canaan, during which he assembles an army and, after receiving favorable divine omens, travels by sea to assume the throne in Alalakh.

Finally, the rise to power and the career of Esarhaddon as reconstructed from his inscriptions and extant prophetic oracles show that Esarhaddon fled into exile in order to escape his brothers, who had seized power upon the death of their father Sennacherib, despite his designation of Esarhaddon as his successor.[28] The accounts of Sinuhe, Idrimi, and Esarhaddon attest the widespread geographical (Egypt, Levant, Assyria) and chronological (over a thousand years; nineteenth and seventh centuries B.C.E.) use of the motif of the hero's "flight" and sojourn in a foreign land. The ancient Near Eastern and biblical contexts surveyed

---

25. On the dating, form, and function of the Idrimi statue inscription, see the discussion and cited literature in Longman, *Fictional Akkadian Autobiography*, 60–66, and John Van Seters, *In Search of History: Historiography in the Ancient World and the Origins of Biblical History* (Winona Lake, Ind.: Eisenbrauns, 1997), 191. This discussion is based on the translation by Tremper Longman (*COS* 1.148:479–80).

26. The image of the statue, now located in the British Museum, can be found in *ANEP*, 156.

27. Instructive too is Idrimi's designation as the "servant" of his deities and the concluding blessing and curse section, which is a conventional conclusion also of the Mesopotamian royal inscriptions and extant ancient Near Eastern treaties.

28. See the survey of Esarhaddon's rise to power in Chapter 2 of this study.

here attest to the widespread familiarity of this motif, which suggest that pentateuchal authors were familiar with this motif and have utilized it in their depiction of Moses' emergence as Israel's heroic savior.

We will now turn to a close analysis of the account of Moses' flight in context of Exod 2:11–22, which can be subdivided into vv. 11–15a and 15b–22. The outer boundary of the narrative that follows the birth of Moses (2:11–15a) is indicated by the phrase "In those days" in v. 11 and the repetition of גדל in v. 11 and ישב in v. 15a. This and the shift of the thematic focus from Moses' identity as a Hebrew "son" in 2:1–10 to his identity as a Hebrew "brother" suggest the coherence of 2:11–15a.[29] The inverse parallelism in v. 11b identifies the focus of this unit:

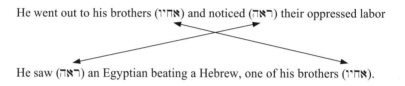

He went out to his brothers (אחיו) and noticed (ראה) their oppressed labor

He saw (ראה) an Egyptian beating a Hebrew, one of his brothers (אחיו).

The sequence of seeing (ראה), striking (נכה) in v. 11 is reproduced in v. 12, where Moses "strikes" the Egyptian after "seeing no one around." The failure to understand Moses' royal role as God's empowered agent has led numerous commentators to view Moses' actions as a premature or abortive attempt to deliver the Hebrew community. Although the Hebrew text does not explain the motivation for Moses actions, subsequent interpreters have rationalized Moses' actions (e.g. Philo, Acts 7)[30] and placed the blame on the Hebrew community's rejection of Moses' leadership as the reason for the aborted attempt. Others (e.g. Augustine) focusing on psychological and ethical aspects of Moses' action view Moses' act as premature and impulsive. The biblical narrator, however, is not interested in the psychological or ethical dimensions of Moses'

29. Propp suggests that the seven occurrences of איש ("man"; 2:11 [×2], 12, 14, 19, 20, 21) serve to unify 2:11–22 as a parallel to ילד ("child"), also used seven times in 2:1–10 (*Exodus 1–18*, 146). The parallels do not work because the noun ילד refers to Moses seven times in vv. 1–10, while איש is applied to Moses only in vv. 14, 19, and 20. Instead, the solidarity among the Hebrew community (עברים/עברי, vv. 11, 12), indicated by אח (2:11 [×2]) and רע ("companion," v. 13) constitutes the main focus of 2:11–15a, in contrast to 2:15b–22 where the focus shifts to Moses' in-law relationship with the Midianites.

30. *On the Life of Moses* 1.44. Here, I am dependent on Childs's sketch of the "History of Exegesis" (Childs, *Exodus*, 40–42). Childs also applies this view to the text (p. 31). However the primary concern in 2:11–15a is establishing the identity and qualifications of Moses as God's chosen agent (cf. Acts 7:25, "God through him was rescuing them") before the actual rescue from Egypt.

actions. The failure to read the Moses account as an "official" or public account, which is a fundamental characteristic of ancient biography according to Klaus Baltzer,[31] has prevented an adequate understanding of the role of this text in its portrayal of Moses. Instead of addressing the modern concerns that are often brought to the text, the text answers the crucial question of the identity of the rescued baby. Now that he has grown up (vv. 10–11), what specifically is the public nature of his royal and divine destiny that has been alluded to in 2:1–10?

This passage develops the introduction of Moses as a royal figure in 2:1–10 by narrating how Moses will act on God's behalf and engage in complementary actions with God in the Hebrew community. Thus the sequence of "seeing" and "striking" describes also God's action of "seeing" the plight of the Hebrew community (Exod 2:25; 3:7, 9; 4:31; 5:19) and "striking" the Egyptians (Exod 3:20; 7:17, 25; 9:15; 12:12, 13, 29).[32] Moses' actions can more appropriately be viewed as an anticipation of his role as God's agent in saving the Hebrews from Egyptian oppression (Exod 1–15) in conjunction with the role of judging internal disputes (Exod 18). Rather than an abortive attempt, Moses' actions in 2:11–15a are best viewed as "an initial deed in a smaller scope" that will preview Moses' public role as Israel's royal savior.[33]

This episode then functions in a manner similar to the public contests that serve to introduce the hero into the public arena. Based on a comparison of Moses with the public emergence of David or Jeroboam, Moses' act of killing the Egyptian should be viewed as an act of insubordination or insurrection against Pharaoh. In contrast to Sinuhe and David, Moses makes an attempt to prevent his actions from gaining public recognition. Moses' actions of looking for potential witnesses and burying the dead Egyptian indicate that he understood the serious implications of his deed if it were to become public. The murder of an Egyptian supervisor would confirm Pharaoh's fear of an uprising by the Hebrew slaves (Exod 1:10) and motivate him to eliminate any threat to his power over the Hebrew community. The flight of Moses from Pharaoh, then, is best understood as the flight of a political fugitive to safety in anticipation of a return in a position of power upon the death of the rival king.

31. Klaus Baltzer, *Die Biographie der Propheten* (Neukirchen–Vluyn: Neukirchener Verlag, 1975), 20–23.

32. See the discussion in Terence E. Fretheim, *Exodus* (IBC; Louisville: John Knox, 1991), 42–43. His citation of Exod 5:19 should be changed to Exod 5:21.

33. Smend, *Yahweh War*, 126. His comparison of the public emergence of Moses and Jeroboam will be discussed in more detail later in this chapter.

Exodus 2:11–15a decisively resolves the identity of Moses and the issue of where his loyalties lie. Although he is a member of an Egyptian court, his Hebrew identity, clearly established in 2:1–10, means that Moses is squarely on the side of the Hebrews in their oppression.[34] Moses' action of rescuing his Hebrew "brother" by killing the Egyptian and attempting the next day to arbitrate an ostensibly internal legal dispute[35] receives interpretation by one of the Hebrew community who designates Moses' actions in v. 14 as consistent with the office of a "judge" (שׁפט) and "ruler" (שׂר). The designation "judge" (שׁפט) is a synonym for "king" (מלך) in a number of passages (e.g. Isa 16:5; 33:22; Ps 2:10; Hos 7:7; 13:10; Amos 2:3; Mic 5:1) and designates the major function or responsibility of a king (e.g. 1 Sam 8:5, 6, 20; 2 Sam 15:4. cf. Gen 18:25; Judg 11:27; Prov 29:14; 2 Chr 26:21). The profile of a "judge" in the book of Judges is virtually identical with the portrayal of an Israelite king with the exception of dynastic succession. According to Jo Ann Hackett,

> The Hebrew word *šōpēṭ* actually describes someone with governing functions over a society, like a king, but without the dynastic implications of an inherited kingship. A *šōpēṭ* is a "charismatic" leader, meaning that he or she leads because the people being led see something persuasive and powerful in that person's self-presentation rather than agreeing to leadership by a particular family.[36]

In the book of Judges, the noun שׁפט occurs only in Judg 2:17–19. This passage suggests a comparison of the profile of Moses in Exodus with the judges in Judg 2:11–23. In addition to שׁפט, we have the cry of the oppressed (נאקתם, "their cries," Judg 2:18 // Exod 2:24; cf. 3:9), a "raising" (קום) of a "judge" to save (ישׁע) the Israelites "from the hand of" their oppressors (Judg 2:16, 18; cf. Moses "raising" [קום] to "save" [ישׁע] the daughters of Reuel and delivering them "from the hand of" the shepherds; Exod 2:17, 19), God's presence and empowerment of the judges (Judg 2:18 // Exod 3:12), and the issue of obeying (שׁמע) the judge (Judg 2:17 // Exod 3:18; 4:1, 8; 6:12).[37] These close parallels suggest that

---

34. See, e.g., the concise discussion in S. Dean McBride, "Transcendent Authority: The Role of Moses in Old Testament Traditions," *Int* 44 (1990): 231.

35. So Childs, *Exodus*, 30, based on the legal term לרשׁע.

36. Jo Ann Hackett, "Violence and Women's Lives in the Book of Judges," *Int* 58 (2004): 356–64.

37. Other parallels between Judg 2 and the wilderness episodes include: the stubborn nature of Israel (קשׁה, Judg 2:19; Exod 32:8; 33:3, 5; 34:9), worship of other gods (אלהים, Judg 2:12, 19; Exod 32:4, 8; 34:15–17), anger of God or Moses

Moses' royal vocations include the major activities associated with the office of a judge.[38]

Yet the question raised by the guilty Hebrew "brother" in v. 14 shows that the designation "judge" alone does not fully capture the identity of Moses. In addition to "judge," he includes the designation "ruler" (שׂר). In the Hebrew Bible this term is a general designation for various activities of leadership that must be specified in their immediate literary context. The word has a range of meanings, including military leader (e.g. Gen 21:22; Judg 4:7; cf. Josh 5:14, 15), royal official (e.g. Gen 40:2; Exod 1:11), governor (e.g. Judg 9:30), or prince (e.g. Hos 3:4). This is the standard designation for "king" in Akkadian. The possibility that this word has a royal connotation must not be ruled out given the substantial points of contact between the Sargon Birth Legend and accounts of the birth of Moses.[39] In the immediate literary context of Exod 1–2, this term is used of the Egyptian taskmasters in 1:11. Yet the equivalence is not exact, and the dissenting Hebrew would not raise a question of Moses' authority if he were acting in the capacity of an Egyptian foreman. Instead, the word "ruler" is joined with "judge" in v. 14 to create a hendiadys that expresses a complex concept through the joining of two nouns. Moses is a "ruling judge" or "judging ruler."

The dissenting Hebrew does not doubt Moses' presumptive royal authority. Rather, he questions the basis of that authority, which the narrator later addresses by showing that God is the one who has appointed Moses (Exod 3:1–4:17; cf. Gen 45:8–9). For now, Moses' actions on behalf of God are previewed through his acts of "seeing" and "smiting" (and later as "saving" and "delivering" in vv. 15b–22) on behalf of the oppressed. But the narrator is also previewing Moses' future relationship with Israel. He is destined to arbitrate internal disputes,[40] but with authority that will be questioned or contested by segments of the Israelite community (e.g. Num 12 and 16). Thus Exod 2:11–15a presents a miniature portrayal of the identity of Moses and his

burning against Israel (Judg 2:14, 20; Exod 32:10, 11, 19); God's changing his mind (נחם, Judg 2:18; Exod 32:14), and testing Israel if they keep his commands (נסה, Judg 2:22; 3:1; Exod 15:25).

38. Thus Smend (*Yahweh War*, 128) argues that Exod 1–14 portrays Moses as a "charismatic leader" who plays the role of the "first of the 'major Judges'" and "not as priest, prophet, or such kind."

39. Other parallels between the Pentateuch and various other Assyrian documents are discussed in Otto, *Die Tora des Mose*, 11–33.

40. Note how David's neglect of this important royal responsibility provided the basis for Absalom's rebellion (2 Sam 15:1–6).

relationship vis-à-vis God and Israel that will be developed in following chapters (e.g. Exod 3 and 18).

In addition to Moses' designation as "leader" and "judge" and his flight to Egypt, the crucial role played by Exod 2:11–15a in establishing the royal identity of Moses is also demonstrated by the literary structure of 2:1–22, which further highlights the central placement of the posed question "Who made you a ruler and judge?" That structure is as follows:

A: Born into a Levitical priestly family in Egypt (2:1–2)

    B: Recognized as a Hebrew by Pharaoh's daughter in Egypt after rescue from river (2:6)

        C: Question of Moses' identity: ruler or judge? (2:14)

    B':   Recognized as an Egyptian by Jethro's seven daughters in Midian after rescue at the well (2:19)

A':   Marries into a Midianite priestly family (2:19–22)

Although each of the three units has its own literary design, the arrangement of the three in a palistrophic framework serves to pose the fundamental question of the identity of Moses. Hence the standard view of Exod 2:11–15a as merely a transitional section that functions to move Moses from Egypt to Midian must be firmly rejected.[41] This literary unit in the center presents a particular view of Moses that resists a traditional designation of Moses as a priest, prophet, or judge. Exodus 2 establishes Moses' Levitical and Midianite priestly background without designating him as a priest or clarifying the relationship between his Levitical and Midianite heritage. Moses is not designated as a "prophet" either here or in his subsequent call in Exod 3:1–4:17. Through the juxtaposition of the designations of "judge" and "ruler" in the central verse of this section and the numerous royal motifs described so far, the narrator of Exod 2:1–22 presents Moses as a royal figure as explicitly as possible without using the specific designation "king" (מלך). While such an explicit designation would be premature at this point in the Moses story (but cf. Deut 33:5), Exod 2:1–22 applies various royal features to Moses without reducing him to the Israelite office of "king" (מלך). That is, this

---

41. E.g. Van Seters's comment on 2:11–15a (*The Life of Moses*, 30): "[T]he scene is not complete in itself but merely provides the explanation for Moses' flight and his residence in a foreign land." My view of the structuring of Exod 2:1–22 would further highlight the artistry of Van Seters's "J."

depiction of Moses transcends any attempt to limit him to a discrete office. The use of royal tropes is the most effective way to portray this exaltation.[42]

The literary boundaries of the third and final segment of Exod 2:1–22 is established by the repetition of ישׁב in v. 15 and the transitional section of vv. 23–25. This unit is framed by occurrences of ישׁב in v. 15b and 21 that serve to indicate how the situation of Moses' "sitting" at the well resulted in his "dwelling" with Reuel as a new member of his family. Thematically, the focus shifts away from Moses' relationship with his Hebrew "brothers" in vv. 11–15a to an examination of Moses' entrance into the Midianite community. This move results in the reappearance and readjustment of various themes in the first unit (vv. 1–10) that indicate its bracketing function around vv. 15b–22. In both scenes we have an account of a rescue at a location of water[43] as well as a marriage followed by the birth and the naming of a son. In both scenes, Moses crosses ethnic boundaries. He is recognized as a Hebrew and joins the Egyptian culture through his adoption as a son in vv. 1–10 and is recognized as an Egyptian who joins the Midianite community by becoming a son-in-law to Reuel through marriage to his daughter Zipporah. More precisely, Moses is portrayed as a passive figure in vv. 1–10 (i.e. he is "rescued" and "named" by Pharaoh's daughter) who then emerges as an active figure in vv. 15b–22 who "saves" and "delivers" the daughters of Reuel and later names his son. This movement of Moses from one who is rescued to one who rescues in the structure of vv. 1–22 provides additional confirmation for Gerhards' argument for the portrayal of Moses in v. 10 as the "saved savior" (*Mose als geretteter Retter*).[44]

Exodus 2:15b–22 continues the demonstration in vv. 11–15a of Moses' royal identity as revealed through his actions. In addition to "striking" the Egyptian and adjudicating disputes as a "ruler and judge," here Moses is portrayed as "rising" (קוּם) to "deliver" (ישׁע) Reuel's seven daughters from the shepherds (v. 17) in a manner reminiscent of several of the judges (cf. Judg 3:9, 15; 10:1). This act is described later by the daughters in v. 19 as a "deliverance" (נצל) from the power (מיד)

---

42. This portrayal of Moses is remarkably similar to the way that Philo portrays Moses with the qualities of king, priest, legislator, and prophet as specific attributes of his role as king. See the discussion on Philo's portrait of Moses in Chapter 1 of this study.

43. Cf. the action of drawing from the water in vv. 10 and 16.

44. See the discussion in Gerhards, *Mose*, 136–48. However, the portrayal of Moses' actions of killing the Egyptian and rescuing the daughters of Reuel argue against Gerhards's portrayal of Moses as merely a passive counterpart to the active designs of Pharaoh (pp. 121–29).

of the shepherds. Moses' actions of "delivering" and "saving" anticipate God's "saving" Israel in 14:30 (the only occurrence of the verb ישע after 4:17) through the agency of his servant Moses (v. 31; cf. the noun form in 14:13; 15:2) and "delivering" Israel from the power of Pharaoh and Egypt (18:10; cf. 18:8; 3:8; 5:23; 6:6; 12:27). Both terms also describe actions of a king (ישע in Ps 20:7, 10; 2 Sam 8:6, 14; 1 Chr 18:6, 13; נצל in 1 Sam 14:48; 30:8; 2 Sam 14:16; 19:9 [Eng.]; 2 Kgs 18:29). Gideon, for example, "saves" (ישע) Israel from the power (מיד) of Midian, after which Israel attempted to install Gideon into the dynastic office of "king" (Judg 8:22).[45]

In sum, through the composition and configuration of the three discrete scenes of Exod 2:1–22, several important dimensions of the portrayal of Moses begin to emerge. The numerous indications of the royal identity of Moses ranging from the unusual nature of his birth, the varied depictions of his actions as a savior and deliverer, and the overall literary structure that centers on the designation of Moses as "ruler" and "judge" in v. 14 show how Moses will become God's agent who will rescue Israel. Moreover, this passage anticipates Moses acting on God's behalf. Moses "strikes" the Egyptians and "delivers" the daughters of Reuel. Moses occupies a unique position between God and Israel that will prove to be crucial to the ongoing participation of Israel in the covenant that will be established with Moses in Exod 34. Although replete with activities that are consistent with a royal figure, the specific designation of Moses as "ruler" and "judge" and the literary structure of vv. 1–22 stops short of simply equating Moses with any specific office. In other words, the text serves to highlight the basic identity of Moses as a royal figure without claiming that Moses functioned as an actual king. According to vv. 1–22, Moses is the one who will "rule" and "judge" Israel, "strike" the Egyptians and "save" Israel in the wilderness.

3.4. *"I will be with you":*
Private Commissioning and Divine Empowerment
of a Royal Deliverer (Exodus 3:1–4:17)

Scholars have identified a basic form, usually labelled "the call narrative," which is found in the commissioning accounts of God's prophets and leaders.[46] A comparison of the call of Moses in Exod 3:1–4:17 with

45. The next section will show the close correspondences between the portrayal of Moses in Exod 2–4 with Gideon in Judg 6–8.

46. N. Habel, "The Form and Significance of the Call Narratives," *ZAW* 77 (1965): 297–323; Walther Zimmerli, *Ezekiel: A Commentary on the Book of the*

the call of Jeremiah in Jer 1:1–19 has played a significant role in the classification of Moses as a "prophet" in modern scholarship.[47] While the call of Moses shares some features with the account of Jeremiah's call, a closer examination shows that these similarities are superficial. Significant differences between the two accounts make it unlikely that one of these calls is modeled after the other. This section seeks to demonstrate that the account of Moses' call in Exod 3:1–4:17 shares numerous structural and literary features with the call and portrayal of royal figures, especially Gideon (Judg 6–8) and Saul (1 Sam 9–11). Moreover, Van Seters points out that the account of Moses' call reflects features of Assyrian royal biographies, "In the Assyrian royal inscriptions the king regularly regards himself as commissioned by his God to punish the enemy. By means of an oracle he receives the assurance that God will be with him."[48] Since the call of Moses is too often viewed as a call of a prophetic figure, this section will provide a detailed comparison of the call of Moses with the calls of Jeremiah, Gideon, and Saul in order to demonstrate that the call of a prophet (Jeremiah) is fundamentally different from the call of a royal leader (Moses, Saul, Gideon).

3.4.a. *"You shall put words in his mouth": The Commissioning Accounts of Moses and Jeremiah*
Although both Moses and Jeremiah resisted their call, the specific basis of their objections is different.

> Then I said, "Ah, Lord God! Truly I do not know how to speak, for I am only a boy." (Jer 1:6)

> But Moses said to the Lord, "O my Lord, I have never been eloquent, neither in the past nor even now that you have spoken to your servant; but I am slow of speech and slow of tongue." (Exod 4:10)

Jeremiah does not "know how to speak" because he is a boy (נער; Jer 1:6). Moses states that he is not "eloquent" (lit. "a man of words") and is "slow of speech and slow of tongue" (Exod 4:10). Thus Jeremiah

---

Prophet Ezekiel (Hermeneia; Philadelphia: Fortress, 1979), 97–100; Wolfgang Richter, *Die sogenannten vorprophetischen Berufungsberichte: Eine literature-wissenschaftliche Studie zu 1 Sam 9, 1–10, 16, Ex. 3 f. und Ri 6, 11b–17* (FRLANT 101; Göttingen: Vandenhoeck & Ruprecht, 1970). See also the discussion in Childs, *Exodus*, 53–56, as well as the literature cited in Baltzer, *Die Biographie der Propheten*, 23 (n. 39).

47. E.g. Childs, *Exodus*, 55–56, 59; Van Seters, *The Life of Moses*, 45–46; Propp, *Exodus 1–18*, 229–31.

48. Van Seters, *The Life of Moses*, 44, cites Isaiah's request for King Ahaz to ask for a sign as an example from the Hebrew Bible (Isa 7:10–17).

is not an articulate speaker due to his young age; by contrast, Moses has a physical speech impediment that is in need of healing (cf. v. 11; 6:12, 30).[49]

In addition to the quite different nature of their speaking abilities, God's responses to the two objections are also different. To Jeremiah, God says that he will be with him (אתך אני; Jer 1:8, 19) after which God touches Jeremiah's mouth and says that he will put his words in Jeremiah's mouth. We are told that Jeremiah is sent (שלח) as a prophet with the specific task of speaking God's message to the nations (vv. 5–7; 17). Rather than speaking as a prophet to Israel and the nations, Moses' objection based on his speech impediment is related to speaking to the elders and his anticipation that the elders will not listen to his voice or the "voice" of the three signs of 4:1–9 (cf. vv. 1, 8, 9). God responds initially by stressing again the divine presence with Moses (אהיה עמך; 4:12; cf. 3:12, and see the different expression אתך אני in Jer 1:8, 19). After .Moses' request for God to send (שלח) someone else, God designates Moses as "God" (אלהים) to Aaron (v. 16; cf. 7:1). The vocabulary for "sending" (שלח) is not limited to a prophetic call since it is used elsewhere to describe the sending of God's messenger to lead Israel into the land (Exod 23:20) and of Gideon to save Israel from Midian (Judg 6:14). As "God," and in stark contrast with the account of Jeremiah, Moses is the one who will put words in Aaron's mouth. Aaron thus becomes Moses' "prophet" to the Israelite community, a role that now provides the solution to Moses' resistance to speak to the elders.

God's presence with Moses and Aaron functions differently than the assurance of divine presence with Jeremiah. God assures Jeremiah of God's presence for the purpose of "delivering" Jeremiah himself from the dangers that will result from conveying a controversial message. In contrast, Moses is endowed with the divine presence in response to his perceived inadequacy for the task of confronting Pharaoh and leading Israel from Egypt (3:12). The promise of divine presence that enables Moses to deliver Israel from Egypt corresponds to the role of divine presence in the account of Gideon's call as well as to various ancient Near Eastern accounts of the deity's presence alongside a king in battle.[50]

---

49.   On Moses' physical speech defect, see Jeffrey H. Tigay, "'Heavy of Mouth' and 'Heavy of Tongue': On Moses' Speech Difficulty," *BASOR* 231 (1978): 57–57.

50.   See esp. Mann, *Divine Presence*. The implications of the important theme of the deity's presence alongside the king in the ancient Near East for understanding the portrayal of Moses will be explored in the next chapter.

Finally, the call of Jeremiah lacks two important features of the basic structure of a "call narrative" (which will be discussed in more detail in the next section): an explicit indication of a crisis or need that occasions the call and the giving of a "sign" to confirm the divine authenticity of the call. No impending crisis is detailed explicitly in Jeremiah's account because he is commissioned for the role of "prophet" to deliver God's oracles rather than as a royal deliverer who is divinely designated and empowered to address the crisis (though it is granted that the looming invasion of the "northern foe" might function as an implied crisis here). The request for a sign is expected of a king upon receiving a divine revelation, as indicated by Van Seters, and thus is quite inappropriate for Jeremiah[51] but very appropriate for Moses. To be sure, many features in both accounts are clearly similar, but the *tasks* to which Moses and Jeremiah are called are substantially different. The next two sections will show that the commissioning of Moses shares much closer parallels with the accounts of Gideon and Saul.

3.4.b. *"The Israelites cried to the Lord": The Commissioning of Moses and Gideon*

Wolfgang Richter has provided an extensive comparative analysis of the accounts of the calls of Moses, Saul, and Gideon and has discerned a basic pattern underlying these accounts: (1) indication of a crisis; (2) commission; (3) objection; (4) assurance of help; and (5) sign.[52] However, despite the close structural and verbal correspondences among these three accounts,[53] Richter ultimately concludes that Moses is portrayed as a prophet in "J" and a miracle worker in "E."[54] Recent

---

51. Habel ("Call Narratives," 305, 316) does recognize that the call narrative is not limited to "prophetical" commissions. He describes the commissioning accounts of Gideon and Moses vaguely as the call of "Yahweh's ambassadors" or "ancient mediators of Israel." Nevertheless, he views the account of Moses' call as "prophetical" in his attempt to discern a pattern similar to the calls of Jeremiah and Isaiah, and concludes that "Jeremiah also claims to stand in the prophetic succession of Moses" (p. 306). Habel's speculation that the "sign" element in Jeremiah's call is God's act of touching Jeremiah's mouth (p. 309) is forced and unconvincing, especially since the calls of Moses, Gideon, and Saul all use the specific term for "sign" (אוֹת). Since Jeremiah is not called as a royal deliverer, we should not expect this use of a "sign" here. Rather, the act of touching Jeremiah's mouth represents God's act of inspiring Jeremiah to proclaim the divine word as God's prophet.

52. Richter, *Berufungsberichte*, 139.

53. See esp. Richter's chart (ibid., p. 138), which highlights the common phraseology in all three accounts.

54. Ibid., 131–33.

scholarship has tended to abandon the separation of the account of
Moses' call in Exod 3:1–4:17 into parallel sources (i.e. "J" and "E") and
has instead stressed either a redactional composition[55] or a unified
account.[56] Given the unified account of Moses' call and the portrayal of
Moses as a royal figure in Exod 1–2, to view Moses' call as that of a
royal leader, and not of a prophet, strengthens Richter's observation by
suggesting that in these three accounts there is an underlying pattern of a
divine commissioning of a royal leader during a situation of crisis. The
crisis that will result in the commissioning of Gideon is indicated by
Judg 6:1–6. Israel is under the power of Midian (בְּיַד־מִדְיָן; v. 1), whose
periodic raids of crops and livestock deprived Israel of food. As a result,
Israel cries to God:

וַיִּזְעֲקוּ בְנֵי־יִשְׂרָאֵל אֶל־יְהוָה

…the Israelites cried out to the LORD for help. (Judg 6:6)

וַיֵּאָנְחוּ בְנֵי־יִשְׂרָאֵל מִן־הָעֲבֹדָה וַיִּזְעָקוּ וַתַּעַל שַׁוְעָתָם
אֶל־הָאֱלֹהִים מִן־הָעֲבֹדָה

The Israelites groaned under their slavery and cried out. Out of
the slavery their cry for help rose up to God. (Exod 2:23)

After the account of the crisis, Judg 6:11–40 narrates the divine commissioning and empowerment of Gideon to deliver Israel from Midian
followed by a series of five objections raised by Gideon (vv. 13, 15, 17,
36, 39). The messenger of the Lord appeared to Gideon at the "terebinth"
(אֵלָה) at Orphah where he is secretly threshing wheat in a winepress:

---

55. E.g. Christoph Levin, "The Yahwist and the Redactional Link Between
Genesis and Exodus," in Dozeman and Schmid, eds., *A Farewell to the
Yahwist?*, 131–41.

56. Thus Childs (*Exodus*, 53) concludes that "[I]n spite of the presence of literary
sources, there is more unity in the present text than has been generally recognized."
Although not illustrated by Childs, vv. 7–9 exhibit an artful palistrophic design that
has been obscured by an almost exclusive attention to the apparent doublet in vv. 7
and 9. Other scholars who advocate a basic unity to 3:1–4:17 include Van Seters
(*The Life of Moses*, 35–63), Dozeman ("The Commission of Moses and the Book of
Genesis," in Dozeman and Schmid, eds., *A Farewell to the Yahwist?*, 107–29), and
Blum, who views 3:1–4:18 as unified "D-Komposition" inserted between 2:23 and
4:19 (*Studien zur Komposition des Pentateuch* [Berlin: de Gruyter, 1990], 22–28).
However, Blum has subsequently modified this by viewing 4:1–17 as a post-Priestly
addition to Exod 3 (a view advocated earlier by Brian Peckham, *History and
Prophecy: The Development of Late Judean Literary Traditions* [New York:
Doubleday, 1993], 522, 532, as part of a late [post-P] Dtr redaction of Genesis–
2 Kings). See, e.g., Blum's "The Literary Connection," 91–96, and "Die literarische
Verbindung von Erzvätern und Exodus: Ein Gespräch mit neueren Endredaktions-
hypothesen," in Gertz, Schmid, and Witte, eds., *Abschied vom Jahwisten*, 119–56).

וירא אליו מלאך יהוה

An angel of the LORD appeared to him… (Judg 6:12)

וירא מלאך יהוה אליו

An angel of the LORD appeared to him… (Exod 3:2)

The description of Gideon presenting a sacrifice to the messenger of the Lord on the rock under the terebinth (Judg 6:19–22) and his subsequent construction of an altar and naming of the place ("The Lord is Peace" [v. 24]) suggest an underlying etiology of a contemporaneous holy place in Gideon's hometown of Ophrah in Abiezer.[57] Like Moses, Gideon also is engaged in a routine activity during his encounter with the messenger from the Lord.[58] The messenger begins his message with the affirmation of God's presence with Gideon: "The Lord is with you, valiant warrior!" (cf. Exod 3:12). Then the Lord "turned to Gideon" (Judg 6:14; cf. Exod 3:4) and commanded him: "Go (הלך; cf. Exod 3:10, 16; 4:10) with this power of yours and save Israel from the power of the Midian. Am I not sending (שלח; cf. Exod 3:10, 12, 13, etc.) you?" Gideon then objects to his commission twice by using a phrase identical to that of Moses, בי אדני (Judg 6:13, 15 // Exod 4:10) in contrast to Jeremiah's אהה אדני יהוה (Jer 1:6). Gideon's second objection draws detailed attention to his lowly status as an insignificant member of a poor family; this circumstance is implicit in Moses' first objection (Exod 3:11). God's response to Gideon is identical to his reply to Moses—"I will be with you" (אהיה עמך; Judg 6:16 // Exod 3:12)—in contrast to God's response to Jeremiah's objection (אתך אני; Jer 1:8, 19). This promise of the divine presence will empower Gideon to "strike" (נכה) Midian as "one man."

Following the two initial objections, Gideon asks in Judg 6:17–24 if he "has found favor" with God (cf. Exod 33:12, 13, 17; 34:9). He brings three different types of sacrifices (meat, unleavened bread, and broth) that are consumed by fire in reply to his request for a "sign" (אות) that God is indeed speaking to him. This consumption (אכל) by fire (אש) through the agency of the angel of the Lord also characterizes Moses' encounter with the angel at a bush that is not "consumed" (אכל) by

57. The etiological nature is especially suggested by the notice that the altar continues to exist "to this day" (Judg 6:24). See the discussion in Robert G. Boling, *Judges: Introduction, Translation, and Commentary* (AB 6A; Garden City, N.Y.: Doubleday, 1975), 130, 134.

58. Contra Van Seters, *The Life of Moses*, 44–45. "A theophany in a sacred place" is an accurate description of Gideon's encounter with the messenger of the Lord and thus is not an exclusive characteristic of a prophetic commission that distinguishes it from the basic scheme of the commissioning of a deliverer.

"fire" (אֵשׁ). Both reacted with fear. Moses hid his face out of fear of apprehending the deity (Exod 3:6). Similarly, Gideon cries out that he has seen God "face to face" (Judg 6:22; cf. Exod 33:11; Deut 34:10). Following his endowment with the "spirit of the Lord" (Judg 6:34; cf. Exod 4:16; 7:1), Gideon assembles a militia from the surrounding tribes and requests two additional signs in Judg 6:36–40 to assure him that God will save Israel through him (lit. "my hand"). By this point, Gideon has either objected to or requested a sign five times (vv. 13, 15, 17, 36, 39) in a pattern that is similar to the five objections of Moses. Finally, both series conclude with a description of God's anger. Gideon requests that God's anger not burn against him (יִחַר אַפְּךָ בִּי; v. 39), using the exact construction that is found at the conclusion of Moses' fifth objection (וַיִּחַר־אַף יְהוָה בְּמֹשֶׁה; Exod 4:14).

Following Gideon's victorious rout of Midian as God's empowered agent (7:1–21; cf. the cry "for the Lord and Gideon!" in vv. 18, 20), the Israelites attempt to make him king. Despite Gideon's refusal, he appears to embrace the privileges of kingship though his actions, such as accumulating gold and constructing an ephod, marrying "many wives" and fathering seventy sons, as well as naming one son "My Father is King" (lit. "Abimelech").[59] The subsequent account of Abimelech suggests the beginning of a royal dynasty. The typical clustering of royal motifs provides additional evidence for the royal portrayal of Gideon: the divine commissioning, emergence through controversy, and a decisive military defeat followed by the construction of a cultic object. A comparison of the accounts of the commissioning of Gideon and Moses reveals a number of remarkable parallels that clarify the implicit purpose of the call of Moses.[60] Like Gideon, but in a superior way, Moses is endowed with God's presence to deliver Israel from the power of Egypt as a result of Israel's cry.

59. See esp. the discussion in Dennis T. Olson, "Buber, Kingship, and the Book of Judges: A Study of Judges 6–9 and 17–21," in *David and Zion: Biblical Studies in Honor of J.J.M. Roberts* (ed. Bernard F. Batto and Kathryn L. Roberts; Winona Lake, Ind.: Eisenbrauns, 2004), 208–12.

60. Although it is beyond the scope of the present study, the similarities suggest the possibility of direct literary relationship or common authorship that warrants additional study. Brian Peckham, for example, locates portions of the commissioning of Moses (Exod 3:15–22; 4:1–17) and the account of Gideon as part of the Deuteronomistic redaction of Genesis–2 Kings (*History and Prophecy*, Chapter 5 [cf. 522, 525]).

3.4.c. *"He will deliver my people": Saul and Moses*

Since Saul is commissioned by Samuel and not through a theophany, the account of Saul's rise to power is usually not compared with those of Gideon and Moses.[61] However, the Saul account shares a common cluster of royal motifs with the Moses and Gideon accounts. More precisely, in the Saul account the pattern of a private commissioning of a royal leader is followed by a public affirmation of Saul's reign after his divine empowerment and subsequent rescue of the citizens of Jabesh-Gilead and concluded with a public exaltation of the Lord in 1 Sam 12 that parallels a similar sequencing of episodes in Exod 3–14. If the description of the birth of Samuel in 1 Sam 1 made use of an earlier account of the miraculous birth of Saul, based on the wordplay of the name "Saul" in 1 Sam 1:28 and the close connection between 1 Sam 1:1 and 9:1, then the basic contours of the account of Saul's commission would agree even more with the account of Moses' call in Exod 2–14.[62]

The introduction of Saul in 1 Sam 9:1–2 shares a few general points of contact with the story of Moses. Saul is depicted as "vigorous" (בחור) and the tallest and most handsome person (טוב; cf. Exod 2:2) in Israel.[63] Although Saul does not experience a theophany, in contrast to Moses and Gideon, the following account in 1 Sam 9:3–10:16 portrays the Lord's private commissioning of Saul through Samuel as Israel's ruler (נגיד; 1 Sam 9:16; 10:1). It is the outcome of Saul's pursuit of his father's lost donkeys, an ordinary activity that roughly resembles Moses' activity of shepherding and Gideon's threshing wheat prior to their divine commissioning to lead Israel.

The divine command for Samuel to commission Saul closely resembles the divine speech in Exod 3:7–9:

---

61. Thus George W. Savran, *Encountering the Divine: Theophany in Biblical Narrative* (JSOTSup 420; New York: T&T Clark International, 2005), pays little attention to close parallels that Richter identified between the commissioning of Moses, Gideon, and Saul. Saul receives only brief mention in Habel, "Call Narratives," 300 n. 10, who thinks it represents a "modified call narrative." However, the pattern remains intact if 1 Sam 9:21 is considered as the initial commission rather than 1 Sam 10:1. In any case, the exclusive focus on the "call narrative" section of Saul's account has led Habel and others to neglect the similar phrasing and structure of the larger unit of 1 Sam 9–12 as indicative of a royal biography.

62. See the discussion in P. Kyle McCarter Jr., *1 Samuel: A New Translation with Introduction and Commentary* (AB 8; Garden City, N.Y.: Doubleday, 1980), 63, 65–66.

63. On the character's handsome appearance as a royal motif, see §2.1b of the present study.

רָאִיתִי אֶת־עֳנִי 64 עַמִּי כִּי בָאָה צַעֲקָתוֹ אֵלַי

I have seen the affliction of my people for their cry has come to me. (1 Sam
9:16)

רָאֹה רָאִיתִי אֶת־עֳנִי עַמִּי...צַעֲקַת בְּנֵי־יִשְׂרָאֵל בָּאָה אֵלַי

I have indeed seen the affliction of my people…the cry of the Israelites have
come to me. (Exod 3:7, 9)

As a result of Israel's cry to God, Saul is commissioned privately as
Israel's leader to "save" (יָשַׁע; cf. Exod 2:17; 14:30) Israel from the
power of the Philistines (מִיַּד פְּלִשְׁתִּים; 1 Sam 9:16; cf. Exod 2:19; 3:8).
As with the Gideon and Moses accounts, the private commission of Saul
is followed by the giving of a sign. In this case, 1 Sam 10:1–13 narrate a
series of three signs (אוֹת; cf. the three signs in Judg 6). The MT version
of 1 Sam 10:1 is apparently defective, lacking a significant portion of
text that explains the purpose of the signs. The Old Greek version
preserved the longer text:

> The Lord has anointed you as ruler over his people, over Israel. Thus you
> will rule the people of the Lord and you will save them from the hand of
> their enemies all around. Now this [will be] the sign to you that the Lord
> has anointed you ruler over his inheritance.[65]

This text explains the specific purpose of Saul's commissioning to rule
Israel—to save Israel from their enemies—and the purpose of the sign as
confirmation of this commissioning. Although the nature of the signs in 1
Sam 10:2–13 is different from sign(s) given to Gideon and Moses,[66] the
signs in all three accounts serve the same function by confirming the
divine authenticity of the commission of the appointed ruler. In addition
to the sign, the Saul account also includes two objections of Saul to his
call as ruler. Like Gideon's first objection, Saul's rebuttal to Samuel in

64.   Although harmonization with Exod 3:9 is possible, עֳנִי is restored based on
Old Greek, Syriac, and the Targums. McCarter's discussion (*1 Samuel*, 169) could
have noted the possible loss of עֳנִי due to haplography, triggered by the repetition of
ע and/or י in the sequence עֳנִי עַמִּי.

65.   Author's translation. A Hebrew retroversion of the Old Greek is provided by
McCarter (ibid., 171) who speculates that haplography due to the repetition of the
phrase יהוה לְנָגִיד מְשָׁחֲךָ caused the omission of the intervening material.

66.   The specific sign given to Moses in Exod 3:12 is not entirely clear. See the
discussion in Childs, *Exodus*, 56–60, who speculates that the burning bush is the
sign. However, the reference to the burning bush is quite remote (mentioned only in
vv. 1–6) and is not mentioned in v. 12. Since the phrase "I will be with you"
immediately precedes the phrase "this sign," it is very likely that God's presence
with Moses is the sign (cf. NJPS translation of Exod 3:12: "I will be with you; that
shall be your sign that it was I who sent you").

1 Sam 9:21 highlights his lowly status. Second, during Samuel's public proclamation of Saul's reign in 10:17–27, Saul was chosen by lot but had to be retrieved from hiding (vv. 21–23).

Following the private commissioning of Saul and subsequent public introduction to the people, which closely resembles the sequence of the private commissioning of Moses in Exod 3–4 and his public emergence among the Israelite community in Exod 5, the dramatic demonstration of Saul's divine empowerment by God's spirit (1 Sam 11:6) and his rescue of the besieged inhabitants of Jabesh-Gilead serves to overcome the initial opposition to his rule (1 Sam 10:27; 11:12–13; cf. Exod 2:14; 5:21; 14:11–12).

The installation of Saul as king becomes complete in Samuel's farewell speech in 1 Sam 12. Samuel's address to Israel bears a remarkable resemblance to the description of Israel's salvation at the sea and the consequent exaltation of God and his servant Moses in Exod 14. In addition to serving as concluding affirmations of God's salvation through God's chosen agent, both texts share close verbal correspondence in 1 Sam 12:6, 16, 18 and Exod 14:13, 31.[67] In both we have a speech to the people of Israel commanding them to "stand and see" (התיצבו וראו) "the salvation of the Lord" (Exod 14:13) and "this great thing the Lord will do" (1 Sam 12:16; i.e. sending thunder and rain upon Samuel's command). Finally, we have a statement of the people "greatly fearing the Lord and Samuel" which resembles the description of the people "fearing the Lord and believing in the Lord and his servant Moses." The phrasing is close enough to suggest viewing both texts as a conclusion to the sequence of events in Exod 2–14 and 1 Sam 9–12 that has as its principal topic the selection, public emergence, and dramatic vindication of the Lord's chosen agent.[68]

In sum, the Gideon and Saul accounts suggests that the call narrative is a common component of the account of a royal figure. In all three accounts (Moses, Gideon, Saul), the commissioning is occasioned by a specific crisis that causes the people of Israel to cry to God for rescue. The commissioning is initiated by God either through a direct theophany

---

67. See the discussion in Blum, *Pentateuch*, 30–32, who also notes a comparison with the exaltation of Joshua in Josh 4:14, and views the correspondences as evidence of a D Composition in Exodus.

68. See the comparison of the different contexts of Exod 14 and 1 Sam 12 as part of a larger critique of E. Blum's reconstructed D-Composition in Graham I. Davies, "K[D] in Exodus: An Assessment of E. Blum's Proposal," in *Deuteronomy and Deuteronomic Literature* (ed. M. Vervenne and J. Lust; Louvain: Louvain University Press, 1997), 409–10.

or through a prophet. In all three accounts the commissioning occurred while the protagonist was engaging in a routine or mundane activity.[69] These parallels support an interpretation of Exod 3:1–4:17 as the commissioning of a *royal*, rather than a prophetic, figure. As the discussions of the larger literary contexts of the Gideon and Saul have indicated, a divine and private commissioning of the royal leader is a prelude to a series of events designed to show the public emergence of the chosen leader to convince the community of the legitimacy of the leader's divine commission.

3.5. *Public Emergence and Controversy*

The emergence of the chosen leader from obscurity to public renown is an expected and logical motif since the private and divine selection of a leader must gain support if it is to become effective, particularly in situations of crisis, revolt, or dynastic controversy, which characterize most of the extant biographical depictions of kings and heroes in the Old Testament and ancient Near East. After noting briefly the public emergence of Gideon and Saul, this section will compare in detail the public emergence of Moses and Jeroboam.

The Gideon narrative reports an episode between Gideon's commissioning and his military victory that cements his status as Israel's "king" (Judg 6:25–32). Gideon obeys the divine command to build an altar and offer sacrifices to God after demolishing his father's altar and Asherah pole. This Gideon does in secret at night, but the news reaches the citizens of the community whose subsequent investigation identifies Gideon as the perpetrator. Gideon's father persuades the community to refrain from executing Gideon, after which Gideon became publicly known by a new name, "Jerubbaal." In a manner similar to Moses' secret killing of the Egyptian, this action serves publicly to introduce Gideon, who is now in a position to use his fame to assemble a militia to defeat Midian. In a related, but different manner, Saul was publicly introduced by Samuel to the assembled Israelite community, who acclaimed Saul as their king on the basis of Saul's imposing physical appearance ("head and shoulders taller than any of them"; 1 Sam 9:23). This public emergence of Saul, however, was met with controversy in the community

69. Based on George Savran's development of a typology of theophany in the Old Testament, this routine activity is part of the preparation for the encounter with God, either through a theophany or a prophet that is designed to isolate the protagonist from the public sphere in preparation for a solitary encounter. See Savran, *Encountering the Divine*, 14.

(v. 27) that was resolved only after Saul's rescue of the citizens of Jabesh-Gilead from Ammonite control (11:1–13). Afterwards Saul was publicly and formally installed as king as part of a joyous cultic celebration at Gilead (11:14–15).

Comparing the portrayal of Moses in Exod 5 and Jeroboam in the more original Old Greek version of 1 Kgs 12, Smend concludes that both episodes represent a similar scene of the people of Israel pleading with the king to ease their burdens.[70] In the Old Greek version of 1 Kgs 12, Jeroboam remains in Egypt during the negotiations between the people and Rehoboam.[71] After the negotiations are broken off, the people find out that Jeroboam has returned from his flight to Egypt and install him as their king. In a similar way, Moses (and Aaron) recede into the background in Exod 5:5–19 while the Israelite supervisors make an emotional appeal to Pharaoh to ease their increased burden. In both accounts, Smend argues, there is a sequence of events that is typical of the portrayal of the public emergence of a leader:

> According to the precepts of the narrative art, this course of events is the proper one. A figure destined to help in an emergency (and Jeroboam may also be considered as such) tends to put in an appearance only when it is necessary. Before that he exists only in secret, known to the listener or reader as already appointed and possibly even through an initial deed in a smaller scope as already proved. The moment of suspense consists of when and how the general emergency makes it necessary for the hero to come forth from his seclusion and meet the emergency. It can be verified a hundredfold that this moment is delayed as long as possible. A deliverer seldom comes too early.[72]

Indeed, an examination of the sequence of events following the negotiations with Pharaoh in Exod 5 shows the extent to which the deliverer is ultimately unveiled. While Smend speculates that Exod 5 led into some version of the plague account at an earlier literary stage, in the final form of the text the failed negotiations with Pharaoh, who refused to obey (שמע) the voice of the Lord (Exod 5:2), creates a new situation of intensified labor that also prevents the people from listening to Moses (5:9, 20–21) and thus set the stage for a reaffirmation of Moses' commission in Exod 6:1–7:7. Although not a theophanic encounter on the

---

70. Smend, *Yahweh War*, 124–28.

71. MT adds v. 2 and includes Jeroboam with the Israelite negotiators in v. 3 and 13. With the excision of these verses, the statement that "Israel heard that Jeroboam had returned" in v. 20 becomes clear. Otherwise, how could Israel have heard about Jeroboam's return if he was leading the negotiations all along?

72. Smend, *Yahweh War*, 125.

level of Exod 3:1–4:17, the Lord's second message to Moses follows an inverted structure by sending Moses to speak to Israel (6:1–9) and to Pharaoh (6:10–11; see the chart in the appendix to this study). It also includes another designation of Moses as "God," in this case, to Pharaoh.

The initial speech in 6:1–8 reprises several important themes of the first encounter. Moses is entrusted with the use of the Lord's name, which frames the address in vv. 2–8, and he is commanded to say to the Israelites that the Lord has heard their cries and will deliver them from Egypt and will settle them in the land. In contrast to the people's response in 4:31, here the people do not listen (שמע) to Moses due to their "crushed spirit and oppressive labor (עבדה)." This demonstrates the successful intention of Pharaoh's new strategy to oppress the population of Israel (so 5:9, "Let heavier work (עבדה) be imposed on them; then they will labor at it and not heed to deceptive words.") After Moses calls attention again to his speech impediment, the Lord empowers Moses as "God" with Aaron as his "prophet" in anticipation of Moses' confrontation with Pharaoh, who refuses to listen to the Lord. The principal purpose of Exod 1:1–7:7 is to introduce publicly and to empower Moses as "God" for both Israel and Pharaoh with the goal of securing their obedience to Moses and the Lord. In contrast to other accounts, the public emergence and acknowledgment of Moses' authority as God's chosen agent is a major concern in the depiction of Moses. It is carefully developed to show the acknowledgment and obedience to Moses and God by Pharaoh and the Egyptians. And this is followed by the parallel attempt to secure Israel's belief in and obedience to in Moses in the wilderness.[73]

3.6. *Conclusion*

This chapter has identified four royal motifs attested in biblical and other ancient Near Eastern sources and has examined how they are used in the first major segment of Exodus (1:1–7:7). These four motifs are typically clustered together to introduce and legitimate a candidate for royal or heroic status. The account of Moses' birth utilized the familiar motif of the abandonment and rescue of an infant destined to be king in order to introduce Israel's future savior and leader. The two episodes following the birth of Moses adapted a well-known motif of the flight of a political fugitive and his return to assume power (Exod 2:11–22). Moses' flight and sojourn in a foreign land provided the context for articulating the identity and vocation of Moses. The text carefully avoided equating

73. See the chart above, p. 58.

Moses with a specific role such as prophet, king, or judge by portraying him as the one who will "rule" and "judge" Israel and will "strike" the Egyptians and "save" Israel in the wilderness. The episode that follows Moses' flight used a third royal motif: the private commissioning and divine empowerment of royal deliverer. This motif has been adapted in Exod 3:1–4:17 to stress that Moses' vocation to deliver and lead Israel is the will of God, who has chosen and empowered Moses to act on God's behalf to save and guide Israel. Finally, Exod 1:1–7:7 concluded by narrating the public emergence and the contested status of Moses's leadership before Israel and Pharaoh. At the conclusion of this section, Moses' vocation and role has been affirmed and secured by God. The next chapter will turn to an examination of four additional motifs and how these are used to depict Moses in the wilderness episodes.

Chapter 4

"IT IS AN AWESOME THING THAT I WILL DO WITH YOU": THE PORTRAYAL OF MOSES IN THE WILDERNESS EPISODES

4.1. *Introduction*

This chapter will examine four additional royal motifs in the Pentateuchal depiction of Moses: the exaltation of king and deity; the king as lawgiver and covenant maker; the king as temple builder and cultic overseer; and the death of the king and rise of his successor.

4.2. *"The Lord passed across his face": Exaltation of King and Deity at Sinai*

A major concern in Exodus is the exaltation of Moses as God's empowered servant and Israel's affirmation of this exaltation. This exaltation and affirmation of Moses as God's chosen agent appear at two decisive points in Exodus: at the defeat of Egypt at the Sea and Israel's encounter with God at Sinai. The relevant verses read:

> Israel saw the great work that the Lord did against the Egyptians. So the people feared the Lord and believed in the Lord and in his servant Moses. (Exod 14:31)

> Then the Lord said to Moses, "I am going to come to you in a dense cloud, in order that the people may hear when I speak with you and so trust you ever after." (Exod 19:9)

This section will provide an examination of Exod 32–34 that portrays Moses as a divinized, royal figure in a dramatic narrative, as one who is closely associated with God and becomes a means of extending God's presence to Israel. The principal concern of these chapters is the establishment of God's presence and guidance of Israel through the agency of Moses.[1] This section will provide an overview of how Moses is closely associated with God. Next, this section will examine how Moses' close

---

1. See esp. the discussion in Mann, *Divine Presence*, 154–59.

relationship with God provides a means for Moses to extend God's presence to Israel as the solution to the loss of God's presence that is the result of the sin of the golden calf.

The close association between God and Moses is made in a number of ways in Exod 32–34. First, Israel is described alternately as the people of Moses in divine speech (32:7; 34:10) and the people of God in Mosaic speech (32:11–12; 33:13–16):

> The Lord said to Moses, "Go down at once! *Your people*, whom you brought up out of the land of Egypt, have acted perversely." (Exod 32:7)

> He (the Lord) said, "I hereby make a covenant. Before all *your people* I will perform marvels, such as have not been performed in all the earth or in any nation." (Exod 34:10)

> But Moses implored the Lord his God, and said, "O Lord, why does your wrath burn hot against *your people*, whom you brought out of the land of Egypt with great power and with a mighty hand?… Turn from your fierce wrath; change your mind and do not bring disaster on *your people*. (Exod 32:11–12)

> Moses said to the Lord, "See, you have said to me, 'Bring up this people'; but you have not let me know whom you will send with me… Now if I have found favour in your sight, show me your ways, so that I may know you and find favour in your sight. Consider too that this nation is *your people*." He said, "My presence will go with you, and I will give you rest." And he said to him, "If your presence will not go, do not carry us up from here. For how shall it be known that I have found favour in your sight, *I and your people*, unless you go with us? In this way, we shall be distinct, *I and your people*, from every people on the face of the earth." (Exod 33:13–16)

Second, these chapters portray both God and Moses as the one who brought Israel out of Egypt (Moses—32:1, 7; 33:1; God—32:11):

> The people gathered around Aaron and said to him, "Come, make gods for us, who shall go before us; as for *this Moses, the man who brought us up out of the land of Egypt*, we do not know what has become of him." (Exod 32:1)

> The Lord said to Moses, "Go down at once! *Your people, whom you brought up out of the land of Egypt*, have acted perversely." (Exod 32:7)

> The Lord said to Moses, "Go, leave this place, *you and the people whom you have brought up out of the land of Egypt*…" (Exod 33:1)

> But Moses implored the Lord his God, and said, 'O Lord, why does your wrath burn hot against *your people, whom you brought out of the land of Egypt* with great power and with a mighty hand? (Exod 32:11)

Complicating these portrayals of Moses and God is the depiction of the golden calf in the role of leading the people:

> "Come, make gods for us, who shall go before us..." (Exod 32:1)

> They said, "These are your gods, O Israel, who brought you up out of the land of Egypt!" (Exod 32:4; cf. 32:7)

The role of the golden calf as the one who brought Israel from Egypt and who will "go before" the people suggests that the calf is fashioned in Moses' absence as a substitute for Moses.[2] The complementary role between the calf and God is made clear in the establishment of the "festival to the Lord" shortly after the construction of the calf (32:5–6).[3]

Finally, the close association between Moses and God is also apparent in the destruction of the tablets of the covenant and the composition of the new set of tablets. The depiction of Moses' angry reaction upon his descent with the tablets of the covenant in Exod 32:19 employs the same phrase used to describe the anger of God in 32:9–10:

> The Lord said to Moses, "I have seen this people, how stiff-necked they are. Now let me alone, so that my wrath may burn hot (ויחר אפי) against them and I may consume them; and of you I will make a great nation." (Exod 32:9–10)

> Moses' anger burned hot (ויחר אף משה), and he threw the tablets from his hands and broke them at the foot of the mountain. (Exod 32:19)

Consistent with his portrayal as a royal figure, Moses then proceeds to break the tablets in pieces as the means of nullifying the covenant between God and Israel, an act that is attested in other ancient Near Eastern sources.[4] Thus the common understanding that Moses broke the tablets

---

2.   J. M. Sasson examines the connection between Moses and the calf in Exod 32 and on the basis of Exod 34:29–35 discerns an underlying cult devoted to Moses as a horned deity. In "Bovine Symbolism in the Exodus Narrative," *VT* 18 (1968): 380–87. See also R. W. L. Moberly, *At the Mountain of God: Story and Theology in Exodus 32–34* (JSOTSup 22; Sheffield: JSOT, 1983), 46.

3.   According to Moberly, Moses and the calf represent two different means of the embodiment of God's presence (*At the Mountain of God*, 46–47).

4.   According to Moshe Weinfeld ("ברית," *TDOT* 2:265), "Breaking the covenant tablets means annulment of the covenant (cf. Akk *ṭuppam ḥepû*), and this explains why Moses broke the tablets in Exod 32." Cf. the reference to breaking the tablet of the treaty between Suppiluliuma I of Hatti and Shattiwaza of Mittanni: "If he breaks it, if he changes the words of the text of the tablet—in regard to this treaty we have summoned the gods of secrets and the gods who are guarantors of the oath..." (Gary Beckman, *Hittite Diplomatic Texts* [2d ed.; SBLWAW 7; Atlanta: Scholars Press, 1999], 46).

when he lost his temper is not entirely accurate. Rather, Moses manifested God's wrath, and as God's "royal" agent he deliberately broke the tablets in order to nullify the covenant. Finally, Moses is closely associated with God in the account of the composition of the new set of tablets:

> The Lord said to Moses, "Cut two tablets of stone like the former ones, and I will write on the tablets the words that were on the former tablets, which you broke." (Exod 34:1)

> The Lord said to Moses, "Write these words; in accordance with these words I have made a covenant with you and with Israel." He was there with the Lord for forty days and forty nights; he neither ate bread nor drank water. And he wrote on the tablets the words of the covenant, the ten commandments. (Exod 34:27–28)

In sum, Exod 32–34 attributes a number of features to both Moses and God, namely, the leadership of Israel and deliverance of Israel from Egypt, the angry response to the construction of the calf, and the composition of the new set of tablets. The close association between Moses and God is consistent with the association of the king with his deity and the role of the king as the agent of his deity.

Following the sin of the golden calf, this close association between Moses and God will provide the basis for a solution to the loss of God's presence in Israel. The description of the manufacture of the golden calf as a "terrible sin" (חטאה גדלה; Exod 32:21, 30, 31) indicates the seriousness of the situation that is underscored through the collection of several terms for sin in Exod 34:7, 9 ("iniquity," "transgression," "sin"). Although Moses' attempt to expiate (כפר) Israel's sin in Exod 32:30–35 succeeds in warding off the total destruction of Israel, God effectively removes his beneficial presence from Israel by sending a plague to punish Israel (32:35).

Following the plague, God explicitly denies Israel his immediate presence (33:3, 5). He arranges for Israel to take possession of the land under the agency of the messenger (מלאך, "angel" [NRSV], 33:2). God is no longer able to be with Israel since his immediate presence would consume the people (33:3, 4; cf. 32:10). This new state of affairs sets the stage for the intimate interaction between God and Moses in Exod 33:7–34:35 regarding the status and survival of Israel as God's covenant people.

Exodus 33:7–11 and 34:29–35 frame the intimate dialogue between God and Moses. These two texts focus on the habitual actions of Moses speaking with God and pose the issue of God's presence and guidance, as well as the mediation of God's words to Israel. The first passage,

Exod 33:7–11, depicts how and where Moses regularly communed with
God after the golden calf incident.[5] This text emphasizes that the tent is
now located outside the community of Israel with God's presence
restricted to Moses.[6] Twice this passage notes that the tent is located
"outside" the camp and "far away" from the camp (v. 7). Thus the people
(v. 7) and Moses (v. 8) must "go out" in order to reach the tent. The use
of imperfect verbs indicates the new habitual activity of Moses. He must
now "go out" to the tent that is located at a large distance from the
community. Only when Moses enters the tent does the cloud descend to
the tent as the Lord speaks "face to face" with Moses as with a "friend."[7]
The people are relegated to the margins and can only view Moses entering the tent and the cloud over the tent. In sum, following the rupture of
Israel's relationship with God and the withdrawal of the divine presence,
Exod 33:7–11 describes the standard and unsatisfactory practice of
revealing the divine word only to Moses at a distance from the Israelite
community.

Exodus 33:7–11 establishes the intimacy and freedom of Moses'
reciprocal relationship with God as God's "friend" and thus provides a
transition to the dialogue between Moses and God that follows in Exod
33:12–34:28. This dialogue occurs in two parts. The first part (33:12–23)
occurs presumably at the tent of meeting that has now been constructed.
Here, Moses explicitly rejects God's appointment of the divine messenger as an unacceptable solution. According to Moses, the loss of God's
immediate presence relegates Israel to the status of other nations and thus
negates their status as God's "treasured possession out of all the people"
(Exod 19:5–6). Moses uses his own special relationship with God,
described as "friendship" (33:11), to include Israel into the favored status
currently enjoyed by Moses:

> Now if I have found favor in your sight, show me your ways, so that I may
> know you and find favor in your sight. Consider too that this nation is *your
> people*.

> For how shall it be known that I have found favor in your sight, *I and your
> people*, unless you go with us? In this way, we shall be distinct, *I and your
> people*, from every people on the face of the earth. (Exod 33:13, 16)

5. Moses performs the kingly role of constructing a sanctuary by taking the "tent
and pitching it outside the camp." Cf. Van Seters, *The Life of Moses*, 322, who calls
attention to 2 Sam 6:17, "They brought the ark of the Lord, and set it in its place,
inside the tent that David had pitched for it."

6. See Moberly, *At the Mountain of God*, 63–64.

7. Jacqueline E. Lapsley, "Friends with God? Moses and the Possibility of
Covenantal Friendship," *Int* 58 (2004): 117–29.

Moses urgently requests God's presence with both Moses *and* the people in order to distinguish the people of Israel from the rest of the nations.

God finally agrees to this request in Exod 33:17–23 and gives a series of promises to Moses that will be fulfilled later at Sinai in 34:1–8.[8] The command addressed to Moses, "be ready" (היה נכון; Exod 34:2), echoed the earlier command to the people who are now noticeably absent (היו נכנים; Exod 19:11; היו נכנים; Exod 19:15). The difference here is that this command is addressed only to Moses in the singular and anticipates the ratification of the new covenant primarily with Moses. This is carefully emphasized in v. 3, where only Moses is to go up on the mountain:

> No one shall come up with you, and do not let anyone be seen throughout all the mountain; and do not let flocks or herds graze in front of that mountain. (Exod 34:3)

Other individuals who have previously accompanied Moses (Aaron, Nadab, Abihu, elders, Joshua) are noticeably absent. The prohibition against the presence of Israel's animals (which may have been allowed to feed near the mountain earlier [Exod 19:2]) before the giving of the first covenant is also heightened here. These intensifications of the Lord's earlier directives to Israel in ch. 19 serve to isolate Israel from the Lord and ensure that only Moses will enter the Lord's presence.

Although the precise identification of the subjects performing the actions of 34:5–6a is unclear, contextual connections with Exod 33:19–23 suggest that Moses is standing before the Lord and that the Lord takes the initiative to proclaim his name twice.[9] Just as the Lord initiated the conversation and the subsequent revelation of his name at the burning bush in Exod 3, so here the Lord reveals his attributes to Moses by using an extended string of adjectives that function to explain the divine name:

> The Lord, the Lord: a God merciful and gracious, slow to anger, and abounding in steadfast love and faithfulness. Although he keeps steadfast love for the thousandth generation, and forgives iniquity and transgression

8. According to Donald E. Gowan, these fulfilled promises include: (1) Moses' request to see the Lord's glory (33:18), which is answered by the Lord's descent in a cloud (34:5); (2) the Lord's command to Moses to stand on the rock (33:21), which is fulfilled when Moses presented himself before the Lord at Sinai (34:2, 5); (3) the passing by of the Lord's goodness and glory (33:19, 21), which is fulfilled in 34:6; (4) the Lord's pronouncing his own name (33:19; 34:6); (5) the brief theological exposition of the Lord's name in 33:19b, which is expanded in 34:6a–7. See Donald E. Gowan, *Theology in Exodus: Biblical Theology in the Form of a Commentary* (Louisville: Westminster John Knox, 1994), 233.

9. For a recent discussion and bibliography, see Widmer, *Moses*, 170–75.

and sin, *he will certainly not clear the guilty.* He will visit the iniquity of the parents upon the children and the children's children, to the third and the fourth generation. (Exod 34:6–7; author's translation)

This explanation of the divine name begins with a series of attributes that emphasize the merciful and compassionate nature of God. Nevertheless, the lone finite verb in v. 7 (נקה; lit. "acquit") indicates the accent on God's justice despite his merciful nature. The message God conveys to Moses is that although God's mercy outweighs God's justice, God will by no means acquit the guilty. The guilty party in this case is Israel. This reading, which leaves unresolved the forgiveness of Israel, explains the urgency of Moses' reaction to this explanation of God's nature:

Moses quickly bowed his head towards the earth, and worshipped. He said, "If now I have found favor in your sight, O Lord, I pray, let the Lord go with us. Although this is a stiff-necked people, pardon our iniquity and our sin, and take us for your inheritance." (Exod 34:8–9)

In spite of the emphasis on God's justice, Moses falls to the ground to implore God to forgive Israel on the basis of his favored status with God. Moses appeals to God's merciful nature with a three-fold request for God's immediate presence, for forgiveness of a "stiff-necked people," and for God to receive Israel as his inheritance. Moses now explicitly identifies himself with Israel by switching from the first person singular, which has predominated throughout his dialogue with the Lord, to the first person plural ("let the Lord go with *us*"; "pardon *our* iniquity and *our* sin, and take *us* for your inheritance"). This shift significantly alters the dynamic of the Lord's relationship with Israel because it will now be through Moses that Israel has any hope of sustaining a viable relationship with the Lord through his continued presence.

To appreciate fully the Lord's response to Moses' request in vv. 8–9, the text of 34:9–10, 27–34 will be translated with the crucial terms italicized:

(9) And he (Moses) said, "If I have found favor in your eyes, O Lord, let Yahweh go *in our midst.* Although this is a stiff-necked people, forgive our iniquities and sins and then take us for your inheritance."

(10) And he (Yahweh) said, "Behold I am establishing a covenant. Before all your people, I will perform miraculous acts which have not been accomplished in the whole earth or all the nations. Because you (Moses) are *in their midst*, all the people will see the work of Yahweh, for it is *a terrifying thing* which I will do with you (Moses)."

(27) And Yahweh said to Moses, "Write these words, for by the speaking of these words I am establishing a covenant with you (Moses) *and with Israel.*"

(28) And he was there with Yahweh forty days and forty nights. Food he did not eat. Water he did not drink. And he (Moses) wrote the words of this covenant—the ten words.

(29) And as Moses went down from Mount Sinai—the two tablets of the testimony were in the hand of Moses—when he went down from the mountain, Moses did not know that the skin of his face "shone" when he spoke with him (the Lord).

(30) And Aaron and all the people of Israel saw Moses and that the skin of his face "shone." *And they were afraid to approach him.*

(31) Moses called out to them, and Aaron and all the leaders of the congregation returned to him and Moses spoke to them.

(32) After that, *all the people of Israel approached* and he commanded them all which Yahweh spoke to him on Mount Sinai.

(33) When Moses finished speaking with them, he placed over his face a "covering."

(34) Whenever Moses would go before Yahweh to speak to him, he would remove the "covering" and would come out to speak to the people of Israel what he had been commanded (35) so that the people of Israel would *see the face of Moses* that the skin of Moses' face "shone." Then Moses would return the covering over his face until he came in to speak with him (Yahweh).

These verses describe the dialogue that occurs immediately after the Lord passed across Moses' "face" (v. 6). This event caused Moses' face to shine and transforms him so that he can now become the means of extending the Lord's presence in the midst of Israel. And after this transformation, Moses remains on the mountain without food or drink for forty days and engages in the divine activity of inscribing the "ten words" (v. 28; cf. v. 1). Moses' bearing the divine presence in the midst of Israel is described as a "terrifying" deed of the Lord that will enable the nations to see that the Lord through Moses is indeed in the midst of Israel.[10]

Thus a resolution of the "great sin" of the golden calf and the loss of God's presence in the midst of Israel has been achieved that is consistent with God's justice and merciful nature as described in vv. 6–7. The current generation of Israel can never again fully enjoy the Lord's direct, immediate presence despite Moses' plea in v. 9. Based on the favored status between Moses and the Lord as "friends," Moses becomes the sole party of the covenant and is the one who will be in Israel's midst. The partner of the covenant is left ambiguous in v. 10, but the Lord makes it clear in v. 27 that the covenant is established primarily with Moses and, by extension, with Israel.

The concluding section of 34:29–35 illustrates the dramatic change of affairs from the dislocation of God's presence in 33:7–11 by describing

10. Cf. Propp, *Exodus 19–40*, 612–13.

the new habitual activity of Moses. Rather than appearing to Moses in a location far removed from Israel, God is now present in Israel's midst through Moses, who functions to extend God's presence to Israel. Moses' descent from the mountain is described as a theophany. He descends to Israel from Sinai. His face radiates gloriously and causes a reaction of fear (cf. v. 10) from Aaron and the Israelites who are afraid to approach Moses. After Moses' speech, Aaron and the leaders, followed soon after by the rest of the community, eventually approach Moses to receive the words from the Lord. According to Propp, "Moses may be regarded as a walking Tabernacle, manifesting and yet concealing the Lord's splendor."[11] No longer relegated to the margin, Israel now can encounter God and receive a divine word from God who dwells in their midst through the agency of Moses.[12]

To sum up the profile of Moses in Exod 32–34, Moses' close association with God allows him to speak and act to God on behalf of Israel as well as to embody God and God's presence in the midst of Israel. In short, we see an exalted Moses in the nexus between God and Israel, which is precisely the role of the king in the ancient Near East.

4.3. *"I have made a covenant with you and with Israel":*
The Royal Tasks of Lawgiving and Covenant-making

An important way for a king to secure and maintain justice and peace is through the promulgation of laws and the establishment of covenants and treaties. Hammurabi's law code, for example, shows that Hammurabi claims to have a divine mandate to rule justly and maintain order.[13] The prologue to this code begins by describing the purpose of Hammurabi's election:

---

11. Ibid., 621.

12. According to Rolf P. Knierim (*The Task of Old Testament Theology: Substance, Method, and Cases* [Grand Rapids: Eerdmans, 1995], 367), Lev 1:1 signals the beginning of a new phase of the revelation of God that is now mediated to Israel at the tent of meeting through the agency of Moses: "Lev 1:1 signals the highest level in the macrostructure of the Sinai pericope... The Sinai pericope aims at the book of Leviticus. This book is the center of the Pentateuch."

13. For a more detailed discussion of justice as a royal responsibility in Israel in the context of the ancient Near East, see Keith W. Whitelam, *The Just King: Monarchical Judicial Authority in Ancient Israel* (JSOTSup 12; Sheffield: JSOT, 1979). See esp. Chapter 1, "The Ideal," and Chapter 11, "The King as Law-Giver," where Whitelam suggests that Moses and Joshua, in contrast to the Israelite kings in the monarchic period, are portrayed as the "royal legislator" (p. 218).

> To make justice prevail in the land, to abolish the wicked and the evil, to prevent the strong from oppressing the weak, to rise like the sun god Shamash over all humankind, to illuminate the land.[14]

This stress on justice reappears at the conclusion of the prologue:

> When the god Marduk commanded me to provide just ways for the people of the land (in order to attain) appropriate behavior, I established truth and justice as the declaration of the land, I enhanced the well-being of the people.[15]

This law code is one of three extant ancient Near Eastern codes with a prologue that attributes the laws to the king, who is seen as the source of justice.[16] The other two codes are Lipit-Isthar, about two hundred years before Hammurabi, and Ur-Namma, about four hundred years before Hammurabi. The prologue to the law code of Lipit-Isthar begins with the description of the divine election of Lipit-Isthar, called the "wise shepherd," in order to "establish justice in the land, to eliminate cries for justice, to eradicate enmity and armed violence, to bring well-being to the lands of Sumer and Akkad."[17] A similar stress on justice also appears at the beginning and end of the prologue of the law code of Ur-Namma, who was king of Ur around 2100 B.C.E.[18]

In addition to lawgiving, another way for kings to establish peace and security is negotiating treaties. The extant ancient Near Eastern treaties have received much scholarly attention and have been compared to the legal literature in the Pentateuch, especially in the classic studies of Mendenhall, McCarthy, Baltzer, Hillers, and Cross. Consequently, the

14. Roth, *Law Collections*, 76.

15. Ibid., 80–81.

16. On the role of the king as lawgiver, see, e.g., Crüsemann, *The Torah*, 15, and the literature cited there. Although he carefully discerns the major differences between biblical and ancient Near Eastern law, Crüsemann notes that ancient Near Eastern law comes from the king and is named after the king. See also the literature cited in Eckart Otto, "The Pentateuch in Synchronical and Diachronical Perspectives: Protorabbinic Scribal Erudition Mediating Between Deuteronomy and the Priestly Code," in *Das Deuteronomium zwischen Pentateuch und Deuteronomistischem Geschichtswerk* (ed. Eckart Otto and Reinhard Achenbach, FRLANT; Vandenhoeck & Ruprecht, 2004), 16–17, who states on p. 17, "In the Ancient Near East the codification of law was a royal task, which King Hammurapi was a prototype for, that the Pentateuchal scribes transferred with anti-babylonian intentions 'subversively' to Moses." Cf. also John Van Seters, *The Edited Bible: The Curious History of the "Editor" in Biblical Criticism* (Winona Lake, Ind.: Eisenbrauns, 2006), 388.

17. Roth, *Law Collections*, 25.

18. Ibid., 15–17.

role of the king in establishing treaties and covenants in the ancient Near East is well known.[19] Treaties were the means of maintaining stability by establishing an alliance between two kings on behalf of their states. Of the approximately 35 extant Hittite treaties, two treaties represent a "parity" agreement between two kings of equal power (e.g. Hatti and Egypt), while the remaining treaties are classified as examples of a "suzerainty" treaty that is unilaterally imposed by the "Great King" of a prevailing empire of the day upon a king of a smaller and weaker state.[20] Other examples include a seventh-century inscription, where Azatiwada narrates how he was designated to rule on behalf of the king Awariku and then "smashed the rebels" and "crushed all evil which was in the land" and "made peace with every king."[21] An inscription dated to 1200 B.C.E. narrates how Idrimi became king over Alakah and then established peace by negotiating a treaty with the overlord Barrattarna and by defeating other kings.[22] These examples show that ancient Near Eastern treaties were typically established between two kings. Other examples show that treaties can also be made between a king and his subjects, such as the vassal treaty of Esarhaddon, or between a king and a deity, such as the establishment of a covenant between Assur and Esarhaddon as the outcome of a series of events that eventually culminated in Esarhaddon's enthronement.[23]

The role of a king in establishing a covenant with God and the people is also well-documented in the Old Testament. Kings who have established a covenant with God or the people include David (2 Sam 23:5; cf. 7:1–17), Joash (2 Kgs 11), Hezekiah (2 Chr 29:10), and Josiah (2 Kgs 23:1–3). In particular, the account of Josiah establishing a covenant with Judah closely resembles Moses' actions in Deut 29. In both accounts, the narrative emphasizes the complete assembly of Israel and their leaders (2 Kgs 23:2; Deut 29:10–11). Both establish a covenant with the entire community on behalf of the Lord and the community is portrayed as actively joining the covenant (Deut 29:12 [11]—עבר בברית; 2 Kgs 23:3—עמד בברית). In a study of the king as a covenant maker, Kathryn

19. See esp. the literature cited in Kathryn L. Roberts, "God, Prophet, and King: Eating and Drinking on the Mountain in First Kings 18:41," *CBQ* 62 (2000): 632–44.

20. I am relying on the information provided in Beckman, *Hittite Diplomatic Texts*, 1–6.

21. "The Azatiwada Inscription," translated by K. Lawson Younger, Jr. (*COS* 2.31:149).

22. "The Autobiography of Idrimi," translated by Tremper Longman III (*COS* 1.148:479).

23. See the discussion of the career of Esarhaddon in Chapter 2 of this study.

Roberts notes the account of Joash where the renewal of the covenant was made between God and the king and people (2 Kgs 11:19), and also between the king and the people (v. 17).[24] She suggests the role of the king as the intermediary between God and the people. In a study of Elijah's command to King Ahab to eat and drink in 1 Kgs 18:41, she argues for understanding Ahab as a sacral king who is required to eat and drink as the logical completion of the pattern of cultic reform. Although Roberts does not view Moses in the role of a sacral king, the pattern of covenant-making and covenant-renewal followed by eating and drinking explains the actions of Moses establishing a covenant with the people followed by a ritual meal in Exod 24:1–11.

In sum, a survey of the role of kings in establishing covenants in the ancient Near East and Old Testament illustrates the different kinds of relationships underlying these agreements, between a king with another king, with the king's subjects, or with the king's deity. This role of the king provides an illuminating point of comparison with the figure of Moses. Porter argues that Moses, who is portrayed as a vassal king, receives the covenant from God, who is portrayed as suzerain. Moses later imposes the covenant on Israel through the covenant ceremony (Exod 24:4–8).[25] Moses is not merely a third-party messenger or mediator.[26] Rather, Moses makes a covenant on behalf of Israel in a private encounter with God, in the role of a vassal king over Israel who is designated as the nation of Moses in Exod 32:7 and 34:10.[27] Porter argues that the covenant between a vassal and an overlord also explains the covenant established between God and Moses in Exod 34:10.[28] In Deut 29–31, Moses acts in the role of a king who establishes a covenant with the assembled people of Israel, in a manner similar to Esarhaddon and Josiah. In all of these examples, the king acts as the intermediary between God and the people and the people are connected to the covenant through their submission to the king's authority.

The rest of this section will provide an examination of the portrayal of Moses as lawgiver and covenant-maker in three episodes located between the exaltation of Moses at the Sea and Israel's arrival at Sinai (Exod 15:22–17:7). These episodes feature the royal identity of Moses as

24. Roberts, "God, Prophet, and King."

25. Porter, *Moses and Monarchy*, 16–17.

26. As argued, for example, by Roberts, "God, Prophet, and King," who views Moses as a covenant mediator.

27. Porter, *Moses and Monarchy*, 17.

28. Ibid., 17 n. 52. He compares this covenant with the covenant made with David (he does not cite a passage, which is presumably 2 Sam 23:5).

lawgiver and covenant-maker in the creation of the new community of
Israel. The first episode, Exod 15:22–27, portrays Moses as God's agent
who speaks and acts in harmony with God to such a degree that it is
sometimes difficult to distinguish them. According to 15:25–26,

> He (Moses) cried out to the Lord. The Lord showed him a tree. He cast
> (the tree) into the water, and the water became sweet. He imposed for
> them there statutes and laws (חק ומשפט) and tested them there. He said,
> "If you will surely obey the voice of the Lord your God, and do what is
> right in his eyes and listen to his commands and keep all his statutes, I
> will not bring upon you any of the diseases which I brought upon Egypt
> for I am Yahweh, your healer.[29]

Moses is apparently the subject of the actions of promulgating the statues
and laws for Israel after crying to the Lord and casting the wood into the
water. However, the subject of verb "imposed" (שים) is ambiguous and
could refer to the Lord. In addition, the speech switches from the third
person to the first person and gives the impression that Moses and the
Lord are speaking harmoniously or in a complementary manner.[30] This is
one of several texts throughout the Moses narrative where similar
ambiguities are encountered (e.g. Exod 19:25–20:1; 34:1, 27–28).[31]

In a detailed study, Victor Turgman calls attention to the royal portrayal of Moses in Exod 15:22–27.[32] He argues for viewing Moses as the
subject of v. 25b–26 and that the principal concern of this passage is to
establish the authority of Moses who then promulgates the law.[33] In
particular, Turgman notes how the actions of Moses in giving the statues
and laws (חק ומשפט) resemble the actions of David in 1 Sam 30:25, as
well as the actions of Joshua establishing a covenant and the statutes and
laws in Josh 24:25. He argues that Joshua's challenge to the people
regarding their readiness and ability to be faithful and loyal to God
explains Moses' "testing" of Israel.[34] Thus Turgman concludes that
Moses' action of giving the law in vv. 25b–26 is consistent with the role
of the king in promulgating the law.

---

29. Author's translation.

30. On this phenomenon, see esp. McBride, "The Essence of Orthodoxy:
Deuteronomy 5:6–10 and Exodus 20:2–6," *Int* 60 (2006): 140.

31. On the ambiguity of the speaker of 19:25–20:2, see Benjamin D. Sommer,
"The Source Critic and the Religious Interpreter," *Int* 60 (2006): 12–15, who argues
that different views of precise nature of the promulgation of the law at Sinai were
intentionally preserved in the received text.

32. Victor Turgman, *De l'autorité de Moïse, Ex 15,22–27* (Eilsbrunn: Ko'amar,
1987).

33. Ibid., 15–18.

34. Ibid., 16.

The speech of Moses in vv. 25b–26 stresses the importance of obeying the voice of the Lord and doing what is right in order to secure God's blessing in order to avoid the "diseases" that have previously afflicted the Egyptians. Van Seters notes the prominence of healing and diseases in the ancient Near Eastern vassal treaties and thinks that the role of God, who alternately heals or brings diseases, reflects the covenant accent of blessing and curses.[35] The conclusion to the Book of the Covenant (Exod 23:20–33) repeats and develops the various themes announced at Marah. In particular, Israel is commanded to obey the voice of God (the voice of the "messenger" in Exod 23:21, 22) in order to secure God's blessing and avoid the curse (described in 23:25 as "disease"; מחלה, which occurs in the Pentateuch only here and in 15:26).[36] The statement in 23:25 follows the same shift from third person to first person speech in 15:25b–27 and can be read as a summary of the preceding episodes at Marah and Massah/Meribah as God's covenant blessing of Israel:

> You will serve the Lord your God so that he may bless your food and your water; and I will take disease away from among you. (Exod 23:25)

Thus the short episode at Marah, the first episode after the escape from Egypt, plays a strategic role in the narrative. It serves as a transition from Egypt to the wilderness where Moses exhorts Israel to avoid Egypt's fate by obeying the Lord's statutory decrees. Moses gives these decrees in a way that mirrors and intertwines with God. This episode also introduces important themes that will be developed throughout the Pentateuch— testing, obedience, and the development of Moses' royal identity that now includes intercession for Israel and the promulgation of the law in context of the covenant. The formation of Israel into a cultic and political community is stressed by the designation of Israel now as a "congregation" (עדה) in the itinerary notices in 16:1 and 17:1. This designation is intentional especially in light of its absence in the station list in Num 33 and its repetition in 16:2. In addition, the standard Priestly designation of Israel before 16:1 is "children of Israel," with the exception of the cultic Passover prescriptions in Exod 12:3, 6, 19, 47, which presuppose the cultic assembly of Israel in their land. Thus, after Marah, Israel through the divine agency of Moses is now formally constituted as a cultic and political assembly under the covenant.

In addition to Marah, the Massah/Meribah account in Exod 17:1–7 also emphasizes the royal role of Moses. In particular, this episode raises the question of divine presence through the agency of Moses. The

---

35. Van Seters, *The Life of Moses*, 179.
36. The word is used outside the Pentateuch only in 1 Kgs 8:37 and 2 Chr 6:28.

question "Is the Lord among us or not?" coupled with the people's complaint against Moses introduces the issue of divine presence that will be developed in Exod 32–34. Why has Moses not continued to embody the divine presence in the wilderness as he did in Egypt? To reaffirm the status of Moses' divine empowerment, the Massah/Meribah episode revisits the issue of faith in Moses as expressed in Exod 4. Thus we have the reappearance of the elders, absent since Exod 4 (except for 12:21), and the staff which has been absent since the deliverance of the sea that concluded with the public affirmation of trust in Moses as the Lord's servant. This staff appears at strategic locations in the narrative of Exodus as a visible emblem of God's power and is intended to legitimate the divine agency of Moses.[37]

In response to the question of divine presence, the Lord tells Moses to "go in front of the people" with "the staff of God" in his hand (17:5). Mann has argued that with the Lord as the subject, the verb עבר (as well as הלך and יצא) with לפני is an expression for divine guidance, as in Deut 9:3 and 31:3.[38] The portrayal of Moses as the subject of verbs typically used for divine activity and movement occurs here and later in the Sinai account.[39] Here, we have Moses paired with the staff[40] as the emblem of the divine presence, proceeding ahead of the people. This fits with the role of the deity or emblem of the deity accompanying the king in the vanguard of the army.[41] Finally, in the Massah/Meribah episode, Moses equates the action of complaining against him with testing of the Lord, "Why do you contend against me? Why do you test the Lord?" (17:2). This statement indicates the close association between Moses and the Lord that we have observed in Exod 14:31 (cf. also Num 14:44). The accounts at Marah and Massah/Meribah demonstrate the covenant blessing of water and frames the covenant provision of food (i.e. manna and quail) narrated in Exod 16.

37. For a discussion of the tradition-historical import of Moses' staff, see Coats, *Moses: Heroic Man*, 186–90.

38. Mann, *Divine Presence*, 255.

39. See the discussion of the portrayal of Moses mirroring the actions of God in Thomas B. Dozeman, *God on the Mountain: A Study of Redaction, Theology, and Canon in Exodus 19–24* (Atlanta, Ga.: Scholars Press, 1989), 81–82, 104, 138–41.

40. Thus the "staff of God" serves a function analogous to the ark as a physical representation of divine presence, as discussed in Mann, *Divine Presence*, 169–71. Cf. the discussion on divine symbols in Chapter 3 of Mann's study, "Mesopotamian Iconography and the Cult."

41. The departing Israelite community is portrayed as an "army" in Exod 13:18 and Num 33:1.

Located between the accounts of events at Marah and Massah/ Meribah is the account of the provision of food (i.e. manna and quail) in Exod 16. Here a detailed demonstration is given of Moses as a lawgiver who provides instructions regarding the provision of food and the Sabbath as a testing (16:4) of Israel's obedience to Moses and God (16:20, 28). Israel's initial failure to obey Moses serves as a transition to the more strident complaining in 17:1–7, but here it results in reissuing the instructions and providing for the placement of manna before the Lord as a physical symbol of God's protection and care in the wilderness. Finally, the issue of Israel's knowledge of the Lord receives stress here (16:6, 12). This chapter thus contains strong covenant and cultic overtones, which have recently been explored by Geller[42] and which fits within the emphasis on Israel's covenant and cultic relationship with God. Although Israel eventually obeys Moses, the emphasis here on Israel's persistent disobedience shows the nation to be in need for continued authentication of Moses' leadership and demonstration of the Lord's power.

4.4. *Temple Building and Cultic Oversight as a Royal Task*

The construction, maintenance, and restoration of temples are prominent responsibilities exercised by kings in the major cultures of the ancient Near East[43] and are well-attested also in the Old Testament (e.g. 2 Sam 7; 1 Kgs 6–8; 2 Kgs 23). A significant sub-category of biographical royal inscriptions is the building inscription, which is represented in all periods of the ancient Near East but especially during the Neo-Babylonian period.[44] Thus a large number of biographical depictions of the king appear in the form of building inscriptions that situate the king's construction of the building (usually a temple) in the context of detailing the memorable deeds of his rule. Hurowitz has provided a comprehensive

42. Stephen A. Geller, "Manna and Sabbath: A Literary-Theological Reading of Exodus 16," *Int* 59 (2005): 5–16.

43. Hurowitz, *I Have Built You an Exalted House*; Arvid S. Kapelrud, "Temple Building: A Task for Gods and Kings," *Or* 32 (1963): 56–62, and "Two Great Rulers and Their Temple Buildings," in *Text and Theology: Studies in Honour of Professor Magne Sæbø: Presented on the Occasion of His 65th Birthday* (ed. Arvid. Tångberg; Oslo: Verbum, 1994), 135–42.

44. For an overview of the royal inscriptions, editions, and secondary literature, see Chapter 12 in Sparks, *Ancient Texts*, 361–416. On the nature and typology of building inscriptions during the Neo-Babylonian period, see Beaulieu, *Nabonidus*, 1, 46, who notes that the king oversees the construction/restoration of temples at the command of Marduk.

investigation of the accounts of temple construction in the literatures of Mesopotamia and the Levant in order to establish a context for his detailed investigation of the account of the construction of Solomon's temple in 1 Kgs 5–9.[45] Hurowitz concludes that the construction and dedication of the tabernacle in Exod 25–40; Lev 8–9, and Num 7 are "a fully developed example of the traditional pattern" of temple building.[46] In a separate essay, he provides a detailed comparison of the tabernacle account in Exodus with 1 Kgs 5–10, as well as with two ancient Near Eastern sources that share a close parallel (i.e. the bilingual "B" inscription of Samsuiluna and the Ugaritic Baal Cycle).[47] He argues that the tabernacle account contains five of the six components of an account of temple building: (1) divine command to Moses to build the tabernacle based on the divinely provided plan (Exod 24:15–31:18); (2) acquisition of materials and securing workers (Exod 35:20–36:7); (3) description of the temple (Exod 36:8–40:33); (4) dedication (Exod 40:34–38; Lev 8–9); and (5) blessing of the king (Lev 9:22–23; the royal blessing of the people in Exod 39:43 should be included here).[48] Although Hurowitz does not investigate the role of Moses in his abbreviated discussion of the tabernacle, the typical account of the building shows Moses acting in the role of the king who receives the divine instruction to build the sanctuary,[49] arranges and oversees the construction, and blesses the people. The same pattern is mirrored in a similar way by Solomon in 1 Kgs 5–10. Instructive, too, is the Golden Calf narrative in Exod 32, which, according to Hurowitz, follows the pattern in several inscriptions of a rebellion against the king that interrupts the ongoing construction project.[50]

Hurowitz, however, fails to extend the close correspondences of the tabernacle account to other building accounts in the Old Testament/ ancient Near East to the role of Moses, although he implies that Moses is

45. Hurowitz, *I Have Built You an Exalted House*.

46. Ibid., 110–13.

47. Victor Avigdor Hurowitz, "The Priestly Account of Building the Tabernacle," *JAOS* 105 (1985): 21–30.

48. Hurowitz's outline is given here in abbreviated form. See the more detailed outline in *I Have Built You an Exalted House*, 112, in comparison with the basic typology listed on p. 64.

49. However, the direct divine communication to Moses is in contrast to the usual revelation of the command to build the temple through dreams and/or signs. See the discussion in ibid., 143–63.

50. Ibid., 111. See, for example, the discussion of the bilingual royal inscription of Samsuiluna, son of Hammurabi, on pp. 63–65, which narrates a rebellion against the king that must be quelled before the resumption of the construction of the temple for Shamash and the building of Sippar.

acting as a royal leader.[51] And since scholarly study of the composition, genre, and function of accounts of temple building is, in Hurowitz's words, "a rather empty and lonely field,"[52] very little attention has been paid to the role of Moses in the tabernacle account. One recent exception is a brief examination of Moses as a royal temple builder in the literary shaping of Exod 19–40 by Martin Hauge.[53] Yet Hauge's view is problematic because he argues that Moses' royal role has been supplanted by the people.[54] It is true that the tabernacle account presents the people actively and eagerly contributing the materials and labor for the tabernacle, but the people are clearly working voluntarily under the direction of Moses in stark contrast to the taxation (1 Kgs 4:1–19) and forced labor as part of Solomon's corvée (1 Kgs 5:13).[55] This view also results from placing too much emphasis on the contrasts between on Exod 39 and 40. Moses' inability to enter the tent in ch. 40 does not signal the phasing out of his role as the source of divine revelation, especially since Moses continues in this role after Exod 40 according to Lev 1:1. Rather than permanently excluding Moses from the tent, Exod 40:34–35 narrates the initial divine filling of the temple that overwhelms even the temple officials. In a similar situation in 2 Kgs 8:11, the priests were unable to "stand to minister" because of the initial divine entrance into the temple. As with Moses in Exod 40:34–35, so here it is not accurate to suggest the exclusion of the priests from permanent service in the temple. Rather, both texts vividly portray the immediacy of God's presence that overwhelms even the legitimate cultic officials and leaders.

There is clearly a need for a substantial study of Moses as a royal temple builder, a role that must be taken into account in any study of the figure of Moses. Such a focus is outside the scope of this study that seeks here only to suggest that Moses' actions of receiving the divine command along with a plan to build the sanctuary, overseeing the acquisitions of materials and construction of the sanctuary, and blessing the people, fit precisely within the overall profile of the basic biographical

51. Hurowitz, "The Priestly Account," 23.

52. Victor Avigdor Hurowitz, "Restoring the Temple—Why and When?" *JQR* 93 (2003): 581.

53. Hauge, *Descent from the Mountain*, 121–22.

54. See ibid., 120–55, for Hauge's discussion of Moses and the people as royal temple builders.

55. On this contrast, see Helmut Utzschneider, *Das Heiligtum und das Gesetz: Studien zur Bedeutung der sinaitischen Heiligtumstexte (Ex 25–40; Lev 8–9)* (Göttingen: Vandenhoeck & Ruprecht, 1988), 167, and cited by Hauge, *Descent from the Mountain*, 123 n. 38.

depiction of the king in the ancient Near East. Future studies can investigate the role of Moses in constructing the tent of meeting in Exod 33:7–11, a passage that uses language similar to David's tent, in addition to the similar language and focus of their prayers (Exod 32:11–13; 1 Sam 7:18–29),[56] and the close parallels between Moses/Joshua and David/ Solomon in the Chronicler's expanded account of the preparation and construction of the temple (1 Chr 28–2 Chr 7).[57]

A comparison of Moses to Jeroboam is relevant to our study. The previous chapter has called attention to a number of parallels between Moses and Jeroboam in the depiction of their respective divine commissioning in private followed by a flight to a place of security, and eventual public emergence to assume power.[58] The portrayal of both in building and staffing cultic sanctuaries continues this pattern. After attaining power, Jeroboam constructed two molten calves for the presumably pre-existing shrines at Dan and Bethel. He installed non-Levitical priests to officiate at the various sanctuaries he had constructed (בתי הבאמות, "temples on high places," 1 Kgs 13:32; cf. 12:31) throughout the northern kingdom. These actions are mirrored in the account of Moses' emergence as a leader who constructs the tent of meeting in Exod 33:7– 11 followed by a divinely sanctioned portable sanctuary that houses the ark as the emblem of God's authorized presence, an act that explicitly subverts Jeroboam's policies (Exod 32).[59] Moses commissions and installs the Levites as priests (Exod 28–29; 32:26–29; 40:12–15; Lev 8–10), including Aaron and later his son Eleazar as Aaron's successor. And these parallels can be further extended by noting the participation of both Moses and Jeroboam in cultic activities (e.g. 1 Kgs 13:1; Exod 17:15; 24:1–8).

In sum, the comprehensive comparative materials collected and analyzed by Hurowitz support the conclusion that Moses is portrayed in the role a king as temple builder. Attempts to categorize Moses as a non-royal figure will ultimately fail, since this aspect of the work of Moses cannot be adequately accounted for as part of a non-royal role. Rather, in conjunction with the numerous royal motifs highlighted in this study,

---

56. On a comparison of the two, see Aurelius, *Der Fürbitter*, 109–11.

57. See the discussion and cited literature in Hauge, *Descent from the Mountain*, 124 n. 44. In view of the critique of his contrast between Moses and people, his attempt to view the people as the successor of the royal task of temple building in place of Joshua is rejected.

58. See the discussion in §3.3 of the present study.

59. Cf. Moses Aberbach and Leivy Smolar, "Aaron, Jeroboam, and the Golden Calves," *JBL* 86 (1967): 129–40.

Moses as royal temple builder fits well within the various motifs that are typically used to depict the king and is a compelling argument for viewing Moses as a royal figure in the Pentateuch since the activity of temple building is exclusively the prerogative of the deity or king.

4.5. *"You will impart some of your majesty to him":* *Death of the Leader and Succession*

The death of the leader and another's succession are typical features of the depictions of kings in the Old Testament. The Gideon account is distinguished from the depictions of the other judges by the description of Gideon's progeny and his death at an old age, which is followed by an account of how Abimelech succeeds Gideon as "king" over Israel (Judg 8:29–35; 9:1–57). The question of who will succeed David is a major concern in 2 Sam 12–20 and 1 Kgs 1–2 (i.e. the so-called succession narrative). The vassal treaties of Esarhaddon are concerned to assure the transfer of Esarhaddon's royal authority to his son Assurbanipal upon his death in order to avoid the internal strife that characterized his rise to power upon the death of Sennacherib. This section will examine briefly the last stage of the life of Moses and will examine in detail the transfer of Moses' leadership to Joshua.

The accounts of the transition Moses to Joshua in Num 27:12–23; Deut 31; 32:48–52, and 34:1–9 provide additional confirmation of the royal portrayal of Moses. Moses' royal authority is passed down in some measure to Joshua, whose career is explicitly modeled after Moses in the book of Joshua (e.g. Josh 1:5, 17; 3:7; 4:14). Numbers 27 narrates the fate of Moses, who is condemned to share the fate of the older generation in Num 20 (repeated at the beginning of this section in Num 27:12–14). After being commanded to ascend the mountain of Abarim, Moses requests the commissioning of a successor. The appointment of the successor to "come" and "go" *before* (לפני) the people generally recalls the role of the king leading the people in battle (1 Sam 18:13, 16; 29:6; Josh 14:11), as well as the language of the divine vanguard (cf. the formula for divine guidance, עבר לפני, which is applied to both the Lord and Joshua in Deut 31:3). But the language of "coming" and "going" also shows the transition of Moses' office to Joshua since Moses is not able to "come" or "go." That is, God prevents Moses from leading Israel across the Jordan (Deut 31:2).[60] Consequently, Moses must appoint a

---

60. Thus Moses is not "tired and weak" in Deut 31:2, as maintained by Thomas C. Römer and Marc Zvi Brettler, "Deuteronomy 34 and the Case for a Persian Hexateuch," *JBL* 119 (2000): 403, nor must Moses conclude his leadership due to

successor to continue his work and provide the means for ensuring Israel's presence in the land. In contrast to Moses, Joshua's activity of "coming" and "going" before the people is subsumed under the divine word received from the Urim under the authority of the priest (Num 27:31), which indicates the lesser degree of divine access after the death of Moses. Subsequent leaders must follow this model of Joshua by seeking the word of the Lord through priestly or prophetic mediation.

In addition to the role of a military leader, Joshua also assumes Moses' role of "shepherding" the people of Israel (Num 27:17; cf. Exod 3:1). Moreover, Moses installs Joshua into the royal office through imparting some of his majesty (הוד) through the laying of his hands (Num 27:20; cf. Deut 34:9).[61] This term, translated as "majesty" or "power,"[62] is used to describe the deity and the king (Hab 3:3; Ps 8:2; Dan 11:21; 1 Chr 29:25; Pss 21:6; 45:4; Zech 6:13) and is yet another depiction of the exalted, royal status of Moses.[63] However, in contrast to Moses' direct empowerment as "God" through a personal and private theophany (Exod 4:16; 7:7; cf. 34:29–35), Joshua instead receives only a portion of Moses' power, and that only indirectly through the agency of Moses. This transferal of some of Moses' הוד takes place publicly in order to establish the community's *obedience* to Joshua (Num 27:20).[64] Subsequent references to Israel's obedience to Joshua (Deut 34:9; Josh 1:17; 22:2) continue the important theme of Israel's obedience to the Lord.

Joshua is portrayed as the first successor of Moses who faithfully models his leadership after Moses and fulfills the ideal requirements expected of each Israelite king succeeding Moses.[65] Joshua is commanded to meditate on the Torah at all times and "carefully keep the Torah"

"old age and disability" (Nelson, *Deuteronomy*, 358). Rather, Deut 31:2 clearly connects his inability to lead the people into the land to God's command rather than to his feeble health.

61. Noted by Porter, *Moses and Monarchy*, 18, as the "clearest and most decisive indication" of Moses' royal portrayal.

62. So *HALOT* 1:241.

63. On הוד as a royal quality, see the discussion in Marc Zvi Brettler, *God Is King: Understanding an Israelite Metaphor* (JSOTSup 76; Sheffield: JSOT, 1989), 60–61.

64. See esp. McBride, "Transcendent Authority." The transmission of Moses' "majesty" (Num 27:20) and "spirit of wisdom" (Deut 34:9) to Joshua shows the nature of Moses' transcendent authority over the office of king, which supplements a similar authority over the elders, priests, and prophets.

65. Cf. Richard D. Nelson, "Josiah in the Book of Joshua," *JBL* 100 (1981): 531–40.

given by Moses (Josh 1:7) and not to turn from it to the "right or left," which echoes the basic duty of the king as stipulated in Deut 17:19–20. A comparison of Deut 17:18 and Josh 8:32 makes the comparison between Joshua and the ideal king in Deut 17 explicit:

ויכתב־שם על־האבנים את משנה תורת משה אשר כתב לפני בני ישראל

And in the presence of the Israelite community, he wrote there upon the stones a copy of the Torah of Moses which he (Moses) had written. (Josh 8:32)

וכתב לו את־משנה התורה הזאת על־ספר מלפני הכהנים הלוים

And in the presence of the Levitical priests, he (the king) must write for himself a copy of this Torah in a book. (Deut 17:18)

In order to show the continuation of Moses' authority and presence, the book of Joshua portrays Joshua as a Mosaic figure.[66] God commissions Joshua as leader in Josh 1 and promises his divine presence in Joshua's success in conquering the land. Among the numerous parallels between the two figures is the report of Joshua's exaltation at the crossing of the Jordan:

On that day the Lord exalted Joshua in the sight of all Israel; and they stood in awe (ירא) of him, as they had stood in awe of Moses, all the days of his life. (Josh 4:14; cf. 3:7; Exod 34:29–35)

According to Josh 8 and 24, Joshua writes a copy of the Torah, and establishes a covenant with the people, both kingly acts. Finally, the book of Joshua ends with a final testament in miniature form that parallels Moses' last words in Deuteronomy.

Joshua is thus a royal figure whose career is modeled after Moses. Joshua is not merely a figure who completes the work begun by Moses.[67] Rather, Joshua is portrayed in a way that shows the incomparably exalted status of Moses, whose authority is faithfully acknowledged and affirmed by Joshua. At the same time, differences between the two figures suggest that Joshua is a model of a faithful king empowered by Moses and in submission to Mosaic authority as expressed in Deut 17. Based on these

---

66. Since a comparison of Joshua and Moses has often been noted, only a sketch is given here. See esp. the brief discussion and cited literature in the section "The Figure of Joshua" in Richard D. Nelson, *Joshua: A Commentary* (OTL; Louisville: Westminster John Knox, 1997), 21–22.

67. For example, according to Walther Zimmerli (*Old Testament Theology in Outline* [Edinburgh: T. & T. Clark, 1978], 82), Joshua "merely finishes what Moses began." Zimmerli correctly notes that Joshua "never became the specific prototype of any priestly or even prophetic authority" but fails to discern how Joshua functions as a proto-typical king as demonstrated in this study.

observations, I argue that Joshua functions as an "epigone" of Moses.[68]
The greatness and unique status of a leader or a period of time can be
shown in comparison to a succeeding leader or period that is characterized by diminished quality (e.g. a "silver" age following a "golden" age).
Along these lines, the Bible often pairs a great figure with a second or
third figure, as with Moses/Joshua, Saul/David/ Solomon, Elijah/Elisha,
and John the Baptist/Jesus. Thus an "epigonic" relationship characterizes
Joshua and Moses, and it must not be construed as a negative view of
Joshua. Rather, Joshua is praised and exalted precisely because his career
conforms to Moses and he is designated, like Moses, as the "servant of
the Lord" in the accounts of his death in Josh 24 and Judg 2. At the same
time, Joshua is portrayed as an "epigonic" figure in order to highlight the
authoritative and unique status of Moses.

68.   In a study of the portrayal of Elijah in 1 Kgs 1, Rofé (Alexander Rofé, *The
Prophetical Stories: The Narratives About the Prophets in the Hebrew Bible, Their
Literary Types and History* [Jerusalem: Magnes, 1988], 33–34) defines an "epigone"
as "[O]ne who arrives, comes into being, or is created in later times; an heir or
replacement. In the sphere of politics the Diadochi, the heirs of Alexander the Great,
are called epigoni. In literature the term is used to describe authors writing in a post-
classical period, who tend to be less creative, more conformist, imitative, and arti-
ficial then their more inventive predecessors." Rofé's application of this concept to
the two literary strata of 2 Kgs 2 in light of his definition is not entirely clear and is
perhaps more applicable to Elijah's relationship than to Elisha (discussed esp. in
pp. 45–48, 74).

Chapter 5

CONCLUSION:
"MAN OF GOD" AND "SERVANT":
THE PORTRAYAL OF MOSES IN THE PENTATEUCH

5.1. *Moses as Prophet?*

Despite the fact that the Pentateuch does not present Moses clearly and unequivocally throughout as a "prophet," this view of Moses has become entrenched in much of the scholarship and has too often led scholars to minimize or discount the more prominent presentation in the Pentateuch of Moses as a royal, super-human figure.[1] A thoroughgoing view of Moses as a prophet stems, in large part, from a particular interpretation of Deut 18:15–22 and 34:10–12.[2] The view of Moses as prophet, however, becomes difficult to justify upon closer analysis of these texts. Neither of these texts provides an explicit and clear portrayal of Moses as a prophet. Deuteronomy 18:15–22 does seem to associate Moses with the institution of Israelite prophecy: "The Lord your God will raise up for you a prophet like me from among your own people" (18:15).[3]

---

1. The axiomatic understanding of Moses as "prophet" has been assumed in sources too numerous to cite here. See esp. the literature cited in David L. Petersen, "The Ambiguous Role of Moses as Prophet," in *Israel's Prophets and Israel's Past: Essays on the Relationship of Prophetic Texts and Israelite History in Honor of John H. Hayes* (LHBOTS 446; ed. Brad E. Kelle and Megan Bishop Moore; New York: T&T Clark International, 2006), 311–24. Recent representative examples include Herbert Chanan Brichto, *Toward a Grammar of Biblical Poetics: Tales of the Prophets* (New York: Oxford University Press, 1992), 88–121, who includes the portrayal of Moses in Exod 32–34 as one of the "Tales of the Prophets"; E. Theodore Mullen Jr., *Ethnic Myths and Pentateuchal Foundations: A New Approach to the Formation of the Pentateuch* (Atlanta: Scholars Press, 1997); and Aaron, *Etched in Stone*.

2. The prophetic identity of Moses is also derived from Exod 3:1–4:18, which is usually compared with the call of Jeremiah (Jer 1). See, e.g., Widmer, *Moses*, 76–77.

3. Unless otherwise noted, subsequent citations will be taken from the NRSV.

However, the NRSV has re-arranged the syntax by moving the comparative phrase "like me" to modify "prophet." In the Hebrew text, this phrase does not follow "prophet" but rather the phrase "from among your own people." That is, the prophet is like Moses because he is a "fellow Israelite" and is not a foreigner.[4] In this case, according to 18:15 and 18, the prophet must arise from within the Israelite community, as Moses did during the theophany at Horeb (5:26–27).[5] This fits well within the immediate literary context of 17:9–14, where Israel is commanded not to heed the "soothsayers and diviners" from the nations of the land. In contrast, the "prophet" Israel is to obey must be from their community, just as 17:15 says about the king.

It is admitted, however, that the requirement for the Israelite prophet to be an Israelite is not dependent on the "like me," which does not appear in a similar requirement for the king in 17:15. If the phrase "like me" is to be linked with the role of the prophet, it is possible that this phrase indicates that the prophet is to resemble Moses in the manner described in Deut 18:16–22. In this case, the issue is Israel's obedience to God's word (vv. 15, 19) that will continue to be mediated to them following their singular encounter with God at Horeb (vv. 16–18) and the importance of distinguishing this word from false prophecy (vv. 20–22). But the profile of this future prophet that will convey these true oracles from God is different from the role Moses has elsewhere in the Pentateuch. The prophet in Deut 18:15–22 functions as God's "mouthpiece" with the principal task of conveying God's message to the people. The fulfillment of the prophet's oracles will provide proof of the authenticity of his message, after which the people are to listen to the prophet.[6] The profile of Moses, however, surpasses that of the "prophet" in Deut 18:15–22. Moses is never described in the Pentateuch as a "mouthpiece," which is a role that is instead given to Aaron (Exod 4:15–16; 7:1). Rather, Moses has the super-human ability to enter God's presence and speak to the people on God's behalf at Sinai:

---

4. So S. Dean McBride, in *The HarperCollins Study Bible, Revised Edition* (San Francisco: HarperCollins, 2006), 284. Cf. Berman, *Created Equal*, 71–74, who views the requirement of the prophet to be "an ordinary citizen" as evidence for the shift of power from an elite class to the community of Israel.

5. Petersen, "Moses as Prophet," 312–13.

6. Petersen (ibid., 312) suggests that one possible interpretation of the comparative phrase "like me" is that it refers to obedience at the end of v. 15: "the prophet whom Yahweh will raise up will be like Moses in authority, that is, someone whom the people are to obey."

> For who is there of all flesh that has heard the voice of the living God
> speaking out of the fire, as we have, and remained alive? Go near, you
> yourself, and hear all that the Lord our God will say. Then tell us every-
> thing that the Lord our God tells you, and we will listen and do it. (Deut
> 5:26–27; cf. 5:4–5)

Rather than a mouthpiece to convey divine oracles to the people, Moses
functions as an intermediary commissioned by God to transmit and teach
the commandments, as well as to teach Israel to observe them for their
well-being (Deut 5:31; 6:1; cf. 4:1–2, 5, 14, 40). Furthermore, Israel's
"trust" in Moses is secured not by the fulfillment of oracles as in the case
of the prophet in Deut 18:15–22, but rather through their experience of
God's speaking to Moses at Sinai (Exod 19:9) as well as the "mighty
deeds and terrifying displays of power" Moses performs on behalf of
God (Deut 34:12; Exod 4:1–9; 14:31). To summarize this view, Deut
18:15–22 assigns to a future prophet the more limited role of an oracular
messenger that is modelled after one aspect of the work of Moses at
Sinai and as such cannot be used as a warrant for viewing Moses princi-
pally as a "prophet."

Deuteronomy 34:10–12 also appears to provide a warrant for viewing
Moses as a prophet: "Never since has there arisen a prophet in Israel like
Moses, whom the Lord knew face to face." Yet even here Moses is not
explicitly described with the title of "prophet."[7] The profile of Moses
summarized in vv. 10–12 is sharply distinguished from the office of the
prophet as defined in the Pentateuch. God knew Moses "face to face,"
while prophets ordinarily receive a word from God indirectly through
dreams or visions (cf. Num 12:6–8; Exod 33:11). No oracular prophet
such as Isaiah or Jeremiah was empowered by God to perform "signs and
wonders" and "terrifying displays of power" to liberate Israel from
Egypt.[8] The closest association between the prophet and the "signs and
wonders" in the Pentateuch is made in Deut 13:1–2. However, the focus
there is on the *prediction* by a prophet of "signs and wonders." In
contrast, Moses actually performs "signs and wonders" on behalf of God
before Egypt and Israel (Deut 34:11–12; cf. Exod 4:21). Deuteronomy
34:10–12 is a retrospective description made long after the career of
Moses and those who succeeded him. The incomparability formula in
Deut 34:10 functions to highlight the uniqueness of Moses by asserting

---

7. Rather, he is the Lord's "servant" (34:5), a royal title that will receive close
attention later.

8. The profile of the prophet in Deut 34:11–12 would be more appropriate of
Elijah and Elisha. A comparison of Elijah and Elisha with Moses will receive attention in §5.2, below.

that, contra Deut 18:15–22, no prophet has ever arisen (קום) who was "like" Moses in terms of his power and intimacy with God.[9] These verses provide an apt summary of the identity and work of Moses, especially as narrated in the plague and wilderness segments in Exodus. Rather than a "prophet,"[10] Petersen concludes that "the author of Deut 34:10–12 has turned Moses into a demigod, attributing to him acts that elsewhere only Yahweh has accomplished."[11]

Finally, if it is granted that Deut 18 and 34 classifies Moses as a prophet, the reconstructed profile of Moses ought to give weight to the more extensive texts that portray Moses as a royal figure through the use of numerous motifs surveyed in this study. The precise question then would be, "Why would prophetic attributes be attributed to a royal figure?" Further analysis could examine prophetic motifs attributed to kings, such as the following prophetic oracle uttered by David:

9.   On the use of the incomparability formula to highlight the unique features of Solomon, Hezekiah, and Josiah in Deuteronomistic History, see Gary N. Knoppers, "'There Was None Like Him': Incomparability in the Books of Kings," *CBQ* 54 (1992): 411–31. It is significant that the incomparability formula is used with reference to *kings* in the Deuteronomistic History. The application of this formula to Moses suggest that he is viewed more as a "king" than a "prophet," or more precisely, as one who exhibits the ideal traits to be modelled by subsequent leaders in Deuteronomistic History, beginning with Joshua. The role of Moses as both the *authority* and *model* for Israel's leaders was previously examined in Chapter 4 of this study.

10.   Before categorizing Moses as a "prophet," this designation must be precisely explained. Unfortunately, a vague conception of the office of prophet is often applied uncritically to Moses. One important exception is Klaus Baltzer's view of Moses functioning as a prophet in the role of the "vizier" of God, patterned on the model of the Egyptian office of "vizier" who acts as the agent of Pharaoh, ruling Egypt on his behalf (*Die Biographie der Propheten*, 136–49). "Vizier" is actually an Arabic word, and the office lacks a specific Egyptian title. The office of "vizier" in Egypt includes a wide range of activities and responsibilities that Baltzer thinks provides the best explanation for the portrayal of Moses. The "vizier" functions as Pharaoh's second-in-command or deputy who exercises the full range of administrative, judicial, cultic, and foreign responsibilities. While Baltzer's view of Joseph as Pharaoh's "vizier" is cogent and convincing, his attempt to classify Moses in the same role needs attention. It is true that Moses assumes the full range of responsibilities on behalf of God that resemble the duties of a "vizier." Nevertheless, other aspects of the Pentateuchal portraiture of Moses, particularly the stories of his birth, flight, and rescue of Israel, are more at home with Mesopotamian accounts of the rise and reign of kings (e.g. Sargon II, Esarhaddon, Nabonidus). The account of the installation of the vizier resembles more the commissioning of Isaiah and Ezekiel, in stark contrast to the commissioning of Moses.

11.   Petersen, "Moses as Prophet," 317.

> The oracle (!) of David, son of Jesse, the oracle of the man whom God exalted, the anointed of the God of Jacob, the favorite of the Strong One of Israel: The Spirit of the LORD speaks through me, his word is upon my tongue. The God of Israel has spoken, the Rock of Israel has said to me: One who rules over people justly, ruling in the fear of God, is like the Light of the morning, like the sun rising on a cloudless morning, gleaming from the rain on the grassy land. (2 Sam 23:1–4)[12]

5.2. *"Man of God"*

Rather than a "prophet," the Pentateuch presents Moses as the "Man of God" and the Lord's "servant." Although used of Moses only once in the Pentateuch (Deut 33:1) and five times elsewhere (Josh 14:6; 2 Chr 23:14; 30:16; Ezra 3:2; Ps 90:1), the description of Moses as the "Man of God" in Deut 33:1 (אִישׁ הָאֱלֹהִים) recalls the designation of Moses' empowerment as "God" (אֱלֹהִים; Exod 4:16; 7:1) and summarizes the human and divine aspects of his nature at his death (Deut 33:1). Based on this portrayal of Moses at crucial places in the Pentateuch (Exod 4:16; 7:1; 34:29–35), אלהים should be taken as an adjective resulting in the translation "divine man." Moses will embody the qualities of both humanity and divinity. According to Deut 34:7, Moses is fully alive and in perfect health at the maximum age allotted to a human being;[13] consequently Moses can die only at the command of the Lord (lit. "by his mouth"; Deut 34:5).[14]

The description of Moses' health at the time of his death, especially his advanced age, good eyesight, and a body that is full of vitality, resembles the autobiographical stela of Adad-guppi.[15] Although she was the mother of Nabonidus, King of Babylon, the autobiographical narrative resembles the basic form of the royal autobiography[16] that was most likely composed by Nabonidus after her death in order to exalt himself as Sin's choice to rule Babylon and rebuild his sanctuary.[17]

---

12. Cf. Philo's view of Moses discussed in Chapter 1 of this study. It appears that Philo viewed the prophetic role of Moses to function as an attribute of Moses' more fundamental identity as a king.

13. Albeit from a non-Priestly view, since Aaron lived to be 123!

14. Cf. Auerbach, *Moses*, 170: "God ordered him to die, and die he did in full vigor."

15. On long life as a royal quality, see Brettler, *God is King*, 51–53.

16. See the comparative analysis in Longman, *Fictional Akkadian Autobiography*.

17. See the discussion in ibid., 103. The full translation of the stela is found on pp. 225–28. Noteworthy also is the request for the gods' presence alongside Nabonidus for the defeat of his enemies (i.e. the vanguard motif) and Nabonidus as the means for restoring the gods' presence in Babylon.

He (Sin) raised my head; he gave me a fine reputation in the land, long days and years of well-being he added to me. From the period of Assurbanipal, king of Assur, until the ninth year of Nabunaid, king of Babylon, my offspring, they established for me 104 years in the worship of Sin, the king of the gods. He kept me alive and well. My eyesight is clear and my mind is excellent. My hands and feet are healthy. Well-chosen are my words; food and drink still agree with me. My flesh is vital; my heart is joyful. My little ones living four generations from me I have seen. I have reached a ripe old age. (II.14–33)[18]

In a prayer recorded later in the stela, Adad-guppi requests that Nabonidus also live to a similar old age through the same power of Sin.

This understanding of the function of the title "Man of God" resembles the designation of Azatiwada with a similar expression in the opening lines of the eighth-/seventh-century[19] bilingual Phoenician and Hieroglyphic inscription discovered in three extant copies in southeast Turkey.[20] An examination of the portrayal and role of Azatiwada in these inscriptions can shed some light on the portrayal of Moses as "Man of God" and "Servant of the Lord." Azatiwada is described with three titles in the opening lines, one of which is the "servant of Baal" (*ʿbd bʿl*) and the other "a mighty man of Awariku" (*ʾš drʾ ʾwrk*). Although the rest of the inscriptions describe Azatiwada's royal career as a king by narrating his military successes, fortifications of his kingdom, building projects, and era of peace, the inscription does not designate Azatiwada as king and rather portrays him as an individual promoted by Awariku, the king of the Danunians (*mlk dnnym*) as an agent (perhaps as a vassal) ruling on behalf of the king. The phrase "a mighty man of Awariku," in Shade's translation,[21] is translated by Younger as "whom Awariku, king of the Danunians, empowered."[22] The translation of the hieroglyphic version provided by Hawkins is "whom Awariku the Andanawean king promoted."[23] Although not described as a "king," Azatiwada is nevertheless portrayed royally as the agent chosen and empowered to rule on behalf of Awariku.

---

18. Ibid., 101–2.

19. On the dating of the three extant inscriptions, see the discussion and cited literature in K. Lawson Younger, "The Phoenician Inscription of Azatiwada," *JSS* 43 (1998): 12–13 n. 6.

20. The Hieroglyphic version is translated by J. D. Hawkins (*COS* 2.21:124–26). The Phoenician version is translated by K. Lawson Younger, Jr. (*COS* 2.31:148–50).

21. Aaron Schade, "A Text Linguistic Approach to the Syntax and Style of the Phoenician Inscription of Azatiwada," *JSS* 50 (2005): 4.

22. *COS* 2:149.

23. *COS* 2:125.

The references to Moses as "Man of God" must then be interpreted in light of the portrayal of Moses in the Pentateuch and critically distinguished from a quite different use of this title in reference primarily to Elisha (some 29 times) as well as to Elijah (8 times)[24] and the "man of God" in 1 Kgs 13 (18 times).[25] Dijkstra observes that about seventy percent of the usage of this title occurs to describe these three figures.[26] In reaction to the tendency to view this title as a (northern) prophetic title and then importing this meaning to Moses,[27] Coats has provided a detailed study of the title and argues that it functioned as a general epithet that describes a relationship between the man and God and was applied to varied figures such as Moses or David in popular storytelling circles.[28] While a helpful corrective against viewing this epithet as merely a northern prophetical designation, Coats is unclear about the precise relationship between איש and אלהים.

A closer examination of the function of this title in the Elisha/Elijah narratives reveals a use that is quite different from its use in relationship to Moses. Rofé provides a helpful suggestion here in his examination of a series of short Elisha episodes in 2 Kgs 4–8 that all recount a number of miraculous acts of Elisha as "Man of God" in contrast to the miracles performed by magical action or the word of God that "attest merely to the supernatural power of the Man of God who performs them."[29] Based on these observations, Rofé concludes that for Elisha, the title "Man of God" functions to describe a holy figure who must be treated with veneration and those who encounter him are in the danger of "swift and terrible punishment."[30] The Man of God contains "hidden energy which

24. See the list given in Coats, *Moses: Heroic Man*, 181. Based on these statistics, among other observations, Rofé thinks that "Man of God" is Elisha's principal title that was secondarily transferred to Elijah (*The Prophetical Stories*, 14 n. 2, 133).

25. Meindert Dijkstra, "Moses, the Man of God," in *The Interpretation of Exodus: Studies in Honour of Cornelis Houtman* (ed. Riemer Roukema in collaboration with Bert Jan Lietaert Peerbolte, Klaas Spronk, and Jan-Wim Wesselius; CBET 44; Dudley, Mass.: Peters, 2006), 22.

26. Ibid.

27. So Werner Lemke ("The Way of Obedience: I Kings 13 and the Structure of the Deuteronomistic History," in *Magnalia Dei: The Mighty Acts of God* [ed. Frank Moore Cross and et al.; Garden City, N.Y.: Doubleday, 1976], 313–14; cited in Coats, *Moses: Heroic Man*, 181, and Tigay, *Deuteronomy*, 318. Cf. also David L. Petersen, *The Roles of Israel's Prophets* (JSOTSup 17; Sheffield: JSOT, 1981), 42–43, who thinks that the title was applied to Moses due to his wonder-working status shared with Elisha and Elijah. This position will be critiqued below.

28. Coats, *Moses: Heroic Man*, 179–82.

29. Rofé, *The Prophetical Stories*, 14.

30. Ibid., 14 n. 2.

never dissipates" and consequently can effect miracles even after death
(2 Kgs 13:20–21).[31] Rofé discerns a genre of *legenda* comparable to
orally transmitted miracle stories of Christian saints or Jewish personali-
ties. These describe the numerous miracles of the Man of God that were
transmitted orally in the northern kingdom and underlie the condensed,
written version in the received text of Kings.[32]

The contrast between the profile of the "Man of God" in the Elisha/
Elijah traditions with Moses could not be clearer. Moses does not
himself possess a quality of holiness or divinity that is intrinsic to his
being. Rather, God is the source of Moses' power, with the signs and
wonders performed by Moses as an agent of God (cf. Exod 4:21). Rather
than a collection of various miraculous episodes designed to glorify
Moses as a wonder-working holy man, as is the case with Elijah, the
portrayal of Moses resembles the selection, exaltation and empowerment
of a ruler in the Hebrew Bible and the ancient Near East.[33]

5.3. *"Servant of the Lord"*

Scholarly discussions of the title "servant of the Lord/God" in relationship to Moses have tended to focus on its usage in the Old Testament
without paying much attention to extra-biblical material. Coats, for
example, follows the extensive study of Zimmerli and adopts his
conclusion that the title describes a relationship between the person and
God.[34] Coats then views the setting and function of this phrase in a
manner similar to the title "Man of God" as another general title drawn
from the popular setting applied to famous heroes of the past with a close
relationship with God (e.g. Abraham, David, Joshua, Caleb, Job) without
referring to a specific role or office. However, it is not clear that the term
"servant" is heroic in nature. Such a view forces Coats into a convoluted
view of the merger of the heroic qualities of Moses with the mighty acts
of God in his discussion of the function of Moses' designation as
"servant" in Num 12.[35] Rather, the term, as Zimmerli notes, refers to a
subject under the authority of a master,[36] which explains its frequent
usage—approximately eight hundred times—to depict individuals and
groups in a variety of settings (e.g. slave[s], prophet[s], Israel, Abraham,

31. Ibid., 22–23.
32. Ibid., 19–22.
33. The title is applied to David three times (2 Chr 8:14; Neh 12:24, 26).
34. Coats, *Moses: Heroic Man*, 182–85; W. Zimmerli and J. Jeremias, *The Servant of God* (London: SCM, 1957).
35. Coats, *Moses: Heroic Man*, 183.
36. Zimmerli and Jeremias, *The Servant of God*, 12.

David, Jonah). Against Coats, I prefer to understand the designation of Moses' role as "servant" to refer to Moses working under the authority of God as his agent. According to Tigay, this designation indicates Moses as God's "representative and agent in governing Israel... It connotes high status and implies that its bearer is loyal, trusted, and intimate with his master."[37] Although Coats wants to generalize this term, the phrase "servant of the Lord/God" or "my servant" in divine speech is used most often, some forty times each, for Moses[38] and David,[39] which suggests a specific nuance of this designation for these two individuals.

The term "servant" is also a prophetic epithet applied to individual prophets such as Elijah (1 Kgs 18:36; 2 Kgs 9:36; 10:10), Ahijah (1 Kgs 14:18; 15:29), Jonah (2 Kgs 14:25), and Isaiah (Isa 20:3). The phrase "my/your/his servants the prophets" is a standard phrase describing the collective group of prophets some seventeen times, mostly in 2 Kings and Jeremiah.[40] Nevertheless, as with the epithet "Man of God," the precise reference to Moses must begin with the use of this term in context of the Pentateuch and attested use of the term in the ancient Near East. Instructive, too, is that the vast majority of occurrences apply to just two individuals in the Old Testament (Moses and David), which suggests a non-prophetic use of this title.

An examination of ancient Near Eastern evidence shows that the designation "servant" is a common royal epithet.[41] We have previously seen that the vassal Azatiwada was designated as the "servant of Baal." The title also designates the vassal relationship with the Great King, as shown by the designation of Bar-Rakib as "the servant of Tiglath-Pileser (III)" in the Aramaic Bar-Rakib inscription dated to the middle of the eighth century (cf. 2 Kgs 16:7; 24:1).[42] Other suggestive examples include the designation of Kirta as "Servant of El" (*ᶜbd . il*) in the Ugaritic Kirta epic in the second millennium B.C.E.[43] and Idrimi as the

---

37. Tigay, *Deuteronomy*, 337.

38. So Zimmerli and Jeremias, *The Servant of God*, 19.

39. References include 2 Sam 7 ([×10] // 1 Chr 17); 1 Kgs 3:6, 7; 8:24, 26, 66; 11:13, 32, 34, 36, 38; 14:8; 2 Kgs 8:19; 19:34; 20:6; 2 Chr 6:15, 16, 17, 42; Isa 37:5; Jer 33:21, 22, 26; Ezek 34:23, 24; 37:24; Pss 78:70; 89:3, 20; 132:10; 144:10.

40. See the references cited in Zimmerli and Jeremias, *The Servant of God*, 22 n. 52.

41. Of course, the term "servant" has a broad connotation in the ancient Near East as well. See the literature cited by Tigay, *Deuteronomy*, 337 nn. 12, 13.

42. "The Bar-Rakib Inscription," translation by K. Lawson Younger, Jr. (*COS* 2.28:160–61).

43. Simon B. Parker, ed., *Ugaritic Narrative Poetry* (SBLWAW 9; Scholars Press, 1997), 18, 23.

"servant of Adad, Ḫepat, and Isthar" in an inscription dated to 1200 B.C.E.[44] A famous inscription dated to the return of Nabonidus from Teima (539 B.C.E.) reports Marduk's command to restore the sanctuary of Sin in Harran, a task that is now made possible by the defeat of the Medes by Cyrus, designated as Marduk's "young servant."[45] These few citations attest the widespread geographical and temporal use of "servant" as a royal title.

A close examination of the account of the rivalry between Aaron and Miriam against Moses in Num 12 shows a clear contrast between the roles of a "prophet" and "servant":

> Then the Lord came down in a pillar of cloud, and stood at the entrance of the tent, and called Aaron and Miriam; and they both came forward. And he said, "Hear my words: When there are prophets among you, I the LORD make myself known to them in visions; I speak to them in dreams.
>
> Not so with *my servant Moses*; he is entrusted with all my house. With him I speak face to face—clearly, not in riddles; and he beholds the form of the LORD. Why then were you not afraid to speak against *my servant Moses*?"
>
> And the anger of the Lord was kindled against them, and he departed. (Num 12:5–9)

The royal characterization of Moses begins with the depiction of his incomparable humility, which is a typical royal attitude in the ancient Near East (Num 12:3).[46] The divine oracle that follows is ironically given directly to Aaron and Miriam and is replete with royal motifs that stress Moses' uniqueness. Here, Moses is clearly set outside the category of prophets by the virtue of his apprehension of the "form of God"[47] and his direct and clear communication with God "face to face" (lit. "mouth to mouth") without recourse to indirect divine speech through visions or dreams (cf. Exod 33:7–11 and Deut 34:10).

Rather than as "prophet," Moses is designated twice as God's "servant," a well-attested royal title that is Moses' principal title used at

44. "The Autobiography of Idrimi," translation by Tremper Longman (*COS* 1.148:479)

45. See Beaulieu, *Nabonidus*, 107–8, for the text of the inscription, along with bibliographical citations for those scholars who note the connection to the reference to Cyrus as God's servant in Isa 42:1. A general bibliography and a discussion of the dating of the inscription can be found on p. 34.

46. See the discussion of the motif of humility in Chapter 2 of this study.

47. The reference to Exod 33–34 is made clearer in by the substitution of "glory" in place of "form" in the versions (LXX, Syriac).

strategic sections in the Pentateuch (Exod 14:31; Num 12:7–8; Deut 34:5). Here, the description of Moses as "servant" frames the exalted depiction of Moses in vv. 7–8. God describes Moses as God's servant who is "entrusted with all my house" (בכל־ביתי נאמן הוא). Even Van Seters in his attempt to demonstrate Moses' portrayal as a prophet admits that this phrase does not appropriately describe a prophet[48] and likely portrays Moses as a "king" entrusted with Israel as God's "house" and with an access to God more direct than a prophet. In support, Van Seters notes the depiction of Israel's future ruler approaching God in Jer 30:21. Auld calls attention to the usage of נאמן with ב in 1 Sam 22:14 as a possible parallel.[49] There David is described as "faithful" among the servants of Saul (בכל־עבדיך נאמן) and suggest a different understanding of Moses as the faithful servant among God's house. Either possibility highlights the royal nature of Moses' status before God. The divine speech concludes with the forceful admonition "Why are you not terri-fied (ירא) to speak against my servant Moses?" The movement from Moses' exalted and more intimate relationship with God to the response of fear on the part of the community and its leaders is mirrored exactly in Exod 33–34.

In the overall plot of the Pentateuch the designation "servant" is applied four times to Moses at three crucial places (Exod 14:31; Num 12:7, 8; Deut 34:5) and is thus the most frequently used designation of Moses' status in Exodus–Deuteronomy. This designation is applied to Moses at least sixteen times in the book of Joshua and is thus Moses' standard designation[50] throughout the Old Testament (i.e. 2 Kgs 8:53, 56; 1 Chr 6:34; 2 Chr 1:3; 24:6, 9; Ps 105:26; Dan 9:11; Neh 1:8; 9:14; 10:30; Mal 3:2). It is not surprising then that the conclusion of the Pentateuch (Deut 34) and the prophetic canon (Mal 3:2) designate Moses as God's servant.[51]

To sum up the results of this study, the titles "Man of God" and "Servant of the Lord," in conjunction with the clustering of the various motifs used to portray Moses throughout the Pentateuch, suggest that Moses acts in the role of a "vice-regent" exercising temporal sovereignty

48. Van Seters, *The Life of Moses*, 237.

49. A. Graeme Auld, "Prophets Through the Looking Glass: Between Writings and Moses," in *"The Place Is Too Small for Us": The Israelite Prophets in Recent Scholarship* (ed. Robert P. Gordon; Winona Lake, Ind.: Eisenbrauns, 1995), 306.

50. In addition to Josh 1:1, 2, see: Josh 1:7, 13, 15; 8:31, 33; 9:24; 11:12, 15; 12:6; 13:8; 14:7; 22:2, 4, 5.

51. This title is applied also to Joshua at his death (Josh 24:29; Judg 2:8) in an imitation of the portrayal of Moses.

on the LORD's behalf to establish Israel as a discrete nation. Chapters 2, 3 and 4 of this study have identified and examined key features of the portrayal of Moses as a royal figure as they are configured in the Pentateuchal accounts of his birth, his rise to power and major accomplishments, and his death and succession by Joshua.

Although care has been taken not to associate the portrayal of Moses with a specific theory of the formation of the Pentateuch throughout this study, the widespread geographical and temporal setting of the various motifs suggests that any particular model of the composition of the Pentateuch must take the royal view of Moses into account. To illustrate this point, I will now summarize in broad scope how the basic features of the composite portrayal of Moses might be located within the three major documentary strata, or tradition complexes, of the Pentateuch:

5.3.a. *JE Strata (Tenth–Eighth Centuries B.C.E.)*
The close connections between the birth account of Moses and legendary account of the abandonment of Sargon II suggest that the earliest shaping of the portrayal of Moses is to be located during or shortly after the reign of Sargon II. This is also the period of the division of the kingdom and the rise of Jeroboam I. The connections between Moses and Jeroboam and the close linguistic and conceptual similarities between Moses and Joseph noted at various points in this study are all best explained by positing that an early form of the Moses narrative was composed subsequent to Jeroboam's acts of apostasy and with reference to a pre-existing Joseph narrative that was originally supportive of Jeroboam's rule.[52] The composition of the Moses narrative and subsequent linking with the Joseph story now represent a critique of the rule of Jeroboam and his disenfranchisement of the Levites by portraying the rise of a Levitical figure from Egypt that acts as a model king in the manner of, but also superior to, Joseph.

---

52.   On the figure of Joseph as representing the legitimation of the rule of Jeroboam in the early stages of his reign with an emphasis forgiveness and "brotherly solidarity," see David M. Carr, *Reading the Fractures of Genesis: Historical and Literary Approaches* (Louisville: Westminster John Knox, 1996), 274. A recent study that examines the relationship between Moses, Jeroboam, and Sargon is Felipe Wissmann, "Sargon, Mose, und die Gegner Salomos: Zur Frage vor-neuassyrischer Ursprünge der Mose-Erzählung," *Biblische Notizen* 110 (2001): 42–54. Wissmann thinks, however, that the portrayal of Moses served to legitimate the northern kingdom. There might indeed be a basis for this conclusion based on the Joseph narrative and the critique and polemic against Solomon at an earlier stage, but it seems to me that a better case can be made for viewing Moses as an anti-Jeroboam figure based on the connections between the two observed in this study.

At this stage, aspects of the portrayal of Moses would include not only the birth and abandonment story but also other major segments of JE, especially the sketch of his sojourn in Midian as a shepherd (Exod 3:1–4:18) and the account of his actions as Israel's archetypal savior and leader (e.g. Exod 2:11–22) such as the account of his abandonment at birth, his role as Israel's savior and leader, and his portrayal as a shepherd. The conflict between the priestly houses in the aftermath of the fall of the northern kingdom probably underlie the portrayal of Moses as God's intimate and trusted servant in Num 12. Thus at this early stage we can already observe the clustering of motifs that serve to indicate the unique status of Moses as God's trusted servant who is Israel's shepherd, savior, and leader.

5.3.b. *Deuteronomic (Late Eighth–Seventh Centuries B.C.E.) and Deuteronomistic (Sixth Century B.C.E.) Traditions*

The Deuteronomic and Deuteronomistic stages of composition can be identified respectively with the periods from Hezekiah to Josiah and the exile. This stage begins with the Assyrian destruction of the northern kingdom in 722 which led to the migration of various epic traditions to the southern kingdom. At this point Moses now formed a standard for the Judean kings during the Deuteronomic movement. The connections between Moses with Joshua and Josiah probably received the principal shaping in this stage.[53] Moreover, the portrayal of Moses in Deuteronomic and Deuteronomistic sources exhibits close resemblance with the depictions of Esarhaddon's rise to power.[54] Connections have also been discerned between the Vassal treaty of Esarhaddon with Deut 13 and especially with the content and sequence of the curses in Deut 28:23–35.[55] On the basis of these observations, Otto argued that the reign of Esarhaddon provided a point of reference for the composition of a version of the Moses narrative in the seventh century B.C.E.[56] This stage supplements the earlier JE portrait of Moses with material that emphasizes the role of Moses as lawgiver and covenant maker.

---

53. Nelson, "Josiah." On the connections between Moses and Josiah, see Richard Elliot Friedman, *The Exile and Biblical Narrative: The Formation of the Deuteronomistic and Priestly Works* (HSM 22; Chico, Calif.: Scholars Press, 1981), 7–10, presented also in "From Egypt to Egypt: Dtr[1] and Dtr[2]," in *Traditions in Transformation: Turning Points in Biblical Faith* (ed. Baruch Halpern; Winona Lake, Ind.: Eisenbrauns, 1981), 171–73, and later in an updated and accessible form in *Who Wrote the Bible?* (2d ed.; San Francisco: HarperSanFrancisco), 111–16.

54. As noted in Chapter 2 of this study.

55. So Weinfeld, *Deuteronomy 1–11*, 7.

56. Otto, *Die Tora des Mose*, 20–22.

5.3.c. *Priestly Traditions (Sixth–Fifth Centuries B.C.E.)*
The Priestly portions of the Pentateuch might include older material, but the principal work of composition and redaction probably occurred between the late exilic and early Second Temple eras. This stage correlates broadly with the period of conflict between Nabonidus and Cyrus and their competing claims to hegemony over the ancient Near East. The re-constituting of a Judean polity in the postexilic period and promulgation of the Torah during the career of Ezra mark the end of this period. Within this setting, the Priestly edition of the Pentateuch presents Moses as a temple builder and as one who is exalted to become God's incomparable, semi-divine agent to save Israel (e.g. Exod 7:1; 34:29–35).

Thus it becomes clear that over the course of the Pentateuch's compositional development, clusters of motifs have been used to portray Moses as a royal figure. We have observed that, during this same span of time, a number of important Mesopotamian kings have been portrayed in a similar way. What is at stake for ancient Near Eastern kings is ensuring a legitimate claim to the throne. On the basis of the king's elevated status as one who stands between deity and the people, the king receives a divine mandate and power to protect and save their nation from enemies, to ensure the peace and stability throughout the realm through their laws, and to oversee and regulate the proper worship of his deity. Within the context of the claims made by the prevailing empire of the Israel, Pentateuchal authors made use of the familiar clustering of motifs to affirm Moses as a more ancient leader, whose work has resulted in the constitution of the community of Israel. All current structures of leaderships, whether kings, priest, prophets, or elders, derive their authority and empowerment from Moses.[57] In the context of competing affirmations of the might and sovereignty of ancient Near Eastern kings, Israel affirms their identity and being through the authority and legacy of Moses and his work as God's trusted and incomparable servant.

---

57.   On the view of Mosaic authority legitimating the various political offices in Israelite society (i.e. prophet, priest, elder), see McBride, "Transcendent Authority." On the basis of the present study, I would now include the office of "king," especially in view of the authoritative status of the Mosaic Torah affirmed by David (1 Kgs 2:3) and Josiah (2 Kgs 23:3). Cf. Josh 1:7–8 and relationships of these texts with Deut 17:14–20. A different approach has been offered by Joshua Berman (*Created Equal*, Chapter 2), who argues that Deuteronomy divests the human king of power and distributes the power among several political realms (military, cult, judiciary, etc.) to create a balanced separation of powers. I would slightly modify Berman's view by noting that the Pentateuch portrays Moses as an authoritative surrogate king who constructs a polity to ensure the continuation of his several functions (prophetic, military, judicial, royal) among the various political offices of the day.

BIBLIOGRAPHY

Aaron, David H. *Etched in Stone: The Emergence of the Decalogue*. New York: T&T Clark International, 2006.

Aberbach, Moses, and Leivy Smolar. "Aaron, Jeroboam, and the Golden Calves." *JBL* 86 (1967): 129–40.

Ackerman, James S. "The Literary Context of the Moses Birth Story." Pages 74–119 in *Literary Interpretations of Biblical Narratives*, edited by Kenneth R. R. Gros Louis. Bible in Literature Courses. Nashville: Abingdon, 1974.

Anderson, Robert T., and Terry Giles. *Tradition Kept: The Literature of the Samaritans*. Peabody, Mass.: Hendrickson, 2005.

Auerbach, Elias. *Moses*. Translated by Robert A. Barclay and Israel O. Lehman. Detroit: Wayne State University Press, 1975.

Auld, A. Graeme. "Prophets Through the Looking Glass: Between Writings and Moses." Pages 289–307 in *"The Place Is Too Small for Us": The Israelite Prophets in Recent Scholarship*. Edited by Robert P. Gordon. Winona Lake, Ind.: Eisenbrauns, 1995.

Aurelius, Erik. *Der Fürbitter Israels: Eine Studie zum Mosebild im Alten Testament*. Stockholm: Almqvist & Wiksell International, 1988.

Balentine, Samuel E. "The Prophet as Intercessor: A Reassessment." *JBL* 103 (1984): 161–73.

Baltzer, Klaus. *Die Biographie der Propheten*. Neukirchen–Vluyn: Neukirchener Verlag, 1975.

Barclay, John M. G. *Jews in the Mediterranean Diaspora from Alexander to Trajan (323 BCE–117 CE)*. Edinburgh: T. & T. Clark, 1996.

Beaulieu, Paul-Alain. *The Reign of Nabonidus, King of Babylon, 556–539 B.C.* New Haven: Yale University Press, 1989.

Beckman, Gary M. *Hittite Diplomatic Texts*. 2d ed. SBLWAW 7. Atlanta: Scholars Press, 1999.

Beckman, Gary M., and Theodore J. Lewis, eds. *Text, Artifact, and Image: Revealing Ancient Israelite Religion*. Providence, R.I.: Brown University Press, 2006.

Beegle, Dewey M. *Moses, the Servant of Yahweh*. Grand Rapids: Eerdmans, 1972.

Beentjes, Pancratius C. *The Book of Ben Sira in Hebrew: A Text Edition of All Extant Hebrew Manuscripts and a Synopsis of All Parallel Hebrew Ben Sira Texts*. VTSup 68. New York: Brill, 1997.

Begg, Christopher. "'Josephus's Portrayal of the Disappearances of Enoch, Elijah, and Moses': Some Observations." *JBL* 109 (1990): 691–93.

Berman, Joshua A. *Created Equal: How the Bible Broke with Ancient Political Thought*. New York: Oxford University Press, 2008.

Berman, Samuel A. *Midrash Tanhuma-Yelammedenu: An English Translation of Genesis and Exodus from the Printed Version of Tanhuma-Yelammedenu with an Introduction, Notes, and Indexes*. Hoboken, N.J.: KTAV, 1996.

Beyerlin, Walter. *Origins and History of the Oldest Sinaitic Traditions*. Oxford: Blackwell, 1965.

Blenkinsopp, Joseph. *The Pentateuch: An Introduction to the First Five Books of the Bible*. New York: Doubleday, 1992.

Blum, Erhard. "The Literary Connection Between the Books of Genesis and Exodus and the End of the Book of Joshua." Pages 89–106 in Dozeman and Schmid, eds., *A Farewell to the Yahwist?*

——. *Studien zur Komposition des Pentateuch*. Berlin: de Gruyter, 1990.

——. "Die literarische Verbindung von Erzvätern und Exodus: Ein Gespräch mit neueren Endredaktionshypothesen." Pages 119–56 in Gertz, Schmid, and Witte, eds., *Abschied vom Jahwisten*.

Boling, Robert G. *Judges: Introduction, Translation, and Commentary*. AB 6A. Garden City, N.Y.: Doubleday, 1975.

Borgen, Peder. "Philo of Alexandria." Pages 233–82 in *Jewish Writings of the Second Temple Period: Apocrypha, Pseudepigrapha, Qumran Sectarian Writings, Philo, Josephus*. Edited by Michael E. Stone. Philadelphia: Fortress, 1984.

Brettler, Marc Zvi. *God Is King: Understanding an Israelite Metaphor*. JSOTSup 76. Sheffield: Sheffield Academic, 1989.

Briant, Pierre. *From Cyrus to Alexander: A History of the Persian Empire*. Translated by Peter D. Daniels. Winona Lake, Ind.: Eisenbrauns, 2002.

Brichto, Herbert Chanan. *Toward a Grammar of Biblical Poetics: Tales of the Prophets*. New York: Oxford University Press, 1992.

Britt, Brian. *Rewriting Moses: The Narrative Eclipse of the Text*. LHBOTS 402. New York: T&T Clark International, 2004.

Campbell, Antony F., and Mark O'Brien. *Sources of the Pentateuch: Texts, Introductions, Annotations*. Minneapolis: Fortress, 1993.

Carr, David M. *Reading the Fractures of Genesis: Historical and Literary Approaches*. Louisville: Westminster John Knox, 1996.

Cassin, Elena. *La splendeur divine: Introduction à l'étude de la mentalité mésopotamienne*. Paris: Mouton, 1968.

Childs, Brevard S. *Biblical Theology of the Old and New Testaments*. Minneapolis: Fortress, 1992.

——. *The Book of Exodus: A Critical, Theological Commentary*. OTL. Philadelphia: Westminster, 1974.

Coats, George W. *Exodus 1–18*. FOTL. Grand Rapids: Eerdmans, 1999.

——. *Moses: Heroic Man, Man of God*. JSOTSup 57. Sheffield: JSOT, 1988.

——. *The Moses Tradition*. JSOTSup 161. Sheffield: JSOT, 1993.

Collins, John J. *Between Athens and Jerusalem: Jewish Identity in the Hellenistic Diaspora*. 2d ed. Biblical Resource Series. Grand Rapids: Eerdmans, 2000.

——. *Daniel: A Commentary on the Book of Daniel*. Hermeneia. Minneapolis: Fortress, 1993.

Colson, F. H., trans. *Philo*. LCL. Cambridge, Mass.: Harvard University Press, 1935.

Cross, Frank Moore. *Canaanite Myth and Hebrew Epic: Essays in the History of the Religion of Israel*. 1973. Repr., Cambridge, Mass.: Harvard University Press, 1997.

———. *From Epic to Canon: History and Literature in Ancient Israel.* Baltimore: The Johns Hopkins University Press, 1988.

Crüsemann, Frank. *Die Tora: Theologie und Sozialgeschichte des alttestamentlichen Gesetzes.* Munich: Kaiser, 1992.

———. *The Torah: Theology and Social History of Old Testament Law.* Translated by Allan W. Mahnke. Minneapolis: Fortress, 1996.

Dalley, Stephanie. *Myths from Mesopotamia: Creation, the Flood, Gilgamesh, and Others.* Oxford: Oxford University Press, 1989.

Davies, Graham I. "K^D in Exodus: An Assessment of E. Blum's Proposal." Pages 407–20 in *Deuteronomy and Deuteronomic Literature.* Edited by M. Vervenne and J. Lust. Louvain: University Press, 1997.

Dijkstra, Meindert. "Moses, the Man of God." Pages 17–36 in *The Interpretation of Exodus: Studies in Honor of Cornelis Houtman.* Edited by Riemer Roukema. CBET. Dudley, Mass.: Peters, 2006.

Dozeman, Thomas B. "The Commission of Moses and the Book of Genesis." Pages 107–29 in Dozeman and Schmid, eds., *A Farewell to the Yahwist?.*

———. *God on the Mountain: A Study of Redaction, Theology, and Canon in Exodus 19–24.* Atlanta, Ga.: Scholars Press, 1989.

Dozeman, Thomas B., and Konrad Schmid, eds. *A Farewell to the Yahwist? The Composition of the Pentateuch in Recent European Interpretation.* Atlanta: Society of Biblical Literature, 2006.

Engnell, Ivan. *A Rigid Scrutiny: Critical Essays on the Old Testament.* Edited and translated by John T. Willis. Nashville: Vanderbilt University Press, 1969.

———. *Studies in Divine Kingship in the Ancient Near East.* Oxford: Blackwell, 1967.

Even-Shoshan, Abraham. *A New Concordance of the Old Testament Using the Hebrew and Aramaic Text.* 2d ed. Jerusalem: Kiryat Sefer, 1993.

Feldman, Louis H. "The Death of Moses, According to Philo." *EstBib* 60 (2002): 225–54.

———. "Josephus' Portrait of Moses." *JQR* 82 (1992): 285–328.

———. "Josephus' Portrait of Moses: Part Two." *JQR* 83 (1992): 7–50.

———. "Josephus' Portrait of Moses: Part Three." *JQR* 83 (1992): 301–30.

———. *Josephus's Interpretation of the Bible.* Berkeley: University of California Press, 1998.

———. *Judean Antiquities 1–4: Translation and Commentary.* Boston: Brill, 2000.

———. "Philo's View of Moses' Birth and Upbringing." *CBQ* 64 (2002): 258–81.

Ferguson, Everett. *Backgrounds to Early Christianity.* 3d ed. Grand Rapids: Eerdmans, 2003.

Fletcher-Louis, Crispin H. T. *All the Glory of Adam: Liturgical Anthropology in the Dead Sea Scrolls.* STDJ. Boston: Brill, 2002.

Fohrer, Georg. *Introduction to the Old Testament.* Translated by David Green. Nashville: Abingdon, 1968.

———. *Überlieferung und Geschichte des Exodus: eine Analyse von Ex 1–15.* BZAW 91. Berlin: Töpelmann, 1964.

Foster, Benjamin R. *From Distant Days: Myths, Tales, and Poetry of Ancient Mesopotamia.* Bethesda, Md.: CDL, 1995.

Fretheim, Terence E. *Exodus.* IBC. Louisville: John Knox, 1991.

Friedman, Richard Elliott. *The Exile and Biblical Narrative: The Formation of the Deuteronomistic and Priestly Works.* HSM. Chico, Calif.: Scholars Press, 1981.

————. "From Egypt to Egypt: Dtr[1] and Dtr[2]." Pages 167–92 in *Traditions in Transformation: Turning Points in Biblical Faith*. Edited by Baruch Halpern. Winona Lake, Ind.: Eisenbrauns, 1981.

————. "Torah (Pentateuch)." *ABD* 6:605–22.

————. *Who Wrote the Bible?* 2d ed. San Francisco: HarperSanFrancisco, 1997.

Fuchs, Andreas. *Die Inschriften Sargon II. aus Khorsabad.* Göttingen: Cuviller, 1994.

Gager, J. G. *Moses in Greco-Roman Paganism*. SBLMS 16. Missoula, Mont.: Scholars Press, 1972.

Geller, Stephen A. "Manna and Sabbath: A Literary-Theological Reading of Exodus 16." *Int* 59 (2005): 5–16.

Gerhards, Meik. *Die Aussetzungsgeschichte des Mose.* WMANT 109. Neukirchener Verlag, 2006.

Gertz, Jan Christian, Konrad Schmid, and Markus Witte, eds. *Abschied vom Jahwisten: Die Komposition des Hexateuch in der jüngsten Diskussion.* BZAW 315. New York: de Gruyter, 2002.

Gitin, Seymour, and Mordechai Cogan. "A New Type of Dedicatory Inscription from Ekron." *IEJ* 49 (1999): 193–202.

Godley, A. D., trans. *Herodotus*. LCL. New York: G. P. Putnam's Sons, 1931.

Goodenough, Erwin R. *By Light, Light: The Mystic Gospel of Hellenistic Judaism*. New Haven: Yale University Press, 1935.

————. "The Political Philosophy of Hellenistic Kingship." *Yale Classical Studies* 1 (1928): 55–102.

Gowan, Donald E. *Theology in Exodus: Biblical Theology in the Form of a Commentary*. Louisville: Westminster John Knox, 1994.

Graupner, Axel, and Michael Wolter, eds. *Moses in Biblical and Extra-Biblical Traditions*. BZAW 372. New York: de Gruyter, 2007.

Greenberg, Moshe. "The Redaction of the Plague Narrative in P." Pages 243–52 in *Near Eastern Studies in Honor of William Foxwell Albright*. Edited by Hans Goedicke. Baltimore: The Johns Hopkins University Press, 1971.

Gressmann, Hugo. *Mose und seine Zeit: Ein Kommentar zu den Mose-Sagen*. FRLANT 18. Göttingen: Vandenhoeck & Ruprecht, 1913.

Griffiths, J. G. "The Egyptian Derivation of the Name Moses." *JNES* 12 (1953): 225–32.

Habel, N. "The Form and Significance of the Call Narratives." *ZAW* 77 (1965): 297–323.

Hackett, Jo Ann. "Violence and Women's Lives in the Book of Judges." *Int* 58 (2004): 356–64.

Hamilton, Mark W. *The Body Royal: The Social Poetics of Kingship in Ancient Israel*. Boston: Brill, 2005.

Hauge, Martin Ravndal. *The Descent from the Mountain: Narrative Patterns in Exodus 19–40*. JSOT 323. Sheffield: Sheffield Academic, 2001.

Hay, David M. "Moses Through New Testament Spectacles." *Int* 44 (1990): 240–52.

Holladay, Carl R. *Fragments from Hellenistic Jewish Authors*. Vol. 1, *Historians*. Chico, Calif.: Scholars Press, 1983.

————. *Fragments from Hellenistic Jewish Authors*. Vol. 2, *Poets*. Atlanta: Scholars Press, 1989.

————. *Fragments from Hellenistic Jewish Authors*. Vol. 4, *Orphica*. Atlanta: Scholars Press, 1996.

————. *Theios Aner in Hellenistic-Judaism: A Critique of the Use of This Category in New Testament Christology*. SBLDS 40. Missoula, Mont.: Scholars Press, 1977.

Hughes, Paul E. "Moses' Birth Story: A Biblical Matrix for Prophetic Messianism." Pages 10–22 in *Eschatology, Messianism, and the Dead Sea Scrolls*. Edited by Craig A. Evans. Studies in the Dead Sea Scrolls and Related Literature. Grand Rapids: Eerdmans, 1997.

Hurowitz, Victor Avigdor. *I Have Built You an Exalted House: Temple Building in the Bible in the Light of Mesopotamian and North-West Semitic Writings*. JSOT 115. Sheffield: JSOT, 1992.

———. "The Priestly Account of Building the Tabernacle." *JAOS* 105 (1985): 21–30.

———. "Restoring the Temple—Why and When?" *JQR* 93 (2003): 581–91.

Hurtado, Larry W. *Lord Jesus Christ: Devotion to Jesus in Earliest Christianity*. Grand Rapids: Eerdmans, 2003.

———. *One God, One Lord: Early Christian Devotion and Ancient Jewish Monotheism*. Philadelphia: Fortress, 1988.

Jacobson, Howard. *The* Exagoge *of Ezekiel*. New York: Cambridge University Press, 1983.

Johnstone, William. *Chronicles and Exodus: An Analogy and Its Application*. JSOTSup 275. Sheffield: Sheffield Academic, 1998.

———. "Reactivating the Chronicles Analogy in Pentateuchal Studies, with Special Reference to the Sinai Pericope in Exodus." *ZAW* 99 (1987): 16–37.

Kapelrud, Arvid S. "Temple Building: A Task for Gods and Kings." *Or* 32 (1963): 56–62.

———. "Two Great Rulers and Their Temple Buildings." Pages 135–42 in *Text and Theology: Studies in Honour of Professor Magne Sæbø: Presented on the Occasion of His 65th Birthday*. Edited by Arvid Tångberg. Oslo: Verbum, 1994.

Knierim, Rolf. *The Task of Old Testament Theology: Substance, Method, and Cases*. Grand Rapids: Eerdmans, 1995.

Knight, Douglas A. *Rediscovering the Traditions of Israel*. Missoula, Mont.: SBL, 1973.

Knoppers, Gary N. "'There Was None Like Him': Incomparability in the Books of Kings." *CBQ* 54 (1992): 411–31.

Kugler, Rob. "Hearing the Story of Moses in Ptolemaic Egypt: Artapanus Accommodates the Tradition." Pages 67–80 in *The Wisdom of Egypt: Jewish, Early Christian, and Gnostic Essays in Honour of Gerard P. Luttikhuizen*. Edited by Anthony Hilhorst and George H. Van Kooten. Boston: Brill, 2005.

Kushelevsky, Rella. *Moses and the Angel of Death*. New York: Lang, 1995.

Lanfranchi, Pierluigi. *L 'Exagoge d'Ezéchiel le Tragique: Introduction, texte, traduction et commentaire*. Boston: Brill, 2006.

———. "Reminiscences of Ezekiel's *Exagoge* in Philo's *De Vita Mosis*." Pages 144–50 in Graupner and Wolter, eds., *Moses in Biblical and Extra-Biblical Traditions*.

Lapsley, Jacqueline E. "Friends with God? Moses and the Possibility of Covenantal Friendship." *Int* 58 (2004): 117–29.

Lemke, Werner E. "The Way of Obedience: I Kings 13 and the Structure of the Deuteronomistic History." Pages 301–26 in *Magnalia Dei: The Mighty Acts of God*. Edited by Frank Moore Cross and et al. Garden City, N.Y.: Doubleday, 1976.

Levin, Christoph. "The Yahwist and the Redactional Link Between Genesis and Exodus." Pages 131–41 in Dozeman and Schmid, eds., *A Farewell to the Yahwist?*

Lewis, Brian. *The Sargon Legend: A Study of the Akkadian Text and the Tale of the Hero Who Was Exposed at Birth*. Cambridge, Mass.: American Schools of Oriental Research, 1980.

Lierman, John. *The New Testament Moses: Christian Perceptions of Moses and Israel in the Setting of Jewish Religion.* WUNT 173. Tübingen: Mohr Siebeck, 2004.

Lohfink, Norbert. "The Deuteronomistic Picture of the Transfer of Authority from Moses to Joshua: A Contribution to an Old Testament Theology of Office." Pages 234–47 in *Theology of the Pentateuch: Themes of the Priestly Narrative and Deuteronomy.* Minneapolis: Fortress, 1994.

———. "Die deuteronomistische Darstellung des Übergangs der Führung Israels von Moses auf Josue." *Scholastik* 37 (1962): 32–44.

Longman, Tremper. *Fictional Akkadian Autobiography: A Generic and Comparative Study.* Winona Lake, Ind.: Eisenbrauns, 1991.

Macchi, Jean Daniel. "La naissance de Moise (Exode 2/1–10)." *ETR* 69 (1994): 397–403.

MacDonald, John. *The Theology of the Samaritans.* London: SCM, 1964.

Machinist, Peter. "Kingship and Divinity in Imperial Assyria." Pages 152–88 in Beckman and Lewis, eds., *Text, Artifact, and Image.*

———. "Literature as Politics: The Tukulti-Ninurta Epic and the Bible." *CBQ* 38 (1976): 455–82.

Mann, Thomas W. *Divine Presence and Guidance in Israelite Traditions: The Typology of Exaltation.* Baltimore: The Johns Hopkins University Press, 1977.

Marcus, Joel. *Mark 1–8: A New Translation with Introduction and Commentary.* AB 27. New York: Doubleday, 1999.

McBride, S. Dean. "Deuteronomy, Book of." Pages 108–17 in vol. 2 of *The New Interpreter's Dictionary of the Bible.* Edited by Katharine Doob Sakenfeld. 5 vols. Nashville: Abingdon, 2007.

———. "The Essence of Orthodoxy: Deuteronomy 5:6–10 and Exodus 20:2–6." *Int* 60 (2006): 133–50.

———. "The God Who Creates and Governs: Pentateuchal Foundations of Biblical Theology." Pages 11–28 in *The Forgotten God: Perspectives in Biblical Theology; Essays in Honor of Paul J. Achtemeier on the Occasion of His Seventy-Fifth Birthday.* Edited by A. Andrew Das and Frank J. Matera. Louisville: Westminster John Knox, 2002.

———. "Polity of the Covenant People: The Book of Deuteronomy." *Int* 41 (1987): 229–44.

———. "Transcendent Authority: The Role of Moses in Old Testament Traditions." *Int* 44 (1990): 229–39.

McCarter Jr., P. Kyle. *1 Samuel: A New Translation with Introduction and Commentary.* AB 8. Garden City, N.Y.: Doubleday, 1980.

McCarthy, Dennis J. "An Installation Genre?" *JBL* 90 (1971): 31–41.

McKenzie, Steven L. "Deuteronomistic History." *ABD* 2:160–68.

Meeks, Wayne A. "Moses as God and King." Pages 43–67 in *Religions in Antiquity: Essays in Memory of Erwin Ramsdell Goodenough.* Edited by J. Neusner. Leiden: Brill, 1968.

———. *The Prophet-King: Moses Traditions and the Johannine Christology.* NovTSup 14. Leiden: E. J. Brill, 1967.

Moberly, R. W. L. *At the Mountain of God: Story and Theology in Exodus 32–34.* JSOTSup 22. Sheffield: JSOT, 1983.

Muilenburg, J. "The Intercession of the Covenant Mediator (Exodus 33:1a, 12–17)." Pages 159–81 in *Words and Meanings: Essays Presented to David Winton Thomas.* Edited by Peter R. Ackroyd and Barnabas Lindars. Cambridge: Cambridge University Press, 1968.

Mullen Jr., E. Theodore. *Ethnic Myths and Pentateuchal Foundations: A New Approach to the Formation of the Pentateuch.* Atlanta: Scholars Press, 1997.

Nelson, Richard D. *Deuteronomy: A Commentary.* OTL. Louisville: Westminster John Knox, 2002.

———. *Joshua: A Commentary.* OTL. Louisville: Westminster John Knox, 1997.

———. "Josiah in the Book of Joshua." *JBL* 100 (1981): 531–40.

Newman, Murray Lee. *The People of the Covenant: A Study of Israel from Moses to the Monarchy.* New York: Abingdon, 1962.

Nicholson, Ernest W. *The Pentateuch in the Twentieth Century: The Legacy of Julius Wellhausen.* Oxford: Clarendon, 1998.

Nissinen, Martti. *Prophets and Prophecy in the Ancient Near East.* SBLWAW 12. Atlanta: Society of Biblical Literature, 2003.

Nohrnberg, James. *Like Unto Moses: The Constituting of an Interruption.* Indiana Studies in Biblical Literature. Bloomington: Indiana University Press, 1995.

Noth, Martin. *A History of Pentateuchal Traditions.* Translated by Bernhard W. Anderson. Englewood Cliffs: Prentice-Hall, 1972.

Olson, Dennis T. "Buber, Kingship, and the Book of Judges: A Study of Judges 6–9 and 17–21." Pages 199–218 in *David and Zion: Biblical Studies in Honor of J. J. M. Roberts.* Edited by Bernard F. Batto and Kathryn L. Roberts. Winona Lake, Ind.: Eisenbrauns, 2004.

Oppenheim, A. L. "Akkadian *pul(u)ḫ(t)u* and *melammu.*" *JAOS* 63 (1943): 31–34.

Osswald, Eva. *Das Bild des Mose in der kritischen alttestamentlichen Wissenschaft seit Julius Wellhausen.* Berlin: Evangelische Verlagsanstalt, 1962.

———. "Moses." In *RGG* 4:1151–55.

Otto, Eckart. "The Pentateuch in Synchronical and Diachronical Perspectives: Proto-rabbinic Scribal Erudition Mediating Between Deuteronomy and the Priestly Code." Pages 14–35 in *Das Deuteronomium zwischen Pentateuch und Deut-eronomistischem Geschichtswerk.* Edited by Eckart Otto and Reinhard Achenbach. FRLANT 206. Göttingen: Vandenhoeck & Ruprecht, 2004.

———. *Die Tora des Mose: Die Geschichte der literarischen Vermittlung von Recht, Religion und Politik durch die Mosegestalt.* Göttingen: Vandenhoeck & Ruprecht, 2001.

Parker, Simon B., ed. *Ugaritic Narrative Poetry.* SBLWAW 9. Scholars Press, 1997.

Parpola, Simo. *Assyrian Prophecies.* SAA 9. Helsinki, Finland: Helsinki University Press, 1997.

Peckham, Brian. *History and Prophecy: The Development of Late Judean Literary Traditions.* New York: Doubleday, 1993.

Petersen, David L. "The Ambiguous Role of Moses as Prophet." Pages 311–24 in *Israel's Prophets and Israel's Past: Essays on the Relationship of Prophetic Texts and Israelite History in Honor of John H. Hayes.* Edited by Brad E. Kelle and Megan Bishop Moore. New York: T&T Clark International, 2006.

———. *The Roles of Israel's Prophets.* JSOTSup 17. Sheffield: University of Sheffield, 1981.

Porter, J. Roy. *Moses and Monarchy: A Study in the Biblical Tradition of Moses.* Oxford: Blackwell, 1963.

———. "The Succession of Joshua." Pages 102–32 in *Proclamation and Presence: Old Testament Essays in Honour of Gwynne Henton Davies.* Richmond: John Knox, 1970.

————. "The Succession of Joshua." Pages 139–63 in *Reconsidering Israel and Judah: Recent Studies on the Deuteronomistic History*. Edited by Gary N. Knoppers and J. Gordon McConville. Winona Lake, Ind.: Eisenbrauns, 2000.

Propp, William H. C. *Exodus 1–18: A New Translation with Introduction and Commentary*. AB 2. New York: Doubleday, 1998.

————. *Exodus 19–40: A New Translation with Introduction and Commentary*. AB 2A. New York: Doubleday, 2006.

Rad, Gerhard von. *Moses*. World Christian Books. London: Lutterworth, 1960.

————. *Old Testament Theology*. Vol. 1, *The Theology of Israel's Historical Traditions*. New York: Harper, 1962.

————. *The Problem of the Hexateuch, and Other Essays*. Edinburgh: Oliver & Boyd, 1966.

Redford, Donald B. "The Literary Motif of the Exposed Child." *Numen* 14 (1967): 209–28.

Rendsburg, Gary A. "Moses as Equal to Pharaoh." Pages 201–19 in Beckman and Lewis, eds., *Text, Artifact, and Image*.

Richter, Wolfgang. *Die sogenannten vorprophetischen Berufungsberichte: Eine literaturwissenschaftliche Studie zu 1 Sam 9, 1–10, 16, Ex. 3 f. und Ri 6, 11b–17*. FRLANT 101. Göttingen: Vandenhoeck & Ruprecht, 1970.

Roberts, Kathryn L. "God, Prophet, and King: Eating and Drinking on the Mountain in First Kings 18:41." *CBQ* 62 (2000): 632–44.

Rofé, Alexander. *The Prophetical Stories: The Narratives About the Prophets in the Hebrew Bible, Their Literary Types and History*. Jerusalem: Magnes, 1988.

Römer, Thomas C., and Marc Z. Brettler. "Deuteronomy 34 and the Case for a Persian Hexateuch." *JBL* 119 (2000): 401–19.

Sasson, J. M. "Bovine Symbolism in the Exodus Narrative." *VT* 18 (1968): 380–87.

Savran, George W. *Encountering the Divine: Theophany in Biblical Narrative*. JSOTSup 420. New York: T&T Clark International, 2005.

Schade, Aaron. "A Text Linguistic Approach to the Syntax and Style of the Phoenician Inscription of Azatiwada." *JSS* 50 (2005): 35–58.

Schenck, Kenneth. *A Brief Guide to Philo*. Louisville: Westminster John Knox, 2005.

Seebass, Horst. *Der Erzvater Israel und die Einführung der Jahweverehrung in Kanaan*. BZAW 98. Berlin: Töpelmann, 1966.

————. *Moses und Aaron, Sinai und Gottesberg*. Bonn: Bouvier, 1962.

Smend, Rudolf. *Das Mosebild von Heinrich Ewald bis Martin Noth*. Tübingen: J. C. B. Mohr, 1959.

————. *Yahweh War and Tribal Confederation: Reflections Upon Israel's Earliest History*. Translated by Max Gray Rogers. Nashville: Abingdon, 1970.

Smith, Mark S. *The Origins of Biblical Monotheism: Israel's Polytheistic Background and the Ugaritic Texts*. Oxford: Oxford University Press, 2001.

————. *The Pilgrimage Pattern in Exodus*. JSOTSup 239. Sheffield: Sheffield Academic, 1997.

Sommer, Benjamin D. "The Source Critic and the Religious Interpreter." *Int* 60 (2006): 9–20.

Sparks, Kenton L. *Ancient Texts for the Study of the Hebrew Bible: A Guide to the Background Literature*. Peabody, Mass.: Hendrickson, 2005.

Tabor, James D. "'Returning to the Divinity': Josephus's Portrayal of the Disappearances of Enoch, Elijah, and Moses." *JBL* 108 (1989): 225–38.

Talbert, Charles H. "The Concept of Immortals in Mediterranean Antiquity." *JBL* 94 (1975): 419–36.

Thackeray, H. St. J., trans. *Josephus*. LCL. Cambridge, Mass.: Harvard University Press, 1930.

Thompson, Thomas L., and Dorothy Irvin. "The Joseph and Moses Narratives." Pages 149–212 in *Israelite and Judean History*, edited by John H. Hayes and J. Maxwell Miller. Philadelphia: Westminster, 1977.

Tiede, David Lenz. *The Charismatic Figure as Miracle Worker*. SBLDS 1. Missoula, Mont.: Scholars Press, 1972.

Tigay, Jeffrey H. *Deuteronomy: The Traditional Hebrew Text with the New JPS Translation*. The JPS Torah Commentary. Philadelphia: Jewish Publication Society, 1996.

———. "'Heavy of Mouth' and 'Heavy of Tongue': On Moses' Speech Difficulty." *BASOR* 231 (1978): 57–57.

Turgman, Victor. *De l'autorité de Moïse, Ex 15,22–27*. Eilsbrunn: Ko'amar, 1987.

Utzschneider, Helmut. *Das Heiligtum und das Gesetz: Studien zur Bedeutung der sinaitischen Heiligtumstexte (Ex 25–40; Lev 8–9)*. Göttingen: Vandenhoeck & Ruprecht, 1988.

Vancil, Jack W. "Sheep, Shepherd." *ABD* 6:1187–90.

Van Seters, John. *The Edited Bible: The Curious History of the "Editor" in Biblical Criticism*. Winona Lake, Ind.: Eisenbrauns, 2006.

———. *In Search of History: Historiography in the Ancient World and the Origins of Biblical History*. Winona Lake, Ind.: Eisenbrauns, 1997.

———. *The Life of Moses: The Yahwist as Historian in Exodus–Numbers*. Louisville: Westminster John Knox, 1994.

———. "The Report of the Yahwist's Demise Has Been Greatly Exaggerated!" Pages 143–57 in Dozeman and Schmid, eds., *A Farewell to the Yahwist?*

Watts, James W. *Reading Law: The Rhetorical Shaping of the Pentateuch*. Sheffield: Sheffield Academic, 1999.

Weinfeld, Moshe. *Deuteronomy 1–11: A New Translation with Introduction and Commentary*. AB 5. New York: Doubleday, 1991.

———. "Deuteronomy, Book of." *ABD* 2:168–83.

———. "Judge and Officer in the Ancient Israel and in the Ancient Near East." *Israel Oriental Studies* 7 (1977): 65–88.

Wells, Bruce. "The Covenant Code and Near Eastern Legal Traditions." *Maarav* 13 (2006): 85–118.

Whitelam, Keith W. *The Just King: Monarchical Judicial Authority in Ancient Israel*. JSOTSup 12. Sheffield: JSOT, 1979.

Widengren, Geo. *The King and the Tree of Life in Ancient Near Eastern Religion*. Uppsala: Lundequistska Bokhandeln, 1951.

Widmer, Michael. *Moses, God, and the Dynamics of Intercessory Prayer: A Study of Exodus 32–34 and Numbers 13–14*. FAT 2/8. Tübingen: Mohr Siebeck, 2004.

Wiseman, D. J. *The Vassal-Treaties of Esarhaddon*. London: British School of Archaeology in Iraq, 1958.

Wissmann, Felipe. "Sargon, Mose, und die Gegner Salomos: Zur Frage vor-neuassyrischer Ursprünge der Mose-Erzählung." *Biblische Notizen* 110 (2001): 42–54.

Wright, David P. "The Laws of Hammurabi and the Covenant Code: A Response to Bruce Wells." *Maarav* 13 (2006): 211–60.

———. "The Laws of Hammurabi as a Source for the Covenant Collection (Exodus 20:23–23:19)." *Maarav* 10 (2003): 11–87.

Younger, K. Lawson. "The Phoenician Inscription of Azatiwada." *JSS* 43 (1998): 11–46.

Zimmerli, W. *Ezekiel: A Commentary on the Book of the Prophet Ezekiel.* Hermeneia. Philadelphia: Fortress, 1979.

———. *Old Testament Theology in Outline.* Edinburgh: T. & T. Clark, 1978.

Zimmerli, W., and J. Jeremias. *The Servant of God.* London: SCM, 1957.

Zlotnick-Sivan, H. "Moses the Persian? Exodus 2, the 'Other' and Biblical 'Mnemo-history'." *ZAW* 116 (2004): 189–205.

INDEXES

INDEX OF REFERENCES

2 Chronicles		89:3	145	25:34–38	54
1:3	147	90	2	30:21	147
6:15	145	90:1	141	33:21	145
6:16	145	105:26	147	33:22	145
6:17	145	132:10	145	33:26	145
6:28	127	144:10	145	50:6–7	54
6:42	145				
7	132	Proverbs		Ezekiel	
8:14	144	24:21	65	34:1–31	52, 54
19:5–11	71	29:14	96	34:23	145
23:14	141			34:24	52
24:6	147	Isaiah		37:24	145
24:9	147	7:10–17	101		
26:21	96	9:5	63	Daniel	
29:10	124	16:5	96	1:4	49
30:16	141	20:3	145	9:11	147
30:18	74	33:22	96	11:21	134
		37:5	145		
Ezra		40:11	54	Hosea	
3:2	141	42:1	146	3:4	97
		44:24–45:1	85	7:7	96
Nehemiah		63:11	11, 51, 52	13:10	96
1:8	147				
9:14	147	Jeremiah		Amos	
10:30	147	1	55, 137	2:3	96
12:24	144	1:1–19	101	9:14–15	52
12:26	144	1:5–7	102		
		1:5	55	Micah	
Esther		1:6	55, 101,	5:1	96
2:5	74		105	5:5	54
2:7	49	1:7	55		
10:2	74	1:8	55, 102,	Nahum	
10:3	74		105	3:18	54
		1:9–10	55		
Psalms		1:9	62	Habakkuk	
2:10	96	1:17–18	55	3:3	134
8:2	134	1:17	102		
18:16	50	1:19	55, 102,	Zechariah	
20:7	100		105	6:13	134
20:10	100	2:8	54	9:9	72
21:6	134	3:15	54	9:16	54
23:1	54	7:16	74	10:2–3	54
45:2	49	10:21	54	11:4–17	54
45:4	134	12:10	54	12:8	63
45:6	63	14:11–12	74		
77:20	52	15:1	74	Malachi	
77:21	16	22:22	54	3:2	147
78:70	145	23:1–8	54		

INDEX OF AUTHORS